War and Faith

THE LEGACY OF THE GREAT WAR

A Series sponsored by the Historial de la Grande Guerre Péronne-Somme

General Editor
JAY WINTER

Previously published titles in the Series

Antoine Prost
IN THE WAKE OF WAR
'Les Anciens Combattants' and French Society

Patrick Fridenson
THE FRENCH HOME FRONT 1914–1918

Stéphane Audoin-Rouzeau
MEN AT WAR 1914–1918

Gerald D. Feldman
ARMY, INDUSTRY, AND LABOR IN GERMANY 1914–1918

Rosa Maria Bracco
MERCHANTS OF HOPE

Adrian Gregory
THE SILENCE OF MEMORY
Armistice Day 1919–1946

Ute Daniel
THE WAR FROM WITHIN
German Working-Class Women in the First World War

WAR AND FAITH
The Religious Imagination in France, 1914–1930

BY ANNETTE BECKER

TRANSLATED FROM THE FRENCH BY HELEN MCPHAIL

FOREWORD TO THE ENGLISH EDITION BY KEN INGLIS

Oxford · New York

English edition
First published in 1998 by
Berg
Editorial offices:
150 Cowley Road, Oxford, OX4 1JJ, UK
70 Washington Square South, New York, NY 10012, USA

Originally published by Armand Colin Publishers as *La Guerre et la foi. De la mort à la mémoire (1914–1930)* in 1994. © Armand Colin Publishers, 1994.

English edition © Berg Publishers 1998

Translated by Helen McPhail with the financial support of the Historial de la Grande Guerre, Péronne-Somme.

Berg is an imprint of Oxford International Publishers Ltd.

Library of Congress Cataloging-in-Publication Data

A catalogue record for this book is available from the
Library of Congress.

British Library Cataloguing-in-Publication Data

A catalogue record for this book is available from the British Library.

ISBN 1 85973 173 2 (Cloth)

Typeset by JS Typesetting, Wellingborough, Northants.
Printed in the United Kingdom by Biddles Ltd, Guildford and King's Lynn.

To Sarah-Laure, Frédéric and Dolores, they know.

Contents

a prayer to God on behalf of another

Abbreviations

ARAC   Association Républicaine des Anciens Combattants
           (leftist association, mainly communist after 1920)
BDIC   Bibliothèque de Documentation Internationale
           Contemporaine. (Nanterre or Hôtel des Invalides, Paris)
CGT   Conféderation Générale du Travail
PFNSP   Presses de la Fondation Nationale des Sciences Politiques
RHMC   Revue d'Histoire Moderne et Contemporaine
SHAT   Service Historique de l'Armée de Terre, Vincennes

Foreword

This book explores through all its intricacies the relationship between religious faith and the French experience of the Great War. Most studies of religion in that war centre on institutions. Becker's first and last concern is the faith of the laity, the fears and hopes, the sufferings and consolations, of soldiers and their families. 'Everyday religion' is a famously elusive subject, and Becker is energetic, ingenious and sensitive in pursuing it.

She finds a kind of 'awakening' in the early weeks of war, a fire of revival not wholly extinguished by 1918 as people at the front and at home – even the anti-clerical – are sustained by the Christian patriotism, the patriotic Christianity, embodied in the resonant term *'union sacrée'*. She discerns a similar notion in the United States of 1917–18. For Americans as for the French, Becker suggests, the war provoked an awakening, comparable to the revivals of earlier days. Explicitly here, implicitly elsewhere, her comparison invites pursuit by other scholars. This translation challenges readers in English-speaking countries to do their own comparative history.

Did the United Kingdom experience a wartime awakening? If so, not for long, at any rate among civilians. 'There was a remarkable increase in church-going, in the use of prayer, and especially of intercession,' writes the editor of the *English Church Review* in February 1916. 'But this religious movement has seriously subsided. Everywhere the complaint is heard that few attend the services of intercession. Churches are no longer thronged.'[1] Here and there, novel expressions of religiosity encouraged hope, such as the neighbourhood shrines inside and outside churches which began to appear at the end of 1914, honouring men from the district, sometimes incorporating a cross or even a crucifix. 'They serve the double purpose of keeping in mind the absent and the departed', said a Church of England committee,

> and of bringing the recognition and remembrance of God and of the Cross of Christ out into the open . . . In these days of sorrow and danger the spectacle of men and women in the street engaged in prayer, it may be as night is falling,

---

1. Quoted in S. P. Mews, 'Religion and English Society in the First World War', Ph.D. thesis, University of Cambridge, 1973, p. 50.

has often brought to the passers-by the atmosphere of the unseen world, and the sense of the presence of the great Father in Whom is their consolation and defence.[2]

But such signs are few. Was evidence from the front more encouraging? The Revd Herbert Hensley Henson, Dean of Durham, convinced himself that a new link between the Church of England and the nation would be 'forged in the furnace of affliction': 'The ancient churches, where the flags of the regiments have been treasured, and whose walls will carry many names of comrades sleeping on the battlefields or beneath the ocean, will seem natural homes of religion to the soldiers and sailors returning at last from the long war.'[3]

At first something like that may have happened, among the territorial forces and the volunteers of Kitchener's army. But at last, no. The evidence was presented in 1919 in a thorough, careful and inter-dominational study, *The Army and Religion: An Enquiry and its Bearing upon the Religious Life of the Nation*. As summarized by a bishop, the conclusion was devastating. 'Christianity and the Churches have failed, are out of it, are disliked, and *not* for righteousness' sake.'[4] By 1918 British churches harboured a well-grounded dismay that they had derived so little reward from the nation's commitment to war.

Wondering why, some clergymen listened wistfully to reports of religious revival in France (and, more perplexingly, in Germany). 'They tell us that we suffer greatly in this matter by comparison with the French people,' says the vicar of St Barnabas', Pimlico, in 1916. I wonder what he would have made of evidence cited by Becker that English soldiers, few of them Catholic, asked the nuns of Albert, on the Somme, for medals and crucifixes and even pocket rosaries, and wrote letters to Sister Thérèse of Lisieux. It became common knowledge that Tommies who may never before have seen crucifixes were attracted to the wayside calvaries they came across in France and Belgium, and some war memorials in English churchyards were modelled directly on them. One young British officer writes enviously that in France soldiers disfigured by wounds provoke not repulsion, as in his own country, but high honour as 'Les Glorieux'. 'With the French', he reflects, 'a man's wounds are

2. Quoted in A. Wilkinson, *The Church of England and the First World War*, London SPCK, 1978, p. 300. See also C. Moriarty, 'Christian Iconography and First World War Memorials', *Imperial War Museum Review*, 6, 1991, pp. 63–75.

3. Quoted in A. Marrin, *The Church of England in the First World War*, Durham, NC, Duke University Press, 1974, p. 202.

4. Ibid., p. 204.

like decorations, they are tokens of the new religion of sacrifice. With us they are still horrible.'⁵

'Religion of sacrifice' is a notion central to Becker's book. Was Catholic Christianity more amenable than Protestant varieties to the sacralizing of war? Nobody listening to the Anglican Bishop of London, A. F. Winnington-Ingram, would have thought so. For him, says his biographer S. C. Carpenter, there was a sacredness about England which was beyond argument. He proclaimed unequivocally the holiness of the war, and like French Catholics cited by Becker he embraced the doctrine, more Islamic than Christian, that warriors who die in a good cause go straight to heaven.⁶ He was by no means alone; but misgivings about such identification of Church and nation seem to have been more audible in England than in France, both within and beyond the Church of England.

Becker makes much of a new ecumenicism in wartime France, incorporating Protestants and Jews. People interpreting the absence of religious revival in wartime England lamented the persistence of denominational and theological divisions which inhibited spiritual solidarity behind the national cause. Ecumenical commitment in France, Becker shows, required Catholics to forget the Catholics of Germany and Protestants to disown Martin Luther. In Paul Claudel's formulation of the *Union sacrée*, the German invaders were 'the armies of the Devil, the Lutheran hordes'. Léon Bloy diagnosed 'the Lutheran abcess, ripening over four centuries'. In the United States Becker notes efforts to disconnect Calvinism from Lutheranism; but that was not easily done. Joseph Odelin addresses Germans as 'Giants born of Luther, and nephews of Calvin'. Across the Channel, where Calvin was the spiritual father of John Knox, Martin Luther became on 4 August 1914 a conundrum for Protestants: patron of the German churches whose commitment to the cause of the Kaiser was every bit as strong as British churches' to the cause of his cousin King George V, yet a model in Sunday School history of brave Protestant individualism ('Here I stand'). More generally, the wartime alliance posed difficulties of spiritual interpretation on each side: 'Protestants hate the Holy Virgin', said Claudel, while Britons learned at school and even at university a history in which the triad of Protestant Christianity, liberty and empire enabled and guaranteed their nation's hegemony.

5. *The Love of an Unknown Soldier. Found in a Dug-out*, London, John Lane, 6th edition, 1918, pp. 7–8.
6. On Winnington-Ingram see Wilkinson, *Church of England, passim*.

Foreword

Becker provokes us to think about the efforts of remembering and forgetting necessary to preserve the Entente Cordiale. She prompts us also to compare the relationships between Church and State. Two connected elements in the French story have no counterpart in Anglophone countries. First, the defeat of 1870–1 and the clericalist interpretation of this disaster as a judgment on the nation. Second, the formal separation of Church and State in 1905, making militant clergy feel that they had been branded as pariahs. The *Union sacrée* represents a making of common cause between the Church and the Republic, an accommodation of a kind which never had to be worked for in England, where a more or less established Church coexisted more and more peaceably with Nonconformists, Methodists and Catholics, and the monarchy was congenial to all parties. There is no parallel in British rejoicing (not even over the 'Angel of Mons') with the distinct but harmonious voices of republicans and clericals celebrating the Miracle of the Marne.

Post-war commemorations are also shaped by the different relations between Church and State. You might come across war memorials incorporating a cross anywhere in the United Kingdom, but in France the law of 1905 forbade its use anywhere except close to churches and in cemeteries.[7] The Tomb of the Unknown Warrior could be located in Westminster Abbey without much dissent, while France's *Inconnu* had to be installed in the secular territory of the Arc de Triomphe. The French ceremony nevertheless had an element bizarre to Anglo-Saxon eyes, which cannot be understood without reference to the cult of the Sacred Heart, whose wartime importance Becker vividly elicits. In their solemn journey through Paris on 11 November 1920 the bones of the *Inconnu* were accompanied by the heart of Léon Gambetta, maker of the Republic, exhumed from the grave and transported alongside the anonymous representative of the republic's saviours. Becker's quotation from *L'Humanité* is wonderfully eloquent: 'What should we really think of the republican hero whose venerated guts are promenaded around and who will end up by establishing the new cult of the secular and republican Sacred Heart?'

Protestant Christianity was too iconophobic to generate any such symbol. Nor did the day itself, 11 November, have the associations which made it in France a day of the dead. For Catholics the ending of the war

---

7. On war memorials in various countries, as on much else relevant to Becker's theme, see J. Winter, *Sites of Memory, Sites of Mourning*, Cambridge, Cambridge University Press, 1995.

so soon after the days of All Saints and All Souls, and on the very day of
St Martin, was a comforting, perhaps providential, coincidence. In the
United Kingdom and its empire, people everywhere paused for two
minutes' silence on Armistice Day to remember the dead and then got
on with their lives.[8] In France, *Le Onze Novembre* became a national
holiday – *the* national holiday, in the judgement of Antoine Prost, who
reads its rituals as constituting the one actual case of what Rousseau had
in mind by 'civil religion' and remarks on the striking similarity between
its liturgy and that of the Catholic Church. Differences in the meanings
of that day were created also by policies on the disposition of dead bodies,
the British prohibiting their return, the French, after indecision and
conflict, allowing it, making 11 November in France (not as in the United
Kingdom) a day for actually visiting the graves of men honoured on the
monument aux morts as sons of this town, that village.

Around the *monument aux morts*, at the mass for their souls, beside
their bodies in the local cemetery, these men are addressed as saviours
of their own land. British tributes to the absent dead celebrate sacrifice
in another land and therefore dwell more on such abstractions as
freedom, loyalty and honour, and the generality of service in the cause
of a challenged empire rather than an invaded motherland.

Who knows how the religious imagination of England would have
responded spiritually to a German invasion? In these days of counter-
factual history and other modes mixing fact and fiction, Becker's book
could well stimulate some enterprising scholar to imagine that outcome.

Ken Inglis
Australian National University

---

8. See A. Gregory, *The Silence of Memory. Armistice Day 1919–1946*, Oxford, Berg,
1994.

Introduction

Qu'écrire pour moi c'était comme pleurer. Qu'il n'y avait pas de livre joyeux sans indécence. Que le deuil devrait se porter comme s'il était à lui seul une civilisation, celle de toutes les mémoires de la mort décrétée par les hommes . . .

That writing was like weeping. That no joyful book could exist without immodesty. That mourning should appear a whole civilisation in itself, made up of all the memories of death decreed by men . . .

Marguerite Duras, *Yann Andréa Steiner*

This book stands at the junction between two fields of historiography, religion and the First World War. Its purpose is to describe a cultural turning point which until now has been insufficiently appreciated: amidst the great slaughter of the war, death does not become ordinary, it remains unbearable. Individuals and societies are left in a long-lasting and persistent state of shock.

Focusing on religious faith between 1910 and 1930, this study finds its natural setting within the long term reflections of historians of religion.[1] The nineteenth and early twentieth centuries show on the one hand a certain distancing from religious ordinances among Christians and Jews and, on the other, conversions and renewals of belief, particularly among intellectuals. Converts generally tended towards extremely traditional practices. Among French Catholics we therefore find a growing indifference to religion, perhaps even dechristianization, often well under way since before the French Revolution. This was matched by a renewal or rebirth of devotion which might focus on the Sacred Heart of Jesus or the Virgin Mary, whose many appearances attracted varied and substantial pilgrimages.

From the religious point of view, does the war represent a logical step along these two paths of the nineteenth century or should it be seen as part of a break with the past?

---

1. J. M. Mayeur, (ed.), *Histoire du christianisme*, vol. XI, *Modernisation, industrialisation et expansion territoriale,* vol. XII, *Guerres mondiales et totalitarismes, 1914–1958,* Paris, Desclée/Fayard; P. Joutard (ed.), *Histoire de la France religieuse*, vol. III, *Du roi Très Chrétien à la laïcité républicaine*, 1991, Paris, Seuil; R. Rémond (ed.), *id.*, vol. IV, *Société sécularisée et renouveaux religieux, xxᵉ siècle*, Paris, Seuil, 1992.

1

Introduction

Although the prevailing historiography of the First World War has long seen the war as a time of break or change, today's approach tends to challenge this unilateral view and to stress the continuities as well as – perhaps even more than – the ruptures. In every respect, some developments are held back by war and others made possible.

An example of this is that recent publications and thinking on the élite and 'the masses' have substantially clarified artistic creativity during the war. Our clearer view of the cubist avant-garde, popular unsophisticated illustrative art (*images d'Epinal*) and mass-produced war memorials offers us a fresh approach to social and cultural environments both during and after the war. Kenneth Silver[2] shows that during the war the cubists of 1905–14 deliberately chose to abandon techniques that did not appear sufficiently 'French' or could even be perceived as German, such as drawing in the same style as Ingres. Pablo Picasso, Juan Gris and Jean Cocteau deliberately chose to retreat artistically in order to conform to standard French patriotism, or their view of it. At the same time, however, camouflage techniques benefited from cubist fragmentation and promoted hitherto unknown avant-garde art at the front.[3] The image of the combatants as generally recorded in war memorials is largely the natural legacy of the nineteenth century's grandiloquent passion for statues.[4]

This kind of historical assessment, which has been thorough in the case of art and perhaps less complete for literature and poetry,[5] has not yet been attempted for religion. It seemed to me that it was time to do so.

Important studies have of course been devoted to the French Churches in the First World War, but they have been wholly or mainly concerned with the Churches alone. For example, of the Catholic 'trilogy' – the papacy, the clerics and the faithful – only the first two aspects have been

2. Kenneth E. Silver, *Esprit de Corps, the Art of the Parisian Avant-Garde and the First World War, 1914–1925*, London, Thames & Hudson/Princeton, Princeton University Press, 1989.

3. Danièle Dellouche, 'Cubisme et camouflage', in Jean-Jacques Becker, Jay Winter, Gerd Krumeich, Annette Becker, Stéphane Audoin-Rouzeau (eds), *Guerre et cultures, 1914–1918*, Paris, Armand Colin, 1994, pp. 239–50.

4. See the most recent bibliography on this subject in Annette Becker and Philippe Rivé, *Monuments de mémoire, monuments aux morts de la Grande Guerre*, Paris, Secrétariat d'Etat aux anciens combattants et victimes de guerre, 1991.

5. Modris Eksteins, *Rites of Spring. The Great War and the Birth of the Modern Age*, New York, Bantam Press, 1989; Elisabeth Marsland, *The Nation's Cause, French, English and German Poetry of the First World War*, London, Routledge, 1991.

much explored.[6] But in order to understand the Great War from within, it is surely essential to approach the majority of combatants and their families; this is in accordance with René Rémond's proposition that 'Styles of behaviour never reveal more than part of the personality: religious belief remains the most intimate part of the being and structured manifestations reveal it only indirectly.'[7]

Alphonse Dupront's typology of collective religious experience in his authoritative book *Du Sacré*[8] seems to me very useful. It defines the burgeoning of religious observance during the war, indicating that what he calls 'everyday religion', firmly shaped by the Church – the Churches – continued to form the basic framework for most believers. But, faced with an extraordinary situation, the war, the faithful logically reacted in extraordinary ways. Certain devotional practices marginal to the Church began to multiply, in terms both of frequency, outside the feast-days of the liturgical calendar, and of physical setting: the presence of death adds unaccustomed significance to every apprehension of the divine.

In such uncertain times, when everyday matters are transformed by the absence of loved ones and the dangers they constantly suffer, there is a need for spiritual fringes where sacred manifestations (apparitions, prophecies) and collective devotions (cults of saints and relics, pilgrimages) offer an immediate response.

Finally, when the 'everyday' and the 'extraordinary' both fail to bring reassurance, there is recourse to 'superstition' outside the Churches. Yet, as we know in relation to the nineteenth century – the cradle, after all, of the soldiers of the First World War – it may be very difficult to separate Churches from beliefs.[9]

It is undeniable that beyond the visible return to church attendance in the early weeks of the war, beyond the rapid growth of confession and communion among Catholics and positive religious observance

6. Annette Becker, 'The Churches and the War', in Jean-Jacques Becker, *The Great War and the French People*, Part II, pp. 178–91, Oxford, Berg, 1985, pp. 178–91; Jacques Fontana, *Les Catholiques français pendant la Grande Guerre*, Paris, Cerf, 1990; Jean-Marie Mayeur, 'La Vie religieuse en France pendant la Première Guerre mondiale', in *Histoire vécue du peuple chrétien*, Privat, 1979, vol. II, pp. 179–93; Gérard Cholvy and Yves-Marie Hilaire, *Histoire religieuse de la France contemporaine*, vol. II, *1880–1930*, Paris, Privat, 1986.

7. René Rémond, 'Les Structures religieuses du XVIIIᵉ au XXᵉ siècle', *La France et les Français*, Encyclopédie de la Pléiade, 1972, p. 618. A first collective approach to this question can be seen in Nadine-Josette Chaline (ed.), *Chrétiens dans la Première Guerre mondiale*, Paris, Cerf, 1993.

8. Alphone Dupront, *Du Sacré*, Paris, Gallimard, 1987.

9. Joutard, *Histoire de la France religieuse*, pp. 465–6.

among Protestants and Jews, a general intensification of religious practice took root during the first year of the war, and was evident after the conflict. War, wounds, death, the supposedly temporary separation from loved ones that might turn out to be permanent – all these created new and more intense spiritual needs.

The interpretation of 'religion as a lightning conductor in times of great upheaval'[10] and the concept of 'putting one's affairs in order before dying' can be offered, with justification; yet this is rather simplistic as an explanation for the explosion of devotions, both at home and at the front. When a mere modest prayer was sufficient to seek God's protection, why was so much energy and money devoted to religious activity, precisely at a time when both energy and money were wholly committed to the war effort?

Reading soldiers' correspondence and diaries and examining the traces and graffiti left all along the front by these four-year wanderers, concerning 'the great mystical line with so much blood flowing along it',[11] reveals a true spirituality of the front. Reading the letters and other writings of wives and friends, and travelling even today along the pilgrim routes – from Lourdes to Paray-le-Monial, from Lisieux to La Salette, and into the humblest regional or local sanctuaries – also reveals an intense spiritual life of the home front, a spirituality caught up in constant interchange with the front; men on leave or wounded soldiers returned home for a few days or for ever, messengers bringing news of death.

In these exchanges, the clergy – the clergies – certainly played an important role, and they will not be forgotten in this book. But I have tried wherever possible to quote them only in the complete absence of 'non-professional' religious sources. Similarly, the role played by the papacy during the war should not be neglected, but Pius X and Benedict XV will only appear here through the faith of true believers.

My aim in this book has been to reverse perspectives, even though two-way communication between the faithful and the official Church hierarchy was clearly continuous, and the true origins of a prayer are not easy to perceive.

The war that I wish to describe consists of suffering and prayer, neither of which leaves traces that can easily be extracted from the archives. Yet signs of faith, or symptoms of certitude, hope or despair, can be discerned. The sources include much from what may be called the

---

10. Leopold Guillot, agricultural engineer interviewed in July 1915 by *La Grande Revue*, no. 575.

11. Pierre-Dominique Dupouey, *Lettres et essais*, Paris, Cerf, 1935, p. 180, 12 March 1915.

militants of belief, not excluding the etymological sense of the term. Elite lay figures from either the 'left', *Le Sillon*, or the 'extreme right', more especially *Action française*,[12] met in the trenches or acted as mediators with the home front. Men – and some women – skilled in writing set down their experiences and feelings in letters, books and memoirs. Although most of these writings come from a Catholic élite, figurative sources, ex-votos and letters deposited in shrines to the Virgin present us with a wider public, and the numerous illustrations in this book bear witness to them too.

Since the eighteenth century, periodic rebirths of faith have been known as 'revivals' or 'awakenings' in the United States[13] when they touch many people during a given period. American observers of the First World War drew a parallel between their religious tradition and what they thought they understood of France at war. Although the formidable American mobilization of men and energy which began in 1917 might suggest a comparison between the two countries in religious terms, the United States arrived too late, and experienced virtually nothing but the offensive followed by the victory. For the Americans, this war was not a long bruising wait in the face of death. This difference between the two countries is, moreover, quantifiable in the archives: there is a great disproportion between the amounts of source material available on the two sides of the Atlantic. Although this book concentrates primarily on the French experience of the war, the American evidence used here is intended to offset it, to cast a slightly more distant light on its concerns. Men who were largely Protestant can clarify an experience which was largely Catholic. Men who came from across the Atlantic, even if most of them were of more or less recent European ancestry, tell us about

12. *Le Sillon*: a Catholic movement and title of its journal, both founded by Marc Sangnier. The subtitle *Revue catholique d'action sociale* shows clearly the aim of the movement: to be a Christian movement in democracy. Marc Sangnier's ideas had, between 1895 and 1914, a very strong influence on Christian youth, even if they were partially condemned by the pope in 1910. They insisted on an ideal of chivalry and crusade that can be traced through this book.

Action française: nationalist-monarchist political movement, whose paper of the same name, founded in 1899, had a very wide readership among the anti-Dreyfusards and anti-republicans before the war. By entering the *Union sacrée*, they aimed to be at the forefront of the national crusade.

Eugen Weber, *Action Française*, Stanford, Stanford University Press, 1962; Michael Sutton, *Nationalism, Positivism and Catholicism, the Politics of Charles Maurras and French Catholics, 1890–1914*, Cambridge, Cambridge University Press, 1984.

13. 'Revival' is used for limited local movements, 'awakening' for manifestations of very widespread and intense resurgence of faith throughout groups or States.

themselves and about France because they believed they had come to fight on and for French territory – territory which became the bulwark of their patriotic mystique. American volunteers signed up as early as 1914; fighting with the French Foreign Legion, or as nurses or orderlies with the ambulances of the American Field Service, they traced the route of what was to be their compatriots' future active service.

Throughout the war, moreover, Frenchmen travelled to the United States, seeking to persuade Americans to join up on the 'right' side, and later to thank them. These transatlantic exchanges seem sufficiently important to justify a foreign detour, the better to clarify a page of French history.

Every Frenchman between 1914 and 1918 had to hold on, in the longest and most dreadful of wars. Fervour formed a diptych with death. Between 1914 and the 1930s this diptych became a triptych: it reached its peak in commemoration.

In 1915, Victor Basch, a vice-president of the *Ligue des droits de l'homme* (League for Human Rights), concluded his report on *The War of 1914 and the Law* as follows: 'This war is the struggle of free peoples, desirous of freedom, against militarism, against imperialism . . . That is how this terrible war can become a holy war.'[14] Found everywhere and in all kinds of discourse, even among the most anticlerical of French people, this kind of vocabulary – such as 'Sacred Union' (*Union sacrée*) and 'the mystique of the front' (*la mystique du front*) – cannot be dismissed as simple chance. It is this mystique that I wish to account for here. Although difficult to quantify, it is at the very least worthy of description.[15]

14. Quoted by Jean-François Sirinelli in *Intellectuels et Passions françaises*, Paris, Fayard, 1990, p. 39. Victor Basch and his wife were murdered in their old age, in another war, on 10 January 1944. René Rémond (ed.), *Paul Touvier et l'Eglise*, Paris, Fayard, 1991.

15. This book is a reflection of my two fields of activity in the Historial de la Grande Guerre at Péronne and the Université Charles-de-Gaulle/Lille-III. Stéphane Audoin-Rouzeau, Jean-Jacques Becker, Gerd Krumeich, Jay Winter, members of the Executive Committee of the Historial's Research Centre, have observed and fostered this project from its beginnings, together with Jean-Pierre Thierry, the great expert in artefacts and echoes of the Great War. To Etienne Fouilloux, who was the godfather of this book, my warm regards. My colleagues and students at Lille University, Fabrice Bouthillon, Caroline Fontaine, Bénédicte Grailles, Frédéric Gugelot and William Maufroy, discovered stained glass, books, objects, war memorials. Throughout the world, historians are working on associated projects. In Ireland, Australia, Israel and the United States I have profited from communication with Avner Ben Amos, Omer Bartov, John Horne, Ken Inglis, George Mosse and Emmanuel Sivan. I would like to express here my warmest gratitude. For this English version, all my deep thanks to Dolores Burdick and Helen McPhail.

1

Belief and Death: 'All Wars are Wars of Religion'

In 1915, the writer Jacques Rivière was a prisoner in Germany. Following his conversion to Catholicism in 1913, he tried to convince his comrades in captivity that the war had a meaning, and that this meaning must be sought in God: 'Man goes to war for a certain way of seeing the world. All wars are wars of religion. And indeed, who would not rather die than see good and evil, beauty and ugliness, through our enemies' eyes?'[1]

Jacques Rivière's militant certitude as a religious neophyte in 1915 – 'All wars are wars of religion' – makes a good point of departure for my reflections on faith at the time of the First World War. Like Jacques Rivière, millions of Frenchmen – and millions of other people throughout the world – knew that they were fighting and holding out for a particular way of seeing the world, which had absolutely no connection (or so they were convinced) with the way of fighting, of holding out, of their enemies – in this case, the Germans.

These men and women knew that they were involved in a struggle of and for civilization. In 1918, Americans who had recently come into the war used the same discourse:

> It is primarily a religious war. This can be felt everywhere. And the allies' armies are religious armies, for the men are there in order to make the world a better place. It is a religious army even when it appears profane, for the only blasphemy one hears is a prayer.[2]

> God is on our side: not the side of America against Germany, but the side of humanity against inhumanity. We shall prevail, not because our self-indulgent prayers or our servile services will persuade God to favour our cause, but because we are the allies of humanity, which is the cause of God himself.[3]

1. Jacques Rivière, *A la trace de Dieu*, Paris, Gallimard, 1925, p. 37.
2. John Gardner, *Letters to a Soldier on Religion*, New York, 1918, p. 95.
3. Rev. W. Barton, *The Moral Meanings of the World War*, Oak Park, Illinois, 1918, p. 17. This American certainty that the war was a veritable crusade informs almost all the

7

Obviously what is generally known as propaganda, and what the soldiers of the Great War elegantly described as 'eyewash' (*bourrage de crâne*) played a considerable role in forming these certainties. However, it would be wrong to believe that propaganda issued from above – in this case from Church authorities by way of military chaplains and various publications aimed at the faithful, both adults and children – could have had such an impact on the Great War generation if it did not also answer their expectations. These expectations sprang from the depths of their individual lives and from the recent or distant past of the country for which they were living and dying. A process of slow fusion was in operation between the front lines and the rear, between husband and wife, between news editors and their readers, between the sceptics and the trusting. Anyone who still believed in the possibility of victory and peace when absolutely nothing promised a rapid end to the war – and this means from September 1914 until August 1918 – was performing an act of faith. I would not wish to imply that they never felt doubts or that there was never conflict between them: doubt may itself strengthen faith.[4]

For the militants of the faith the war was a crusade because, as Jacques Rivière tells us, it was a fight against evil, against the devil. The war was, first of all, death: 250,000 Frenchmen died between August and September 1914, a total of 400,000 were dead by December. Although these numbers were not announced (military secrecy was of course essential), the spectacular and unprecedented scale of the slaughter in the summer of 1914 was inescapable. It is therefore possible to assess this burden of death on those who witnessed it. Within the framework of this study, I shall limit myself to those who display faith in an afterlife, whether militant or not.

This is a double vision of death, both negative and positive. On the one hand the enemy is seen as the murderer, bearing responsibility for death. Even in such literary excesses as *Au Seuil de l'Apocalypse*[5] and in

---

documents that bear witness to the period: those of the volunteers who signed up between 1914 and 1917, and those of the men who fought after April 1917. See Annette Becker, 'La foi aux Etats-Unis pendant la Première Guerre mondiale', in Jean-Jacques Becker, Jay Winter, Gerd Krumeich, Annette Becker, Stéphane Audoin-Rouzeau (eds), *Guerre et cultures, 1914–1918*, Paris, Armand Colin, 1994, pp. 183–91.

4. On this topic, see Stéphane Audoin-Rouzeau, 'Bourrage de crâne et information en France, 1914-1918', in *Les Sociétés européennes et la guerre 1914–1918*, Paris, University of Paris-X, 1990, pp. 163-74.

5. Diary of Léon Bloy, vol. IV, *Au Seuil de l'Apocalypse, 1913–1915: La porte des humbles 1915–1917*, Paris, Mercure de France, 1963.

Figure 1. Church War Memorial, Valenciennes (North). Painting by the Catholic artist Lucien Jonas. (The 'good' French imitate Christ, the 'bad' Germans end up in Hell.)

9

his very tendency to exaggeration, Léon Bloy is a cogent witness to this current of thought:

> A nation arose in the nineteenth and twentieth centuries to undertake what has never been seen before since the dawn of history: the extinction of souls. This is known as German Culture.
>
> To degrade and debase souls was no longer enough for the Prince of Darkness. He had to annihilate them, and this he achieved. Prussianized Germany was no longer part of humanity. It became a great savage beast, and threatened the whole world . . . God grant that this book may comfort . . . a few friends of God, a few rare and suffering bearers of that Christian Grandeur and Beauty which they wish to eliminate![6]

From 1914 to 1918, without interruption – although more intensively at the beginning and the end – Germany's war was one of 'atrocities', which, real or invented, were always accepted as historically true, as symbols of the German ethos: moral inferiority, even outright devil worship. In the name of God and of France, the militant faithful fought against this negative and satanic death.

But death was also sacrifice, the death of the martyr who chose this fate for himself, his country, his kin. In this sacrificial aspect, death became a gift. The war of religion embodied this dialectic between the ideal of life in spite of death because of faith in the resurrection – for Christians, the imitation of Christ, and for Jews, eternal life – and the forces of death against which the forces of life were set.

In letters to his priest, expressed in simple words and uncertain spelling, a parishioner of Abbé Maurice Salomon, priest of Saint John the Baptist in Neuilly-sur-Seine, shows all the power of this patriotic Catholicism which is also Catholic patriotism:

> By the grace of God I will do my duty everywhere as soldier and Christian . . . The first morning in getting up, I had great pain in my back, too bad that's war . . . (19 August 1914).
>
> Anyway it's a sacrifice for the nation that we are making, and we must hope that we will soon get to the end of our suffering . . . Let us hope that with God's help this war will soon come to an end for the sacrifices are great and already numerous. I beg you to think of me during your holy Mass . . . (29 November 1914).
>
> I have offered my life as a sacrifice, I am not bargaining, and I would be happy if my wife could take care of herself to bring up the children if it should turn out to be God's wish that I kick the bucket . . . (1 December 1914).[7]

6. Bloy, *Au Seuil de l'Apocalypse*, preface.

7. Archives of the Diocese of Paris, 4 Z Salomon. I am grateful to Monsieur l'Abbé Ploix for his kindness and help.

The Germans: Faithless and Lawless

For most of the French who witnessed the war, German civilization could be summed up as the 'Kultur' of destruction. The argument is simple: the German 'atrocities' in Belgium and in the north and east of occupied France were not the acts of a civilized nation of western Europe. Everything proved that the Germans were a race of barbarians, situated somewhere between the Mongols and the Vandals, and of whom Martin Luther was both descendant and symbol.[8] This hatred was laid out with scholarly care by intellectuals who, from Ernest Lavisse to Jacques Maritain, Joseph Bédier or Emile Durkheim, compete in their learning to wage a verbal war against 'the mad swine'.[9] This war of words was also carefully fostered by the Ministry of War, as the following decoded dispatch shows: 'To lend authenticity to French protests published by our agents in foreign press against actions of German army essential send name of Saxon officer confessing in letter his men behaved like "Vandals" and original document.'[10]

Just after the war, the serious *Dictionnaire de théologie catholique* (Dictionary of Catholic Theology) proclaimed in its article on 'War' that 'Germans have no conscience'. And the philosopher Jacques Maritain analysed at length the role of Luther in this moral and religious disintegration of the German Empire:

> To banish God from social and intellectual life, that is, from what is properly human in man . . . is contrary to nature. The Great War was fated to come out of this. Looking at the war from its philosophical and intellectual aspect, we used to say in 1915 . . . that pan-Germanism is the monstrous but inevitable fruit of the great break in balance of the sixteenth century, Germany's separation from Christianity.[11]

Paul Claudel wrote in similar terms on several occasions of his hatred of Germany, the mother of Protestantism: 'Our Lord will not let this insult to his mother go unavenged. Protestants hate the Holy Virgin so deeply!

---

8. Gabriel Langlois, *L'Allemagne barbare*, 1915. Chapter IV: 'Germany the torturer'; Chapter V: 'The German God, the protector of crimes: Martin Luther'. The book is dedicated: 'In pious offering to the sacred victims of the lands of Belgium and France. In Implacable Anathema to all destroyers of cities, pillagers of corpses and rapists of women.'

9. Bloy, 5 February 1915, op. cit., p. 142. A Committee for the publication of studies and documents on the war, chaired by Ernest Lavisse and with Emile Durkheim as secretary, published several books (Armand Colin) of which the most famous was by Joseph Bédier, *Les Crimes allemands d'après des témoignages allemands*, Paris, Armand Colin, 1915.

10. SHAT, Vincennes, Carton 5N9. Telegram no. 1711, 24 October 1914, to the headquarters at Romilly.

11. Jacques Maritain, *Antimoderne*, Paris, Edition de la Revue des Jeunes, 1922, p. 177.

This is the month of the Rosary which will bring us victory over the armies of the devil, the Lutheran hordes.'[12]

The views of these great minds were spread by lesser minds who none the less displayed the same faith:

> You were the passive scourge of the heavenly plan –
> Giants born of Luther, and nephews of Calvin –
> Your armour is of iron, your feet are but of clay.
> A pebble will soon roll from the Gospel today,
> And will bring you down from your lofty pedestal.[13]

Germany as a national entity was thus at one and the same time a rebel against Catholicism via the monk of Wittenberg, and the champion of a liberal Protestant theology which placed interior conscience before dogma. (Alas for Maritain, this is also the thinking injected by modernism into Catholicism.) In criticizing German spiritual evolution, responsible for these outrages, Maritain was paradoxically not far from certain French Protestant militants facing the challenge of accusations against Luther.[14] In their eyes it was the Churches which had failed. They were Christians, reformed and militant, and the war, far from proclaiming the death of their faith, vindicated the firm basis of their militancy in the face of uncertainties: 'This war is not the failure of Christ, it is the failure of the Christian; for centuries now men have been preaching the Gospels, and these disciples of Christ have never yet achieved enough influence to render such atrocities impossible.'[15] Thus it was not in the Reformation

12. *Correspondance, Claudel, Jammes, Frizeau*, Paris, Gallimard, 1952. Paul Claudel to Francis Jammes, 24 September 1914 and 1 October 1914, pp. 274–5.

13. Joseph Odelin, *Du théâtre à l'Evangile, les étapes d'une conversion 1850–1917*, Paris, Beauchesne, 1919, p. 241. The French original is:

> Vous étiez le fléau passif du plan divin
> Géants né de Luther, et neveux de Calvin
> Votre armure est de fer, mais vos pieds sont d'argile.
> Un caillou roulera demain de l'Evangile,
> Qui vous fera tomber de votre piédestal.

14. At the entry into war of the United States, certain thinkers attempted to prove how far American Calvinism – the major transatlantic faith, as in French Protestantism – differed from Lutheranism. *Etudes*, 1918, articles on the 4th centenary of the Reformation. E. Doumergue, 'Calvin et l'Entente, de Wilson à Calvin', *Revue de Métaphysique et de Morale*, 1918, pp. 807–40.

15. Robert Cazalis (1916), quoted in the article by R. Fabre, 'Un groupe d'étudiants protestants en 1914–1918', *Le Mouvement social*, 1983, no. 122, p. 95. Laurent Gambarotto, *Foi et Patrie, la prédication du protestantisme français pendant la Première Guerre mondiale*, Paris, Labor et fides, 1996, 466p.

that the fault lay, but in Lutheranism, to the extent that it was German and therefore a symbol of barbarism. There was nothing of this in Franco-American Protestant links:

> The Huguenots of France could not be other than brothers of the American Puritans. This brotherhood has united our churches and will prove more powerful than ever in the days ahead, when our soldiers will fight together, closely united on the battlefields, faithful to the spirit of the Reformation, to conquer despotism by insuring the freedom and independence of Nations.[16]

From France's intellectual heights to letters from the humblest backgrounds, the spirit almost everywhere is one of hatred or abusive language, a whole vocabulary chosen to describe the chaos wrought by the Germans. Evidence of regret for this hatred, in the name of Christian love or universal brotherhood, is very rare; this was true even in 1916 and 1917, when the war had become commonplace and lassitude weighed heavily on all minds and spirits.

To be sure, we can find the occasional individual positive gesture towards the enemy, particularly towards those who fell on the field of honour. In his sermon a chaplain might associate the newly fallen German dead with the men whose souls were in his charge. Ferdinand Belmont writes from the Somme in November 1915: 'a little speech by the priest of the village of Méricourt who laid a wreath on the tomb of the French, then another on the tomb of the Germans'.[17]

But these individual acts of recognition of the enemy as a man, even as a man gifted with a soul, were never transformed into a collective vision: the German nation, its political and military authorities, were indeed the collective embodiment of evil. With all his artistry as a Christian poet, Paul Claudel expressed this in *La Nuit de Noël 1914*. He imagines that a certain number of soldiers killed in battle, along with civilian victims of German 'atrocities', are holding Christmas Mass in heaven, while the Germans shell Reims cathedral twelve times. The

16. Frank Puaux, President of the Society for the History of French Protestantism, 23 September 1917. Message entrusted to two military chaplains, Georges Lauga and Victor Monod, touring the United States. *The Churches of Christ in America and France*, 1918, New York, p. 24.

17. Capitaine Ferdinand Belmont, *Lettres d'un officier de chasseurs alpins (2 août 1914–décembre 1915)*, Paris, Plon, 1916, p. 87. Prefaced by Henry Bordeaux, the letters of the strongly Catholic doctor, which were acclaimed with the Prix Montyon of the *Académie française*, were of great importance from the moment they came out and were quickly translated into English. In all Anglophone countries, and particularly in the United States, Belmont became the symbol of the French Catholic soldier of the Great War.

priest, shot down in his church, continues the religious instruction of the parish children in heaven:

> Pardon for all those wretches who, in killing you, are the authors of your bliss . . . Let us pray then for our executioners. But Lord, you know that it is not easy to pray for a German. They are such perfectly honest people, and virtuous, and sure of doing right, even when they murder children . . . When they were killing us, my dear brethren, we were the ones who were guilty of the necessity that forced those good folk to immoderate acts . . . Are their rulers not pious men? . . . And in their empire there is no customs official or police commissioner whose office furnishings do not include the image of the Crucified One![18]

In the same vein, Claude Debussy composed in 1915 a *Noël des enfants qui n'ont plus de maison*, for which he wrote the words himself:

> We have no home any more!
> The enemies have taken everything, taken all, taken all, even our little
>   beds!
> They burned the school, and Master Jesus Christ,
>   and the poor old man who couldn't get away . . .
> Of course, Papa is away at the war and poor Maman is dead, at least she
>   didn't have to see all this . . .
> Noël! Little Noël! Do not go to them, never go to them again,
> Punish them! Avenge the children of France! The little Belgians, the little
>   Serbs and Poles as well . . .
> Try to give us our daily bread again . . .
> Noël, hear us, we have no more little wooden shoes.
> But give victory to the children of France![19]

In its issue of 23 August 1917, the *Etoile Noëliste*, a publication for little Catholic girls, put under its normal cover design – a tranquil baby Jesus in his cradle – a charming picture of a small girl holding a young goat in her arms. The caption is an echo of the motto at the top of the page, 'May God protect France': 'The sweet child has just heard talk of the wolf, or the butcher . . . or the Boche . . . and she is quickly taking her favourite little pet goat to safety.'[20]

---

18. Paul Claudel, *La Nuit de Noël 1914*, February 1915. La Pléiade, Théâtre de Paul Claudel, vol. II, pp. 584-5.

19. I would like to thank Stéphane Patin, who is working on French music and the Great War, for showing me the Debussy text.

20. On publications for young people during the war, see Stéphane Audoin-Rouzeau, *La Guerre des enfants 1914-1918*, Paris, Armand Colin, 1993.

The facile play on words 'Bocherie/boucherie' (Boche/butcher) appears also in the caption of a photograph of the church of Berry-au-Bac (Aisne). Of the plaster Christ that decorated the nave, there remain only two dangling arms: 'Christ on the butcher's block, a German work.'[21] These two examples are typical of the way French Catholics presented the German lack of conscience, respecting neither the innocence of children nor God himself.

It was above all the destruction of churches that unleashed passions. Everywhere, from Reims cathedral to the humble churches of the front line, the shells – incendiary or not, German or not – were destroyers, crucifying again the Christ of the calvaries. 'Our city bears forever the stigmata of their hideous "Kultur". . . . Everything has been swept away, crushed, burned by Teutonic iron. Ruins everywhere, everywhere the silence of the tomb.'[22] The fire which destroyed the library in the Catholic University of Louvain was naturally stigmatized in the same terms. In denouncing the destruction of Reims cathedral, the highest Protestant and Jewish authorities of the land rivalled the more directly affected Catholics in their anti-German patriotism. 'The destruction of the Reims basilica is an odious blasphemy against God, the Father of all, and reveals the absence of all religious and human feeling in its perpetrators.'[23]

Lest anti-German hatred should tend to relax with the length of the conflict, people were urged not to forget. This was the aim of an exhibition on German crimes, organized in 1917 by the commemorative league 'Souvenez-vous'. Jonas designed a poster showing a hellish landscape, red with fire and black with smoke; a German soldier is holding a torch, and a butcher's knife dripping with blood. Drunk with cruelty, he is howling, an incarnation of pure evil. A cathedral is in flames, Reims most probably, while a burning calvary collapses into a pool of blood. The Symbolist painter from Nice, Gustav Adolf Mossa, had been very badly wounded in front of Ypres in November 1914. While having a very long recovery (almost the entire war), he drew two cycles of 'Songeries de la guerre' ou 'Très tristes heures de la guerre' in 1915, and 'Visions de guerre' in 1917. In each of his remarkable miniatures, the barbarous and anti-Christian German is attacked in a reinterpretation of the Bible and Germanic myths – in particular those of Wagner – which

21. Special issue of *L'Art et les artistes*; 'Les Vandales en France', 1915, p. 31.
22. Abbé E. Foulon, *Arras sous les obus*, Paris, 1915, p. 120.
23. Alfred Levy, Chief Rabbi of France, quoted in Vindex, *La Basilique dévastée, Reims*, Paris, Bloud et Gay, 1915, p. 40.

the artist had loved before the war. In his 'Massacre of the Innocents', the ogre/Kaiser is drawn as Herod.[24] The cathedral of Reims appears everywhere in his drawings, still standing but pitiful.

Patriotism during the First World War was of necessity ecumenical, the denunciation of a Germany without conscience or culture reinforcing the idea of a spiritual *Union sacrée*.[25] The insistence on German atrocities against religion, profanations both real and invented, and especially the spreading of more or less imaginary well-chosen anecdotes, was a powerful propaganda weapon.

> You must be as impressed as I am by the clearly satanic character of this war. One small fact among more than ten thousand. Our soldiers, entering a cemetery in Flanders, find themselves in the presence of a great cross. In the place of Christ, a man has been crucified by the Germans . . . This can only be explained by a sort of collective possession of the entire German army . . . it is the Lutheran abscess, ripened over four centuries, which is finally splitting open.[26]

It should not be thought that the immoderate Léon Bloy was distorting what he had heard, to provide better proof that in the war the long-expected Apocalypse had finally come to pass.[27] For him, the Germans were the incarnation of that total denial of Christianity in which the crucifixion of an enemy represented the most insane phase. Although tales similar to Bloy's circulated in the various armies, it was Canada that pushed the exploitation of this conviction the furthest. Starting with a description in *The Times* of 10 May 1915, of the crucifixion of a Canadian soldier, the deed was passed on by word of mouth, buttressed by numerous eye-witness accounts, to the point that, when it came to commemorating the war in 1919, the sculptor Derwent Wood produced a bronze which he entitled *The Golgotha of Canada*. A Canadian is nailed on the door of a barn with four Germans jeering at him and one shaking his fist.[28] In their publications on the atrocities, the French also returned

24. Catalogue of the exhibition *Gustav Adolf Mossa, l'œuvre symboliste: 1903–1918*, Paris, Réunion des Musées de France, 1992, pp. 206–19.

25. The *Union sacrée*, the 'Sacred Union', declared at the outbreak of war in August 1914, was the cross-party expression of national unity.

26. Léon Bloy, *Lettres à ses filleuls*, Stock, 1928. Letter to Pierre Van Der Meer in Walcheren, 13 January 1915, pp. 199–200.

27. See R. Griffiths, *Révolution à rebours, le renouveau catholique dans la littérature en France de 1870 à 1914*, Paris, 1971, pp. 131–3.

28. Maria Tippett, *Art at the Service of War. Canada, Art and the Great War*, Toronto, University of Toronto Press, 1984.

often to the crucified Canadian, emphasizing the jeering laughter of the Germans.[29]

Tales like these have never been proved, as can be seen from the difficulties of the Canadian inquest charged in vain with elucidating the files in the face of the international scandal caused by Wood's sculpture. But, as it is said that the greater the lie, the more chance it has of being believed, the more blasphemous and insane the tales of atrocities, the more witnesses came forth who were themselves convinced and then convinced others.[30]

The same phenomenon reappears with tales concerning children's hands being cut off: blasphemy working against God and the children of God. It is in the form of a prayer that a little girl deprived of her hands demands that in her turn the Kaiser's granddaughter should undergo the same torture. Then she checks herself:

> Lord, I've thought about it. It would be very bad to make the granddaughter of the cruel emperor of the Germans suffer. It isn't her fault if her grandfather and her Papa have ordered the hands of Belgian and French children to be cut off. Do not grant my prayer of last night. Only cut off the hands of the little empress's doll; the little empress must be about my age, so tell her what her grandfather's soldiers have done to a little French girl who is going to die of sorrow![31]

Face to face with the horror of death brought by the Germans – satanic death, manipulating the possessed – there is the death of the French. In 1924, Philippe Barrès edited his wartime meditations, recalling the

---

29. *Le Livre rouge des atrocités allemandes par l'image*, 38 prints by J. G. Domergue, Paris, Escudier/Richepin, 1915, p. 37. *Kultur et Teutonnerie*, 27 drawings by Mauprat, Paris, Plon, 1915; *1914–1916, Crimes Allemands*, 10 etchings by Jeanniot with an introductory poem by the artist.

30. This was a lesson retained by one former German soldier of the Great War, Adolf Hitler. The British propaganda struck him as far superior to that of Germany and in *Mein Kampf* he was already seeking to improve matters: 'Every piece of printed material, from the alphabet teaching children to read up to the latest journal, everything in the theatre or the cinema, every public notice-board and every empty hoarding must be put to use in this unique and magnificent mission.'

31. André Müller, Imprimerie A. Mortier, 1918, Monte Carlo, sold in aid of Red Cross funds (BDIC item 18181). Very few witnesses kept a cool head or in particular dared to oppose what had become the anti-German litany. Gide, however, provided a comforting account in his diary. He was content to describe the horror of a German officer who believed that a child with accidentally mutilated hands was a victim of his fellow countrymen. 'So it's true then, what they accuse us of? This is what our people do? . . . He left the shop abruptly, his hand over his eyes and shaking with sobs.' André Gide, *Journal*, Paris, La Pléiade, vol. 1, 27 December 1915, p. 526.

corpses in the mud: 'the green corpse, as out of place as a Mongol on this French plain, brought low by ferocity, is only a sad humiliated thing next to our dead, so pure, shining as they disintegrate'.[32]

Early in the conflict, this Manichaean approach to spirituality was linked with death and the commemoration of death. Dishonourable death, death due to cowardice, ought to be preserved for its example and could even be used as an instructive contrast with noble death, the death of heroes. In this aim, many advised against the restoration of Reims cathedral. 'It should be left as evidence of Teutonic barbarism. We should transport the bones of dead soldiers there. . . . We must inscribe in gold letters the names of all the heroes who died for their country . . . and every year on the date of signing the peace that proclaims the annihilation of Germany, let France kneel there before her dead.'[33] The instigators of this 'annual ceremony of a new rite' would thus maintain in perpetuity – and in the central location of the spirituality of historic France – the combat between God and Satan, between civilization and barbarism; the combat in which, through the destruction of churches, statues of saints and liturgical objects, 'God is the first victim.'[34]

Noble Death, the Death of a Hero/Martyr

'This is the immense field of the dead. This is the enormous cemetery, the resting place of victims of this hellish war. Their numbers have grown beyond counting. This is the new frontier of France, from Alsace to the North Sea. Beyond it lies the world of the barbarians.'[35] One of these 'barbarians' had three sons, a son-in-law and most of his young disciples in the army of their nation, the Austro-Hungarian Empire. He was Sigmund Freud. Looking beyond this individual experience, in 1915 he reflected as a psychoanalyst on the meaning of this new experience of war and its hundreds of thousands of dead (the millions would come later, after four years had passed and with all calculations done), in a Europe once thought too 'civilized' and where, as life expectancy increased, death had become disregarded. Léon Bloy, like all Frenchmen, had not read *Thoughts for the Times on War and Death* – all barbarian thought was banned, and as for that double barbarity of thought,

32. Philippe Barrès, *La Guerre à vingt ans*, Paris, Plon, 1924, p. 138.
33. 'Les Vandales en France', p. 15.
34. Victor Bucaille, *Lettres des prêtres aux armées*, Paris, Payot, 1916, p. 191.
35. Léon Bloy, *Dans les ténèbres*, 1917. *Œuvres*, vol. IX, Paris, Mercure de France, 1969, p. 319.

psychoanalysis . . .! Freud's conclusions, however, full of solid common sense, could only have been echoed by all parties to the war: 'We remember the old adage: *si vis pacem para bellum*. If you desire peace, prepare for war . . . Today we should bring it up to date: *si vis vitam, para mortem*: if you wish for life, prepare for death.'[36]

In 1920, Freud lost his daughter Sophie in the flu epidemic. Deeply distressed, he wrote to two of his colleagues:

> We know that death is part of life, that it is inevitable and that it comes in its proper hour . . . Yes, to outlive a child is painful. Fate does not even respect the order of precedence . . . For years I prepared myself for the loss of my sons; and now comes the loss of my daughter. In my profound unbelief, I have no one to blame and I know that there is nowhere to lay one's complaint.[37]

It is clear that believers were equally unprepared for this kind of death – mass death, the death of young people – even if for Christians the central message of the passion and resurrection inevitably led them to reflect on death.

The young men described by Agathon, of whom Ernest Psichari – killed in August 1914 full of the fervour he had invoked with his vows and nourished with his literary works – was the best example, were a minority in their generation.[38] After August 1914, the whole generation was swallowed up by the war and by death.

The militant faithful took up the burden of preparing their contemporaries for death.[39] Is not the militant, in the etymological sense of the word, the *miles*, the ordinary soldier? Ernest Psichari, an officer in the colonial artillery who became a Catholic convert in 1913, set the tone: 'I am going to this war as though to a crusade, because I feel we are defending the two great causes to which I have dedicated my life.'[40]

36. S. Freud, *Thoughts for the Times on War and Death*, Complete Works, Standard Edition, Vol. 14, London, Hogarth Press, 1975; Peter Gay, *A Life for Our Time*, London, Dent, 1988; Annette Becker, 'Freud, entre rêves et cauchemars', *14–18, la très Grande Guerre*, ed. Le Centre de Recherche de l'Historial de la Grande Guerre, Paris, Le Monde Editions, 1994, pp. 145–51.

37. Sigmund Freud, letters of 4 February 1920, quoted by Gay, *A Life for Our Time*, p. 451.

38. Agathon, *Les Jeunes-Gens d'aujourd'hui*, Paris, Plon, 1913. Henri Massis and Alfred de Tarde (Agathon), *Les Jeunes Gens d'aujourd'hui*, présenté par Jean-Jacques Becker, Paris, Imprimerie nationale, 1995.

39. As will be seen below, other attitudes to death found a place during the war, spiritualism in particular.

40. Letter to the Abbé Bailleul, quoted by A. M. Goichon, *Ernest Psichari d'après des documents inédits*, Paris, Coharol, 1925, p. 343.

Psichari joyously sacrificed his life for France and for God. He saw this spiritual sacrifice as the supreme religious act, the gift to God in imitation of God. As a Christian he was ready for martyrdom. This sacrifice was a deliberate choice, made precisely because of its extreme price, the cost of life itself. For the new knights of the twentieth century, death was a gift of God in exchange for the gift of their lives. This sacrificial heroism appeared among Catholic militants who were sympathetic to *Action française*, particularly among converts, who found the war a magnificent outlet for their new faith, but also among more moderate Catholics, among every kind of Protestant and – apart from the imitation of Christ – among Jews. 'All Jewish hearts in France are ready for any sacrifice, for any act of devotion. To the invaders who dare trample our sacred soil, and whose every advance is marked by pillage, fire and ruin, the Jews, like all Frenchmen, take their stand as free men against them.'[41]

Jacques Péricard still proclaimed proudly in 1930: 'In 52 months France saw more noble knights like the Chevalier d'Assas, more Bayards, more de la Tour d'Auvergnes than ever before in all her history.'[42] Dupouey agreed:

> I am more and more enthusiastic about the war, about this warrior order that overturns material things, guts houses, razes villages, transforms the idyllic banks of the Yser into oceans of mud, but marvellously re-establishes certain precedents in spiritual matters. I think that this winter in the trenches is going to be an incomparable retreat for a very important part of France.[43]

Contrary to whatever Henri Massis, Henri Bordeaux or *La Revue des Jeunes* might say, coming to the same conclusions as Agathon's study and seeing in the behaviour of soldiers under fire the *a posteriori* proof of those conclusions, youth as a whole was not ready for this unimaginable sacrifice. For every Ernest Psichari or Maurice Ernst, the nation's intellectual mystical élite, how many hundreds of thousands of men remained indifferent? And yet, from the very beginning of the conflict, the theme of sacrifice fills descriptions of the war, it remains ever-present, exactly like death itself, to which it is irredeemably attached. 'I am not

41. Rabbi Samuel Korb to the Nantes synagogue, 20 September 1914. Quoted in Philip Landau, 'Les juifs de France et la Grande Guerre, 1914–1941', unpublished thesis supervised by Michelle Perrot and Pierre Vidal-Naquet, Paris, University of Paris-VII, 1992, 3 vols, vol. 1, p. 271.

42. *Livre d'or du Diocèse de Mende*, 1930, p. vii.

43. Pierre-Dominique Dupouey, *Lettres et essais*, Paris, Cerf 1935, 19 December 1914, pp. 129–30.

afraid to die. Now I can say it in all sincerity: I have sacrificed my life.'[44]

The art of letter-writing flourished – necessarily, in the circumstances; letters of condolence must be sent from the front or from home, to families sorely tried by the loss of their young sons. Friends from pre-war days or comrades from the front did their best to comfort parents. The axiom of the war – the longer you've been in it, the smaller your chances of getting out alive – took on an even more poignant force. Our sources, those who best expressed their message of faith and hope at the moment of losing comrades, would soon be killed in their turn: Ferdinand Belmont, Etienne Derville, Pierre-Maurice Masson.

Masson was busy polishing his thesis on Rousseau between battles and sent his wife a daily offering of faith, humour and love:

> I thought about myself yesterday while reading *Le Temps*: an artillery lieutenant, killed in Champagne, and who had passed the proofs for his thesis on the eve of the attack, was recently named *docteur en Sorbonne*, after his death. So here I am, certain, at least, of a posthumous doctorate . . . the Sorbonic [*sic*] ceremony will take place on Saturday, 4 March . . . You must admire the precision, the bold precision of it! You must admit that it's tempting fate, and grenades and torpedoes, before which I must present myself again tonight. Let us hope they will have some slight respect for 'culture'. Meanwhile, there's the monster – I mean my thesis.[45]

One had to be acquainted with the style of this academic in order to appreciate his reflections as a Christian, sent to the wife of one of his cousins killed at the front:

> What is moving and magnificent in this death is the fact that it was accepted months ago with the most serene courage, and that he seemed to love you as much as he did in order to have more to sacrifice to the duty that claimed him, showing in this final gesture of a Christian knight that there are cases where, to fulfil the beauty of a life, one must know how to lose it.[46]

At the front, or at home, when news arrived, the militant literary believers in the sacrifice were soon confronted with blood and death. What were the soldiers if they were not 'sacrificial victims'?[47] All the

44. Alfred-Eugène Cazalis, letter to his parents, 7 April 1915. The letters of this young Protestant volunteer were published after his death in 1916: *En souvenir d'un jeune soldat de la France et de Jésus-Christ*, Paris, Fischbacher, 1916, p. 43.

45. Pierre-Maurice Masson, *Lettres de guerre, 1914–1916*, Paris, Hachette, 1918. Letters in December 1915 and February 1916, pp. 162 and 209. Masson did not get permission from the Verdun front to present his thesis on Rousseau and was killed on 16 April 1916.

46. *Ibid.*, 22 February 1915, p. 55.

47. Jacques d'Arnoux, *Les Sept Colonnes de l'héroïsme*, Paris, Plon, 1938, p. 418.

victims of war, described by Georges Duhamel in his *Vie des martyrs*, are, in the passive sense, victims of sacrifice. One aim of this book is to understand why these victims designated by their country not only accepted their martyrdom, but, in the main, suffered it without resistance for four years – or more exactly, replaced each other in turn, one year's conscripts after another on 'the nation's altar'.

For our witnesses for faith as a group, sacrifice had a meaning, which was grace. In 1917, Henri Massis published his 'Impressions de guerre', under the accurate title of *Le Sacrifice*. This book is presented as an epilogue to the Agathon inquiry.

Ernest Psichari moves from one work to the next. The living witness of national renewal gave himself as sacrifice in the crusade proclaimed in his own vows of 22 August 1914 and so became the perfect idealized example of what he had advocated during his life. We must not take the extraordinary case of Psichari as typical, nor the writings of Massis as scientific truth: and yet it is from the war memoirs of Henri Massis that I have chosen to quote at length. Written during the first battles of Notre-Dame de Lorette in January 1915, published in 1917, far removed from the enthusiasms of 1914 but at one of the most difficult points of the war, they seem to represent better than any others that mystique of sacrifice which Catholic intellectuals rediscovered in the war:

> It seems that man, through this common suffering, has touched the very core of reality. This is what all wish to preserve and bring back, as the precious tribute of their suffering, the divine lesson of sacrifice. Having found their souls once more and feeling them to be so privileged, they intend to save what saved them . . . Through the war we shall have experienced an incomparable grace . . . Such is the meditation that develops in the cloister of the trenches. No anchorite was ever more ardent in his meditations . . . What monastery, what enclosure can offer such a spectacle of nakedness and abandonment, a deeper, more intense vision of death, such depths of solitude, such a society of fraternal souls sustained by such fervour? The holocaust is complete. Whether he chooses the spade that bites into the earth or the shovel that casts it out, each man here is digging his own grave.[48]

Reading such well-chosen phrases and feeling the literary impulse crafting its metaphors, it is easy to see that Massis's *Sacrifice* would appal Jean Norton Cru. The author of *Témoins*, forerunner of the pacifism that became the norm of writing on the war during the 1920s and 1930s, could only resist this vision of sacrifice by arguing that Massis was not long enough in the trenches. Yet this exalted vision of the war, with its

48. Henri Massis, *Le Sacrifice*, Paris, Plon, 1917, pp. 204–6.

beneficent aspects – even including death – was shared by many long-term combatants. Repeatedly in their writings we find this insistence on the sacrifice in its positive sense of initiation. 'There may be men who would benefit from death. The war seeks them out. They are men who, alone, could not have earned God's mercy. And God finds this means: that they must die so that through this great trance they must endure and through this sudden rape of their souls, they may be saved.'[49] The most eloquent of all was to be the Jesuit Pierre Teilhard de Chardin, who served in the war as a stretcher-bearer. In 1917 he tried to summarize his thoughts on the war in a piece with the revealing title of *La Nostalgie du front*. With great clarity Teilhard attempts to understand his own state of mind, in terms which shocked his later admirers: they failed to find here the scholar's mind open to challenging thought.

> The front casts a spell on me . . . What are, in fact, the properties of this fascinating and deadly line? . . . The unforgettable experience of the front, to my mind, is an immense freedom . . . There is a world of feelings I would never have known or suspected, were it not for the war. Only those who were there can ever experience the memory charged with wonder of the Ypres plain in April 1915, when the Flanders air smelled of chlorine, and shells were cutting down the poplars . . . or the scorched slopes of Souville, in July 1916, with their smell of death. Those more than earthly hours instil into life a tenacious, unsurpassable essence of exaltation and initiation, as if they were part of the absolute. All the enchantments of the Orient, all the spiritual warmth of Paris, are not worth the experience of the mud of Douaumont . . . Through the war, a rent had been made in the crust of banality and convention. A window was opened on the secret mechanisms and deepest layers of human development. A region was formed where it was possible for men to breathe an air drenched with heaven . . . Those men are fortunate, perhaps, who were taken by death in the very act and atmosphere of war, when they were robed and animated by a responsibility, an awareness, a freedom greater than their own, when they were exalted to the very edge of the world, and close to God![50]

Fascination with suffering, fascination with man's capacity to surpass himself, this is a return to Pascal's pairing of human lowliness and grandeur. Pascal was much read in the trenches, and often quoted, by Catholic intellectuals. We certainly see here this tragic way of thinking,

49. Rivière, *A la trace de Dieu*, p. 142.
50. Pierre Teilhard de Chardin, *Ecrits du temps de guerre*, pp. 229-39. Intellectuals were not the only ones to experience this feeling; the same expression comes from an ordinary nursing orderly posted to a hospital at the rear: 'I am already nostalgic for the front but it is God's will' (letter to Abbé Salomon, 11 June 1916, archive quoted).

which to some extent denies time and locates itself elsewhere, outside history. Their vocabulary, with expressions such as 'trance', 'rape of the soul' or 'initiation', recalls ethnological accounts of torture accepted and sublimated in the pursuit of purification, sacrificially intermingling social and religious elements.[51]

The paradox of all these testimonies is that they reveal a state of solitude of the front placed by the writers on a level with monastic solitude when the final vows have been taken. Walking today along the front line, through quarries occupied by fighting men, or grottoes hollowed in limestone, it is impossible not to think of cells in the desert. At the Chemin des Dames near Noyon in Champagne these places of death have been transformed into places of prayer, by a few carvings or sculptures – crucifixes, stones set up to form primitive altars. To choose God, to choose to offer one's life to God at the heart of the most intense suffering and in the closest proximity with certain death, represents a leap of humanity without paradox, because it brings meaning to death in the very act of its denial.

A few hours before he was killed at the front, Dominique-Pierre Dupouey described the horrors of night fighting to his wife. He concludes what was to be his final letter: 'Let us not force ourselves to weep when God shows us only reasons for joy . . . At bottom, the great prayer for each of us to offer is still Claudel's magnificent cry: "Lord, deliver me from myself."'[52]

Dolorisme

In its dedication to Dupouey, 'Hero and Saint',[53] Henri Ghéon's account of his conversion – becoming 'the man born of the war' – connected death in the Great War to the pure and tender love of faith. But in no case could this love be achieved without dereliction. The noble death of naval officer Dupouey, this death worthy of a medieval knight, hailed as exemplary at meetings of *Action française* (of which Dupouey had been a fervent militant), is above all a personal and familial drama. Mireille

51. See, for example, Pierre Clastres, *La Société contre l'Etat*, Paris, Minuit, 1978.
52. Pierre-Dominique Dupouey, *Lettres et essais*, 2 April 1915, p. 199.
53. Henri Ghéon, *L'Homme né de la guerre. Témoignage d'un converti (Yser-Artois 1915)*, NRF, 1919. On Ghéon, see the thesis by Frédéric Gugelot, *Conversions au catholicisme en milieu intellectuel 1880–1930*, Paris, CNRS Editions, 1998, and his contribution 'Henri Ghéon, ou l'histoire d'une âme en guerre', in Nadine-Josette Chaline (ed.), *Chrétiens dans la Première Guerre mondiale*, Paris, Cerf, 1993, pp. 67–93.

Dupouey composed dossiers containing the intimate notes and letters that she continued to write to her dead husband. The historian feels almost intrusive in being privy to such texts, even eighty years after they were written and forty years after they were published. These papers show the continuation of an astonishing dialogue on love and faith, beyond death, between a couple separated by the Great War only in outward appearance.

> Lord Jesus, I have asked for the cross in order to receive love . . . now you are leading me to Calvary, I thank you . . . If you break my heart, may my broken heart adore you . . . There is something higher than the love of the heart, which is the call of France . . . I feel truly that I loved you more, as Pierre the soldier and as Frenchman first of all . . . My love given for France, given up to God's will . . . How did my heart accept such a tearing away? . . . Oh we must love God with a terrifying love in order to make him such a sacrifice. To love him in order to give him my love? To love him more than my love? . . . You are not dead and I am not widowed . . . I have this infinitely precious mourning because deep and changeless black is the image of deep and enduring fidelity . . . Now all contact is over and there is only the sacrifice – but our hearts embrace.[54]

Pierre-Dominique and Mireille Dupouey as husband and wife had passed from the generation of sacrificial victims to the lost generation.

This sublimation of sorrow into a mingled love for France and Christ appears not only among intellectual couples close to *Action française*. The fiancée of butcher's boy Henri Volatier entrusted their letters to their parish priest, who arranged for their publication. This two-year-long dialogue was not printed in full; perhaps only the most edifying pages were selected, those which best corresponded to the Catholicism which the priest had so successfully taught them; but a certain naïveté which sometimes appears – the result of the soldier's youth rather than his lack of education – still gives the correspondence an air of truthfulness. The young hero who offers himself as a martyr also dreams of 'the good wound' that would bring him back to the girl he loves. But if death does not separate them – 'Let us always be united in the heart of Jesus,' she had written on a note he kept in his wallet – it is the one who remains who now suffers the martyrdom. She has passed from the home front to the front lines, like all those who lost a loved one in the war: 'I am one of the war-wounded now, everything is broken, all is wiped out . . . I am

54. Mireille Dupouey, *Cahiers 1915–1919*, Paris, Cerf, 1944: 4 September 1915, 31 December 1915, 20 March 1917, pp. 36, 96, 117.

suffering greatly but I am proud to have had a fiancé who is a martyr for our country.'[55]

This girl who had said a rosary for her fiancé every evening, and who had done the stations of the Cross with special meditation on the war, belonged to the Dolorist school of Catholicism. This held that the imitation of Jesus could only find enlightenment from the miracles and the resurrection by concentrating on the sufferings of the Passion; it was one of the fundamental aspects of Christian faith throughout the war and afterwards, as parish war memorials demonstrate so clearly.

The Great War is seen by the faithful as an immense Good Friday. 'To think He suffered, and a hundredfold worse, what I see my brothers suffering around me: one crushed under sandbags, another beaten, torn to pieces by shells, yet another dying of thirst in a shell-hole, calling out in vain for his mother.'[56] The miracle of the battles was that they made a Christ of each soldier, and a soldier of Christ: 'The smashed marble tombs in the cemetery gaped over black holes. Christ, torn at last from the dark cross standing alone on the flooded plain, now lay on the ground, cold and livid, his arms outstretched. He was sharing the common lot of our men.'[57]

Joyce Kilmer, a New Yorker recently converted to Catholicism and a volunteer in an Irish-American regiment, created a Way of the Cross at the front in a long poem of two-line stanzas; one line describing the sufferings of the soldier is followed by another matching it with Christ's sufferings on his way to Golgotha:

> My shoulders ache beneath my pack
> (Lie easier, Cross, upon His back)
> My rifle hand is stiff and numb
> (from thy pierced palm red rivers come) . . .[58]

Poets, painters and engravers created an infinite number of these imitations of Christ in the trenches. In 1943, in another war, the former Baptist chaplain Gordon Brownville, trying to persuade his parishioners to accept Christ into their lives anew, tells them of his 'rendez-vous with Christ in a shell-hole':

55. Henri Volatier, *Au vieil Armand*, Paris, Beauchesne, 1918, pp. 132 and 187.
56. Ghéon, *L'Homme né de la guerre*, p. 193.
57. *Ibid.*, p. 122. Many artists took up this theme; see illustrations and extracts from poems.
58. Joyce Kilmer, *Poems Essays and Letters*, New York, 1918. 'Prayer of a Soldier in France', p. 108. Kilmer was killed at the front on 30 July 1918.

Figure 2. 'Popular deed of the Mass. For our soldiers who died for their country. Redemption by Calvary.' (Historial de la Grande Guerre.)

It was here in a shell hole, in a ravine outside of the town of Milleau, that I met Jesus Christ . . . saying, it is I; be not afraid . . . Jesus Christ kept a rendez-vous with me . . . so he will keep a rendezvous with all in their time of need . . . Although I received no vision yet I was keenly conscious of the voice of Jesus.[59]

In no man's land, the land of death, he had found 'Every man's land' – the land of the resurrection.

A certain number of Ways of the Cross were written during the war, all constructed on the same model: the fourteen stations were described and adapted for their intended public, priests or laymen. They stressed the power and value of the indulgence that the Church attached to this prayer. When Jeanne Bloy learned that her friend Jean Boussac had been wounded, she hurried to church to offer him a Way of the Cross.[60]

J. Bellouard, a stretcher-bearer corporal from Poitiers, published several poems and songs in 1915 and 1916, 'for wartime'. His *Chemin de croix pour ceux qui sont restés* sums up – not without a certain literary verve – this Dolorist view of the war.

Lord, my calvary is hard. But yours was harder still . . . So I shall mingle my sweat with your sweat, my tears with your tears . . . Ninth station: . . . I am not worthy of him who fell, poor lad, on the brink of the attack . . . I am not worthy of you . . . Twelfth station: Lord, the slopes of Golgotha are peopled once again. There are numberless crosses in the shadow of your cross . . . Fourteenth station: For once, Lord, you are better off than our loved ones. You have a tomb . . . and our war dead? The shells have toppled everything . . . the graves have disappeared . . . Having nothing left of them here below, not even their dust, I ask that the earth which hides them from me be no longer the trap which holds my heart . . . May those who loved each other and were separated be reunited in glory even in death.[61]

Christ on the cross suffered and thirsted and asked why. Then he began to say the twenty-second Psalm, 'My God, my God, why hast thou for-saken me?' This 'why', springing from the Old Testament and relived in the New, was repeated endlessly by the people of the Great War. And the most frequent answer was also the most terrible: nations, like the individuals of whom they consist, are punished by God to make them

59. Gordon Brownville, *With Christ in a Shell Hole*, Boston, 1943. This rendezvous is of course a paraphrase, in the form of homage, of the most famous American poem of the Great War: 'I have a rendezvous with Death' by Alan Seeger, a volunteer pilot killed in 1916.

60. Léon Bloy, *Lettres à Pierre Termier et à Madame Jean Boussac, lettres à les filleuls*, Paris, Stock, 1928, 18 August 1916, p. 259.

61. J. Bellouard, *Le Chemin de croix de ceux qui sont restés*, Niort, 1916.

aware of their sins, of the need for expiation. These arrogant civilizations were confident that they could live both without God and without war. God sent them the most barbarous of wars, fought with the new weapons of this civilization that was so proud of its technological progress, and this war of progress led to more deaths, to the most terrible suffering, caused by machine guns or poison gas. For most believers, the slaughter was meant to re-establish a balance between sin and sanction. War was a punishment. Dupouey saw the destruction as salvation; he was irritated to discover that the owners of the fine houses on the Belgian coast had made off with all their wealth, including the lids of reliquaries from the churches, and that they had abandoned the bones of saints: 'The sight of a sacked town is decidedly very moral, and the humiliations which industrial art suffers under our very eyes are very comforting . . . Those people really deserve the war . . . One thinks one possesses, and finds one is possessed. The war is a great grace . . . Must all become futile again afterward?'[62]

For others, it was not all false Christians who were punished by the war, but specifically the French, who must expiate the crimes of the separation of Church and State. Joseph Lahitton's book *Le Chemin de croix national pour le temps de la guerre*, published in 1914, is typical of this point of view. The fourteen stations of the Cross become so many cries in which the sins of France, the atheistic and anticlerical republican rabble, mingle with the atrocities committed by the enemy.

> Fourteenth station, Jesus is lowered into the tomb . . . Our enemies, O Jesus, have also sworn our downfall; they are trying to eliminate France from the map of the world and shut her in a tomb from which she will never be able to rise again . . . But France is immortal in her crusade against the barbarous racism and scarlet invasion of the godless.[63]

Texts like this, together with some highly unwise words from the pulpit, helped launch the 'wicked rumour' that the Catholics were supposedly behind the war, and that in the war they hoped for the defeat of France, to bring her fiercer punishment. The implication was that these 'traitors' wanted a German victory, and therefore that they had joined the side of barbarity. Edouard Poulain refuted lies such as 'The priests, seeing their churches grow emptier and the faithful withdrawing from their spiritual guidance, unleashed the war in order to reanimate the faith and to take

62. Pierre-Dominique Dupouey, *Lettres et essais*, pp. 160 and 179.

63. Joseph Lahitton, *Le Chemin de croix national pour le temps de la guerre*, Mont de Marsan, 1914. This style is not surprising in view of the author's standpoint before the war.

the helm once again.'[64] The false logic of this argument, as disproved by the conduct of Catholics – and particularly their priests – both under fire and on the home front, convinced enough anticlerical minds willing to spread it around, forcing the Church's high authorities to reply. Some trials condemned priests to a certain amount of public outcry, and some dishonest anticlericals as well. The *Union sacrée* often had its limitations.[65]

Although the attitude of the Catholics throughout the war confirmed the foolishness of the rumour, their inner struggles did little to bring calm. Making the necessary allowances, they could be compared with the Jansenists of the seventeenth century: their longed-for God was hidden, and the monstrous world they wished to escape was more monstrous by reason of the war sent by the hidden God.[66]

By giving His son to mankind, God had offered the gift of hope: the hope of expiation. The Christians of the Great War lived the war day after day in their flesh: imitation of the sufferings of Christ did not bring despair – quite the contrary. The greater the suffering, the greater the conviction that the kingdom of God was near. Not only was the Christian without fear of suffering and death, he longed for them as signs of his election. Dupouey's chaplain confirmed that 'There is no sad death in this war.' In some cases this faith clearly took a messianic turn: 'The torpedo speeds its blows and sounds the hour that Christ announced. It is the tocsin for the end of the world.'[67]

Asserting one's love for this pain, intellectualizing sacrifice through faith, wanting to serve as a model for future generations and especially for one's contemporaries is one thing; finding serenity in the most absolute horror is quite another.

A student at the Catholic University of Lille, Etienne Derville, saw the war as his novitiate. In personal notes published after his death, he expressed clearly the paradox of a wholly pure faith confronting death, far from the whole-hearted and sometimes untenable enthusiasm of those who are persuaded that the love of suffering will enable sublimation of any unforeseen revolutionary impulse in the name of life. 'Why must

64. E. Poulain, *Réfutation décisive des treize rumeurs infâmes*, Paris, Téqui, 1916.

65. See Jean-Jacques Becker, *1914, comment les Français sont entrés dans la guerre*, Paris, PFNSP, 1977, and *La France en guerre, 1914–1918, la grande mutation*, Brussels, Complexe, 1988 (with chapter on the Churches by Annette Becker).

66. Lucien Goldmann, *Le Dieu caché*, Paris, Gallimard, 1955.

67. Léon Cathlin, *Les Treize Paroles du pauvre Job*, Paris, Perrin, 1920, p. 183 (written in 1916).

one be so afraid of death, in spite of oneself? . . . Only one thing makes me suffer, and that is fear. And yet my life here is better because it is harder, nearer to death and to God. Enjoying too many good things makes one risk loving life too much.'[68] One of Abbé Salomon's correspondents, a young father, wavers between his love of life and his involvement in the war on the grounds of his religious convictions:

> I offer all these torments to God each day in expiation of my past sins and to be worthy of his grace through prayer and as proof of my personal abnegation . . . It is a war of attrition and in my view only a clear intervention by God will bring us out of it; let us hope it will come soon, for we are saturated.[69]

Léon Bloy was near the end of his life. Aged and ill, he was deprived of even more resources by the loss of his kin to the war. All his later writings express the pain of having many friends and godsons at the front, knowing them to be in danger, hearing of their deaths. Violently, he accused the German emperor of these 'murders'. The lifting of the priestly exemption, so that from then on priests would bear arms, was denounced by the great Christian anti-conformist. He wondered, 'But when will he finally show himself, the living God, the adorable God of the Manger and of Calvary, the God of the poor soldiers who lie dying in agony and whom no one looks for any more?' In the name of 'the living God', he execrated the abusive utilization of the dead by – a cheap gibe – heralds like Barrès: 'The professionals of devout journalism are determined to open the paradise of the Martyrs to them. According to them, each one . . . gave his life for the love of God, in a supernatural detachment from all earthly affections . . . yes, indeed, poor soldiers abandoned on the bed of freezing mud which will serve as their winding-sheet.'[70] This breach felt by Léon Bloy and other Catholic witnesses to the conflict recalls the reactions of another writer who was, to be sure, far removed from Christianity – Blaise Cendrars: 'God is absent from the battlefields and the dead of the war's beginning, those poor little *pioupioux* in their red trousers, lying forgotten in the grass, splashes as numerous as cow-pats in a meadow, and scarcely more important.'[71]

---

68. Etienne Derville, *Correspondance et notes*, Tourcoing, 1921. 6 August 1915, p. 151.

69. Salomon correspondence, archives quoted. Letters, July 1915.

70. Léon Bloy, *Méditations d'un solitaire en 1916*, XVI, 'It is undeniable that God exists no longer', XVII, 'The poor soldiers who are dying', *Œuvres*, vol. IX, pp. 258–62.

71. Blaise Cendrars, *La Main coupée*, Paris, Folio/Gallimard, repr. 1974, p. 184.

Offering Faith

Behind the front lines fewer priests and pastors remained to attend to a task that grew heavier with the war. They had to replace all their colleagues, in all aspects of their work, who had departed to the front or who were serving in military hospitals. Above all they had to respond to the new spiritual need of the French nation: people were suffering from the temporary break-up of their families, which would become permanent in more and more cases as the war continued and the deaths multiplied. For civilians as for the military, the clergy offered professional consolation and explanation. The vast – and happily preserved – correspondence of Abbé Salomon, in Neuilly-sur-Seine, provides a fascinating example of a parish priest's role during the war. He received letters from battlefields, from children he had baptized or to whom he had given their first communion; they remembered his saint's day and wished him a Happy New Year, asked him to watch over their families, and most especially to pray for them. Little by little, letters edged in black make it easy to guess their often misspelled and ungrammatical contents.

> Dear Monsieur le Curé . . . I belong to a battalion of labourers making trenches and shelters, I count on your good prayers . . . [22 November 1915] . . . My regiment is called to do serious and terrible things. So I ask you to pray fervently every day for God to keep me out of danger . . . [11 October 1915] . . . Maybe you know we have been hit for the second time . . . [4 December 1916].

On each letter the priest noted the date of his own reply, and often the stub of a money order sent with the reply is folded into the letter. The young men wrote to their familiar priest as they would to a friend, and complained occasionally about the lack of chaplains:

> I thank you for praying to God for me. I have already looked for a soldier-priest but in my company we don't have any. [27 January 1915] . . . You encourage me to do my religious duties, it would certainly be a great comfort, but this is impossible because first of all it doesn't fit in with what we have got to do all day, and besides there isn't any soldier-priest or any chaplain . . . [16 June 1915].[72]

Meanwhile, at the front, official chaplains (four clergymen per army corps: two Catholics, one Protestant, one Jew; and one Catholic per

72. Archives quoted. This last-quoted letter was written on the back of a double card of Notre Dame des Brebières in Albert (Somme). The first picture showed the church before the war, the second 'after several German bombardments'. The card was written and sent a year before the official battle of the Somme. The Virgin, bending forward on the top of the spire, appears to be throwing her son into the space below.

infantry or cavalry division) were supported by volunteers obtained through the efforts of Albert de Mun, and by the 25,000 men of the cloth mobilized as ordinary soldiers or officers. A total of 32,699 priests, monks and seminarians were mobilized, with only 1,500 military chaplains among them. France, like Italy, had no exemption from military service for its priests. About half of the Catholic priests served in the medical services, the others fought like all citizens of the Republic, some becoming commissioned or non-commissioned officers.

In geographical terms, most of the priests came – as logic would demand – from dioceses where religious observance was most practised, particularly from Brittany.

From the beginning of the war a number of hagiographic stories circulated, mainly aiming to prove the fallacy of the 'infamous rumours', recounting chaplains' patriotic and spiritual deeds. The faith and devotion of men of the Church were seen as the cement which held together the union aptly qualified as 'sacred': 'The *Union sacrée*, this divine miracle of the war, is the schoolmaster fallen on the field of honour for his country, cared for by the priest, dying under his eyes and in his arms.'[73] Various religious groups were organized to support this apostolate: brotherhoods of the Sacred Heart, the Catholic Association of French Youth, tertiaries.

> The study circle at the front is not a burden or an empty dream. Just discussing together a book that several have read makes one think. As for St Francis of Assisi, he never found a setting more favourable to the practice of the virtues that make for perfect tertiaries. It is up to us to lead the novices, who are already almost formed by the harsh law of the war.[74]

Thus both the Catholic Church and the nation profited from the efforts of Catholics at the front. The Protestants too managed to organize as much as possible. Behind the lines in the Pas-de-Calais, for example, the Protestant church in Verdrel served as a place for meeting and prayer.

Similarly, the Churches made enormous efforts to share in the financial burden of the war. Their aim was to become reintegrated into the nation so that after the war they could escape their position as pariahs since 1905. Father Coubé was one of the priests who spared no effort to prove

73. René Gaël, *Dans la bataille*, Niort, 1916, p. 218. This paragraph underlines the unifying nature of the *Union sacrée*: wariness or open hostility and distrust between priests and schoolteachers had been a very marked element of French life during the Third Republic, particularly after 1905 and the separation between State and Churches.

74. Geoffroy de Grandmaison and François Veuillot, *L'Aumônerie militaire pendant la guerre 1914–1918*, Paris, Bloud et Gay, 1923, p. 284.

that the Church belonged entirely to the State. He wrote a great deal about national intercessors capable of the most extraordinary miracles for France and we shall return later to his commentary on the Miracle of the Marne. He saw connections everywhere: the most determined unbelievers must be touched by faith during such an extraordinary conflict. Father Coubé was present on all fronts, a man of tireless activity, and the Bank of France distributed hundreds of thousands of copies of his sermon 'Gold the Liberator'.

> We have been right to blast idle money, selfish money, cowardly money. But gold that works and struggles for the country, ah! that kind I bless, and I am tempted to sing it a hymn of gratitude . . . It's the money that crackles in rifle-bullets, the money that hums in aeroplane motors, that flies over enemy lines and lets fall punishment and death. Glory to gold the lover of justice, to warrior gold, to gold the liberator![75]

Although the Churches had lost the education battle at the turn of the century, they still remained largely in charge of hospitals and burial services, in spite of the efforts of secular hospitals in the big cities.[76] With the war, this almost institutional solicitude for suffering and death could only get stronger. The Churches could also seek revenge, to recover a little lost ground: if the rise in the number of civil burials before 1914 matched the rise of religious indifference, the revival of religion due to the war and wartime death would logically return a greater share of this element to the Churches as well.

In Neuilly-sur-Seine, Abbé Salomon continued to receive letters from the front: 'Would you be so kind as to say a Mass for the soul of Paul Fonssan, fallen on the field of honour on 29 January 1915?'[77]

All the Churches published prayer-books in which soldiers were invited to reflect on their final endings. The last page, whether from a Catholic, Protestant or Jewish edition, was always worded the same way: 'I belong to such-and-such religion, and as such, in case of wound or death, I ask for a minister of my faith to take care of me.' Some, struck by the religious ignorance of the men, wrote catechisms for the front.

75. Albert-Duléry-Reyval, *Le Clairon de la résistance catholique, le père Coubé (1857–1938)*, Paris, Téqui, 1939, pp. 188–9. Sermon in the hall of Nice municipal casino, 16 April 1916. Père Coubé preached two other sermons on the same subject, forming his 'golden triptych'.

76. See Bruno Dumons and Gilles Pollet, 'Enterrement civil et anticléricalisme à Lyon sous la IIIᵉ République (1870–1914)', RHMC, July 1990. Despite the increase in secular burials without funeral ceremony, they never represented more than 20 per cent of burials, leaving 80 per cent as religious ceremonies.

77. Archives quoted, 30 April 1915.

Figure 3. Burial of two soldiers at the front. (BDIC, B 1392–14.)

Figure 4. Chaplain leading military burials in a destroyed city of north-eastern France.

Some 150,000 copies were distributed of *Le Livre de prières du soldat catholique*, written by Father Lenoir in the public ward of Autun hospital.[78]

The chaplains of the different faiths sought to respect daily, weekly or annual liturgical rhythms at the front, and to have them respected. Saturdays, Sundays, Christmas, Easter, Yom Kippur and Passover were only rarely free of military duties, even when there was no battle going on. If the war made a mockery of the calendar, even that of men of faith, the men of faith must adjust to the war, since the reverse was impossible. 'I am a wandering priest who follows his parish around everywhere, who sets up chapels everywhere he goes, who catechizes big children, who alas buries the young.'[79] One such was Jean Limosin, volunteer chaplain, as he bent over a wounded man:

> Ah! Chaplain, you are so kind to come and find us. It's very brave of you to expose yourself to danger without being obliged to . . . Look at my medal, this is what has protected me . . . Look at the photo of my little boy, do you think I'll see him again? Yes, I went to confession before leaving and I say my prayers every morning.[80]

For Christmas, a celebration for Christians and for children, some chaplains tried to play to the full their double role of men of the Church and of families – the families of all the soldiers. Sometimes the Nativity was acted out in living tableaux, manger scenes with even the Virgin 'incarnated' by a soldier.[81] Louis Lenoir ordered thousands of little packages which he distributed to his men on 25 December 1915, together with a friend dressed up as Father Christmas. 'The bullets are still whistling round; but Santa doesn't worry about bullets, he comes by anyway . . . Midnight approaches. We return to the village . . . The church being half demolished, the service will be sung in a barn. It's a bigger version of the stable at Bethlehem.'[82]

In the dugouts and the quarries, chaplains became troglodyte priests, saying Mass at altars in the depths of caves. One pastor described a company that came to listen to him directly after the arrival of relief troops:

78. Georges Guitton, *Un 'preneur d'âmes', Louis Lenoir, aumônier des Marsoins, 1914–1917*, 1922.

79. Mgr. Liénart, *L'Ame d'un régiment, l'abbé Thiébaut*, Lille, 1928, p. 66; letter of July 1915.

80. Jean Limosin, *Sur le front lorrain*, Paris, Maison de la Bonne Press, 1916, p. 30.

81. See the unpublished paper by Annabelle Melzer on theatre at the front, Péronne conference, July 1992. Also, postcard showing a performance of the Passion, Diocèse de Paris, historical archives.

82. Guitton, *Un 'preneur d'âmes'*, p. 132.

'A fantastic audience, made up of clay statues, flopped down on benches ... The prayer of the psalmist could be repeated literally: "Deliver me out of the mire, and let me not sink: let me be delivered from them that hate me, and out of the deep waters."' (Psalm 69, 14).[83] Some spoke of catacombs, thinking to revive the hidden cult of the early Christians, relegated like themselves to places of burial, at least temporarily. In the Chauffours grotto the names of the dead are still visible, engraved on the sides of the altar.

> Father X and I make our painful way along a narrow tunnel full of water in places, ending up in the cellar of a destroyed house. This is where the Father will say mass. Have we gone back to the days of the early Church? What a miserable temple! ... A few boards stuck on two sticks, that's the altar ... Soon the whiteness of the liturgical vestment hides the threadbare military overcoat ... only the muddy boots, still visible, remind us that this priest is a *poilu* ... Up above, in the trenches, grenades are exploding ... The celebrant continues to recite the psalm: '*Judica me, Deus, et discerne causam meam de gente non sancta* ...' I respond: '*Quia tu es, Deus, fortitudo mea ... dum affligit me inimicus.*'[84] Never have the prophetic words seemed more full of truth than today ... The enemy presses in on us but God sustains us.[85]

The chaplains who were so close to men in mortal danger insisted on being able to administer communion with the last rites. Father Lenoir became one of the most ardent defenders of this practice, for the soldiers, even at rest, could hardly take communion fasting, and might be called to the front line, and thus to their death, at any moment. These chaplains 'hoping to save thousands of souls that were about to appear before God'[86] could be compared to officers who insisted on decorations awarded to their men who were 'known to be in danger of death' being distributed by a special accelerated procedure.[87] Everyone shared in this patriotic and/or religious fervour.

83. Pasteur Taquet, *A la mémoire des officiers, sous-officiers et soldats protestants morts pour la France en Artois, 1914-1916*, Paris, Fischbacher, 1920, pp. 9, 16.

84. 'Judge me, God, and set apart my cause from the impure people. Because you are, God, my courage, while the enemy is trying to destroy me.'

85. Pierre Ladoué, *Ceux de là-haut, récits et impressions d'un combattant*, Paris, Perrin, 1917, pp. 11-12.

86. Le Père Lenoir quoted by Guitton, *Un 'preneur d'âmes'*, p. 534.

87. The SHAT at Vincennes has two cartons containing thousands of requests such as: '3 July 1918, no. 2543: Please give information on conduct under fire, the manner of service, the circumstances of wounding of 1st grade soldier ... penetrating chest wound from shell ... noted as being in danger of death by ambulance medical head 7/13 and give, after enquiry, notice on headings concerned for reward' 'Reply to your messages of 13 July ... enclosed, 12 *médailles militaires*' (19 N 35/36).

Beyond the most difficult material conditions during which the faithful continued to practise their faith, the decision to turn to belief was also symbolic: the war itself was forced to take part in religion. 'My death will be my last Mass, and I will unite my blood with the blood Jesus shed on the cross, which by my priestly hands he caused to flow on the altar so many times.'[88] A bitter humour appears in the tales of some Catholics:

> Now we are baptized. All that's left is confirmation . . . These trenches are a corner of Purgatory, with the comfort of thinking that Heaven isn't far away.[89]

> Have I received my baptism by fire? They say not. Those shells that didn't kill anyone from our company don't count. Baptism by fire is not conferred thus, by sprinkling. That is the opinion of the ablest theologians of the squad. All the same, the ceremony was noisy enough, even if it didn't achieve much . . . What worries me would be extreme unction by fire.[90]

Are these the games of intellectuals who are accustomed to debate about grace, or a reaffirmation of the importance of the sacraments? More probably these soldiers are trying to exorcise ever-present death by any means at their disposal. Humour and morbidity are constant elements in the descriptions.

Death appeared in the liturgical calendar observed at the front. If solemn processions took place before certain attacks, if Christmas[91] and Easter were often mentioned, particularly by those who came to faith

---

88. François Gaquère, *Sous le feu, en ville et à l'institution Saint Vaast de Béthune*, 1928. Will of Abbé Ditte, June 1916, p. 64.

89. Victor Bucaille, *Lettres de prêtres aux armées*, Paris, Payot, 1916, pp. 38, 49.

90. Paul Cazin, *L'Humaniste à la guerre*, Paris, Plon, 1920. Letter to his wife, 24 March 1915, p. 44.

91. Wartime Christmas carol:

> Dans la paille de la tranchée,
> L'armée espérante est couchée,
> Le sang brûlant malgré le gel,
> Et comme l'enfant de l'étable,
> Elle attend l'heure redoutable
> De s'immoler sur un autel . . .

> (In the straw of the trenches,
> The hopeful army lies,
> Despite the cold their blood runs hot,
> And like the infant in the stable
> They await the fearful hour
> Of the altar sacrifice)

George de Lys, battalion commander, *Le Lion d'Arras*, 15 January 1917.

during the conflict, still it was ceremonies for the dead – like burials or like All Saints' Day – which witnesses referred to most. They associated their wives or fiancées with these new experiences of Mass at the front. Their faith and their love would pass together through the war from now on, risking death together.

> 13 May 1915: I was able to go to a very early morning Mass and take communion. How close I felt to you in that most intimate union with Him who sustains us . . . All Saints' Day, 1915: each of us works together at everything, and everything operates for the best, that is, towards God; so that all, without knowing it, are enrolled in that great army of 'saints' of whom God is at once the end-point and the impulse. Please forgive my little sermon which perhaps lacks a wholly theological rigour . . . I bear you close to God. May He be the link of eternity between us.[92]

As for the chaplains, the essence of their task seemed concentrated in their presence and attendance on the dead and dying. Everything written about them emphasizes this role, as well as the accounts of lay people who refer to them. The publishing house of *La Bonne Presse* produced a series of twelve postcards showing chaplains with wounded or dying men, or with men who setting off to give their lives, 'supreme absolution in the trenches'. The chaplains themselves constantly witnessed the dying words of the soldiers they helped or published letters they were charged to send on to the men's families. 'I am fighting for the salvation of France and the nation . . . I am dying reconciled with God . . . We will all meet again in heaven where we will be happy. Lucien your son who dies a Christian.'[93]

The growing numbers of the dead regularly evoked reflections on mortality, for which men of the Church are theoretically better equipped than other men. The Latin text of the Mass for the Dead can be seen on the portable trench altar now in the Historial de la Grande Guerre in Péronne; Psalm 26 is there too, 'The call of the innocent', a supplication of the individual which is surely particularly well chosen as a text to help soldiers of the Great War: 'Gather not my soul with sinners, nor my life with bloody men in whose hands is mischief . . . Redeem me, Lord, and be merciful unto me.'[94]

92. Masson, *Lettres de guerre*, letters to his wife, pp. 95, 151.
93. Quoted in *Etudes*, 20 February 1916, p. 525. The spelling in the original French is uneducated.
94. Psalm 26, verses 9, 10, 11.

If the austere messages of *Dolorisme* and expiation were acceptable to militant practitioners of the faith, did not this dogmatic harshness run the risk of revolting the non-believer and the non-observer? Far from feeling drawn to remorse for their faults, and turning for judgment to a just God, would they not be tempted to rebel against a God who could allow this 'factory of death' to exist?[95]

The Churches themselves, where they were not destroyed, were used for rows of the wounded and the dead. This territory, dedicated to God, was respected neither by the war nor by death. 'They are dead from head to toe. One would say even their overcoats are dead, all sticky with blood as they are . . . The house of God is nothing more than a muck-heap.'[96] The Church described by Cazin had become a metaphor for the entire world. Being a Christian, then, meant remaining in permanent attendance at an immense Mass for the dead, an infinite Requiem. In music composed in France during the war, the themes of death are omnipresent; and it included at least five Requiems, a genre rarely undertaken by French musicians hitherto.[97]

Prayer-books in French and Latin for Catholic soldiers included prayers for the dead, as well as for souls in purgatory. Similarly, texts distributed to Jewish soldiers stressed the Kaddish. Periodicals designed for chaplains included whole pages of little vignettes to cut out and give to the men, which were indulgences. 'A prayer to be recited to gain plenary indulgence at the point of death.'[98] Documented articles informed priests of their obligations in the face of death, particularly in November. An association was even founded out of specific respect for All Saints' Day.

Sources from chaplains or militants of the faith showed no doubts that all soldiers felt the same thing, even if they did not always express it in the same terms. Care must be taken over these necessarily biased reports: true, soldiers attended religious services for their fallen companions, but surely this was for the most part a comradely homage, a collective act of the squad, a way of continuing to live together for a few more minutes? That was how Marc Bloch experienced and understood it: 'I cannot remember without deep emotion the church of La Neuville. More than once I attended services there for men of the 272nd

---

95. Cazin, *L'Humaniste à la guerre*, p. 193.

96. *Ibid.*, p. 197.

97. Stéphane Patin, researches quoted.

98. *Le Prêtre aux armées*, bi-monthly journal for mobilized priests and monks. *Prêtres-soldats de France*, bi-monthly letters of pastoral information and observance.

who had just been killed by the enemy . . . I always felt I was fulfilling a pious duty in commemorating the dead. What did the ritual matter?'[99]

Chaplains took the dead and dying into their care; it is possible to accept and sympathize with their work without necessarily accepting the message that they instilled into their efforts to deliver comfort. Unfortunately, the very abundance of religious source materials conceals indifference or rejection on the part of the majority of soldiers, who did not express themselves on the subject. But the silence of trench journals on the question is very eloquent.[100]

Capably, and with great sincerity, the utterances of the chaplains always connected and combined faith in the nation with religious faith. The latter might be lacking but never the former: the men of the Churches, who participated in the dominant discourse, could not fail to be accepted, if not as clerics then at least as Frenchmen experiencing the same war effort together.

The Historial de la Grande Guerre in Péronne possesses thousands of postcards that were sent or preserved during the war. Forty-two cards out of this collection are pictures of chaplains saying Mass at the front, or presiding over a funeral service. Is this very small number due to mere chance in the process of acquiring material for the museum, or to the writers' real lack of interest in the subject? In any event, it is interesting to analyse this meagre representation. When a Sunday service is shown, there are few soldiers – between two and about ten – gathered around the clergyman. When the subject is a Mass in honour of the soldiers of a particular regiment who have been killed in battle, the number attending is very high. Clearly this is less a matter of 'going to Mass' than of 'paying one's last respects' to friends who feel all the closer because the same fate can be so easily imagined for oneself tomorrow. Out of the forty-two cards, seventeen were written and sent from the front. In fourteen cases the texts bear no connection to the photograph on the card. One soldier simply wrote over his signature, 'Don't look for me', signifying to his correspondent that he was not one of the kneeling men in the picture. And two correspondents noted that, like the soldiers pictured on the card, they too attend religious services. 'I go almost every Sunday, and we pray fervently to come back safe and sound from this war, and for the success of our arms.'

99. Marc Bloch, *Memoirs of War, 1914–1915* (ed. Carole Fink), Cambridge, Cambridge University Press, 1988 (the translation from the French of this passage is mine). Marc Bloch, *Ecrits de guerre, 1914–1918*, textes réunis et présentés par Etienne Bloch, introduction de Stéphane Audoin-Rouzeau, Paris, Armand Colin, 1997.

100. Stéphane Audoin-Rouzeau, *Men at War 1914–1918*, Oxford, Berg, 1992.

Is it possible to look for conclusions on the basis of such slim evidence? These postcards confirm my hypotheses. Because faith and the war were both concerned with death, they were indissolubly linked, consciously by chaplains and practising observers, and unconsciously by everyone else – the majority.

This link with death lies behind the casual ecumenism at the front: the chaplains, whether Catholic, Protestant or Jewish, were engaged in the same work – they consoled, encouraged and helped. Protestant and Jewish chaplains were obviously a tiny minority, and their flocks sparse: 500 clerics and 150 theology students of Protestant confession, 16 Jewish chaplains in 1914, 46 in 1918.

The chaplains themselves were thoroughly surprised at the pleasure they took in the company of their 'colleagues', whom they had ignored, despised or even hated before the war. They were capable of treating this novelty with humour, as for example the anecdote of four men having to share two beds: 'We draw lots: the pastor lies down with the rabbi (the Old and New Testaments) and dogma, which I represent, lies down beside free-thought.'[101]

Protestants and Jews witnessed human qualities in Catholic chaplains, and vice versa; 'in spite of the divergences of our religious opinions'.[102] The future Cardinal Liénart recalled a dinner with a Jewish major in his regiment, at whose request he discussed with the Protestant clergyman the matters that united and separated them in their faith in Jesus Christ. 'It is the only time during the war when I approached ecumenism at the level of doctrine, but this ecumenism was being lived every day among the men.'[103]

For many Catholic observers, the *Union sacrée* meant above all encounters like these, which were rare before the war but which proliferated in the particular circumstances of the front. Not only did believers of different faiths manage to hold a dialogue that had been unthinkable before; even agnostics, even free-thinkers found themselves confronted with faith, even the act of faith. Edifying little stories tell of many a schoolteacher, hardened against mysticism yet breathing his last in the arms of a chaplain. Such things certainly happened; but the sanctification of yesterday's enemies sounds too neatly constructed to satisfy a historian. If it was not a schoolteacher, it was a former pimp, or an 'apache' who discovered the joys of Christian brotherhood in the trenches. The harder

101. Bucaille, *Lettres des prêtres aux armées*, p. 306.
102. Léonce de Grandmaison, p. 135.
103. *La Croix-Dimanche du Nord*, supplement, 17 February 1973.

it seemed for someone to take the new path, the more gratifying it is to describe him taking it. The strip cartoons for children in *L'Etoile Noëliste* repeatedly illustrated remarkable cases.[104] Were children a particularly receptive audience, thought to be naïvely credulous? The arrival of the Americans was used in the same way by *L'Etoile Noëliste*, with drawings rendering an article published in *La Croix*. A 'free-thinking, anticlerical' barkeeper was enthusiastic about the modern ways of the troops from overseas, who 'install telegraphs and telephones in the wink of an eye'. Disappointed on the other hand that they did not drink wine, he hoped that they would not be going to Sunday morning services: 'Then he is witness to such an astonishing spectacle that it almost chokes him . . . Holding a prayer book or a rosary in their hands . . . the Americans, these ultra-modern men, men of science and progress, Americans with big voices and big hearts, were chanting the Credo.'[105] This charming publication still neglected to make it clear that the great majority of these fervent Christians were Protestants!

Lucien Lévy-Dhurmer painted a fascinating picture, showing a rabbi holding out a crucifix to a Christian soldier who had taken him for a chaplain of his own faith. The dying Catholic is wearing a medal of the Sacred Heart around his neck. The Sacred Heart did not protect the soldier from being killed, but his desire to see the crucifix in his dying moments proves that although his imitation of Christ may be over on earth, he is still convinced he will attain the kingdom of the resurrection. At the request of the family of the rabbi (who was killed at the front shortly afterwards) the Jewish painter Lévy-Dhurmer thus represented a man of one faith helping a fellow man, of another faith, to die in the way he wished. Although the painting in its ensemble is tragic, dark and full of the flames of war, the artist also shows a clear view of heaven. The rabbi's tolerance, his determination to offer the dying man a God who was not his own, express hope in spite of death. In his book *Les Diverses familles spirituelles de la France*, Maurice Barrès recounts the same episode, adding the exact date and place: on 29 August 1914, in

104. *L'Etoile Noëliste*, no. 153, 12 April 1917. 'The Death of Charlot the *apache*'. 'André the good Catholic is spending his last night beside Charlot; both are wounded and are going to die. André: 'It is good, don't you see, to die for one's country, and God will accept our sacrifice and wipe away all our wrongs'. Charlot: 'God? I never thought of Him . . .' 'Can you still say the Lord's Prayer?' 'No, I'm not bothered about greeting God when I get there . . .' 'Say it with me . . .' The prayer came to an end; the 'apache' was no longer moaning, he wept gently and murmured, 'I am not suffering enough . . .' 'Don't worry, my friend, you will go to God purified by your tears and your blood.'

105. *L'Etoile Noëliste*, no. 218, 11 July 1918.

Figure 5. Lucien Lévy-Dhurmer, Rabbi Bloch offering a crucifix to a dying Catholic soldier. (BDIC.)

Figure 6. Christ appears to the wounded on the battlefield. Postcard. (Historial de la Grande Guerre.)

the Vosges mountains, the rabbi of Lyons, Abraham Bloch, dies in his turn – in the arms of a Catholic chaplain. Barrès's whole book is a hymn to the *Union sacrée*, through acts of heroism and patriotic piety. That the incident of Rabbi Bloch concludes the chapter on the Jews is important: 'The old rabbi presenting the immortal sign of Christ on the cross to the dying soldier is an image that will not perish.'[106] Beyond the theme set up by Barrès, surely the most important point for the French Jewish community was the fact that the rabbi could die in his turn in the arms of a Jesuit, Father Jamin. Would Lévy-Dhurmer's hope – that, thanks to the war, anti-semitism would die down – outlive the end of the *Union sacrée*?[107]

106. M. Barrès, *Les Familles spirituelles de la France*, p. 73.

107. Pierre Hirsch, a wartime convert, quoted the same episode and concluded: 'Beneath the wooden crosses there sleeps a nation reconciled.' *De Moïse à Jésus. Confession d'un juif*, Paris, La Renaissance du livre, 1933, p. 157. For the full account of the use of Rabbi Bloch's death by the Jewish community and its shift into myth, see the thesis of Philippe Landau, 'Les juifs de France et la Grande Guerre'. On the Jews' patriotic engagement, the drop in anti-semitism in the *Union sacrée* and the persistence of fundamental anti-semitism, see Raphaël, *Histoire de la France religieuse*, vol. IV, pp. 267-9.

This image of a rabbi offering a crucifix or of a Jewish soldier being comforted by a Christian chaplain was taken up and repeated in all the armies. It can be seen in particular among the Australians[108] and the Americans. 'A man was dying; I offered to pray with him, he answered that he was Jewish. "Do we not have the same God? And my Saviour was a Jew," I prayed, commending his soul to God.'[109]

In *La Nuit de Noël* Paul Claudel linked this wartime ecumenism to conversion. Children massacred by the Germans describe from heaven what they see on earth:

> I see a medical officer in the corner of a hospital, who has just converted, and who is trying to say his rosary . . . I see a rabbi on his knees next to a dying man, helping him to kiss the crucifix . . . I see Renan's grandson . . . He is on the ground, his arms outspread like a cross . . . He bears the sign of St Dominic's flock . . . I see a dying man to whom they are bringing Christ, and who is trying to make a military salute . . . I see Charles Péguy falling with his face to the ground.[110]

Discovering Faith: Conversion

In *La Nuit de Noël*, the convert Paul Claudel gives us a virtual typology of wartime conversion. Some non-believers converted during the war, the war operating as either the initiating impulse or the ultimate destination of their spiritual journey; but in addition the important converts of the years following the 1905 separation of Church and State paid 'significant homage to the war',[111] as a corollary of belonging to their particular generation and the force of their convictions. They became intermediary agents, opening the way for others to engage in belief and conversion. There were therefore some who were converted by the war, like Henri Ghéon, whose conversion story is entitled *L'Homme né de la guerre*, and some who became converts at the war; Ernest Psichari, for

108. Michael McKernan, *Australian Churches at War*, Sydney, The Catholic Theological Faculty, 1980, p. 138.

109. Testimony of an American Christian chaplain in *The Committee on the War and the Religious Outlook. Religion among American Men*, New York, Association Press, 1920, p. 97.

110. Claudel, *La Nuit de Noël 1914*, pp. 586–7. Renan's grandson was Ernest Psichari, a convert in 1913 who became a Dominican tertiary. On Catholic chaplains, see the study by Nadine-Josette Chaline in *Chrétiens dans la Première Guerre mondiale*, pp. 95–120.

111. Etienne Fouilloux, 'Un philosophe devient catholique en 1929', *Actes du Colloque Gabriel Marcel*, 1988, p. 94.

example, whose death in turn fostered faith in others. In addition to the recorded conversion of a few dozen famous intellectuals,[112] evidence from chaplains, pious correspondents and religious journals showed numerous wartime conversions of which it is unfortunately impossible to undertake a statistical study. But by revealing here a network of converts and 'facilitators' who were themselves usually converts both to the war itself and within it, we can throw valuable light on spirituality in time of war.

Of course the converts had the ardour of neophytes. When enthusiasm for the war encountered enthusiasm for faith, individuals who were out of the ordinary could be glimpsed; they had the purity of new devotees but also their intransigence and even their intolerance.

Enthusiasm for war was linked to what could be called 'the 1914 momentum'. First published in April 1917, Barrès's *Les Diverses Familles spirituelles de la France* essentially only took into account testimony from the beginning of the war. Along with those whom he called 'the traditionalists', Barrès could have shown interest in the group of his favourite witnesses, in terms of conversion. Although 'Catholics, Protestants, socialists, all of them, in defending France are defending their particular faith',[113] it is possible to see in Barrès the bard of devotion to patriotism, which he saw as natural, innate, for some and a 'conversion' for others.

The same phenomenon was apparent within the different religious faiths. There were the Catholics, the Protestants and the Jews – and those who become them, in 1914 or later. Although the importance of Catholicism in France was such that here too most of our sources concern it, conversions to Judaism and Protestantism during the war were noted. Unfortunately, to date they have been little studied.[114]

Because Catholicism is the principal religion in France, and because conversions often represent a belated return to the baptismal Church, the majority of conversions were to this faith. 'There are some who returned from a great distance. Some had not approached the communion table since renewing their first communion; many others, not since their marriage. And the war offered them the grace of return. There were

---

112. See Gugelot, 'Conversions au Catholicisme'.

113. Barrès, *Les Diverses Familles spirituelles de la France*, chapter heading, ch. 8.

114. One known Protestant example can be seen in a letter from a soldier unaccustomed to writing: 'Before this war I was not among the most well-informed in my religion. Now I recognize that it is only God who protects me and I advance further and further into belief.' Quoted by Taquet, *A la mémoire*, p. 15.

numerous and serious returns, after three, six, twelve or fifteen years, with a certain delicacy of conscience.'[115] Chaplains reporting such conversions were unfortunately rather imprecise. Although Chapter V of Grandmaison and Veuillot's book is entitled '*Conversions*', details go no further than: 'There were wartime converts in droves.'[116] Twenty-one military chaplains contributed their testimony on conversions at the front, all stressing the large number of souls gained or regained for God. 'For them the war became a field for missionaries. It is certain that the war, for many latecomers, will be worth at least ten missions. And each time I am amazed at the returns which I am witnessing.'[117] A statistical study may be impossible, but there exist dozens of testimonials whose contents are waiting to be studied. The chaplains themselves encouraged it, insisting on the veracity of these returns to belief. Above all they wanted to deny any possibility of conversions motivated by the fear of dying, without any true inner struggle.

The conversion account of Naval Lieutenant X, recorded by his chaplain after his death, is exemplary on this point:

> I have neglected myself for a long time . . . I am sorry about that. From the beginning of the war I have had the idea and instinct of putting myself right with God, of confessing, of living completely as a Christian. I didn't do it because I was stopped by a scruple. I thought it would be neither loyal nor honest to seek God now that I needed him under the threat of danger. It would have looked as if I was proposing a bargain, asking him for my life in return for my submission and adoration. He could have thought I was coming to him through fear of death . . . But now here we are back from Dixmude. I faced death there a hundred times. I escaped. Now I can approach God. God will know it isn't through fear of death, nor through love of life, nor for my own sake; but because of Him, of Him alone.[118]

This conversion or act of grace came close to a religious awakening, two elements which should certainly be kept separate in a first attempt at analysis. Even if there is in fact no religious awakening without

---

115. Geoffroy de Grandmaison and François Veuillot, *L'Aumônerie militaire pendant la guerre 1914–1918*, Paris, Bloud et Gay, 1923. Experiences of various chaplains in 1914 and 1915, p. 297.

116. *Ibid.*, p. 295.

117. *Ibid.*, p. 302.

118. 'Une conversion', in *l'Union des armes, 31 août 1915*. The journal published the chaplain's letter to the wife of Naval Lieutenant X after his death at the front. Henri Ghéon, to whom Dupouey had narrated this conversion, has identified the officer as Lieutenant Illiou (*L'Homme né de la guerre*, pp. 69–70).

individual conversions, these must still all take place within a certain time-limit. It is not only the total number of conversions that constitute the awakening, but the lasting quality of a collective phenomenon.

The specificity of conversion to Catholicism also encouraged this distinction. Catholicism was seen, in effect, as the pure religion of the miracle. Conversions were at once responses to the miracle of God and miracles in themselves. There were thus several dimensions to the presence of God, felt by all converts before the war but intensified during the conflict, as is expressed so well by Jacques Rivière, a convert of 1913 who was to spend most of the war in a prison camp:

> Only miracles convert. And so I must track down the portion of my life that is a miracle . . . Yes, it is indeed a miracle, of the same species as the healing of the possessed, which God exercised on me in granting the prayer he himself had placed on my lips: 'My God, make me undergo a great humiliation!' . . . Taking up the traces of God.[119]

Ghéon gave the same explanation in his conversion account:

> Those who are most astonished at my conversion confess that, all in all, they would have understood a considered move on my part to Protestantism . . . 'Are you no longer a free spirit?' – 'No, I no longer have my freedom . . . God gave me an interpreter of his own choice; I shall read God through the eyes of another, as the Church reads him, as Dupouey used to read him, according to Catholic thinking . . . I don't give two pins for a religion that gets rid of the miracle . . . It was starting off with a miracle that brought my new faith to the point of hearing the voice that preaches love.'[120]

Thus the various signs and wonders of God were perceived as calls to conversion, coming through the mediation of the living and the dead. To remain alive in the conflict was a miracle, bringing conversions in its wake; certain deaths were miraculous, because they incited men to conversion.

Henri Ghéon on leave convinced Gide of what was going on at the front: 'Ghéon, who is not a believer, living in the midst of the naval fusiliers, is overcome by that alliance of faith and courage that he sees creating in them a sort of sanctity.'[121]

---

119. Rivière, *A la trace de Dieu*, 27 February 1917, p. 333. The humiliation was the war, life in a prison camp, bullying, etc. On the condition of prisoners, especially their spiritual condition, see Annette Becker, *Des Politiques humanitaires dans la Grande Guerre?*, Paris, Noêsis, 1998.

120. Ghéon, *L'Homme né de la guerre*, pp. 190–1.

121. Letter from André Gide to Charles Dullin, 26 July 1915. *Registres*, vol. III, p. 259.

Courage, the supreme virtue of soldiers, becomes here an act of faith, and courage in the face of suffering was seen as the highest form of sacrifice. In conversion narratives of 1914–18, the war itself is converted, transformed into a spiritual exercise. War, a political and military sphere, is placed on a religious level.

In modern times the Latin aphorism *Cuius regio eius religio* ('the religion of the prince is the religion of the nation') implied mass conversions and did not always hold meaning at the level of personal faith; but effective solidarities linked groups of converts. In accounts from the First World War, it was both the pre-existing solidarity among the men that created conversions and simultaneously the individual experience of conversion at the front that created new solidarities. Every convert immediately became an effective proselytizer, through his attitude and even his writings. Every convert acknowledged his own intermediary on the route to faith, which might be the war itself or the front-line death of someone close to him, and often felt the urgent need to become an intermediary in his turn.

If the war was such an effective intermediary, it was because it brought about the utter dereliction necessary before any real transformation – 'conversion' in the etymological sense – could take place. Suffering, even the sure approach of death, plunged individuals into a favourable psychological atmosphere. A study of psychological trauma – cases of temporary or permanent hysteria created in the trenches – would no doubt be equally fundamental in understanding the soldiers of the Great War.[122]

'After the enthusiasm of the war, I am now experiencing all its horror. And in this hell, who should one turn to?'[123] The soldier was changed by the war, the reality of the front imposed it. Whatever his enthusiasm,

122. See Georges Dumas, *Troubles mentaux et troubles nerveux de guerre*, Paris, Alcan, 1919. These disturbances caused by the war, of which this great psychiatrist had the impression that many had affected men who were 'predisposed by heredity', are a fascinating topic for the cultural historian to study – something which I intend to undertake soon. Letters quoted by Dumas show the full wealth of this documentation: 'Sir [the Kaiser], please would you be so kind as to return to us Alsace and Lorraine and the millions from 1870 and put everything back as it was?' (p. 8). 'General, I am not mad. It is the voice of God which speaks through me. Joan of Arc, whom I have seen in a dream, has told me to find you; thanks to her I knew, three months before the war, all that was going to happen', etc. (p. 19). For a study of the British psychiatrists (as well as of their chaplains and poets), see Laurinda Stryker, unpublished thesis, 'Languages of Sacrifice and Suffering in England in the First World War', Cambridge University, 1992.

123. Henri Ghéon, letter to André Gide, 1 February 1915, in Ghéon, *L'Homme né de la guerre*, p. 72.

his desire to fight, the force of his patriotic convictions, he was unable not to suffer, not to ask for grace. In this sense, every combatant was transformed by the war. This transformation led him – depending on his encounters, his pre-war social and intellectual milieu, his pre-war religious observance, or lack of it – either towards pacifism, socialism, a wait-and-see philosophy, prayer, irony (even cynicism) and loss of faith, or to religious conversion. Gabriel Marcel, a 1929 convert, explained with his customary lucidity the ambiguity which the war created in him, and thus gave us an active example of these paradoxes:

> I am tempted today to wonder what could have been the war's effect on my religious development . . . I think that superficially the war certainly slowed down my access to Christianity, considered in its confessional aspect. I was profoundly shocked to see how adversaries could each claim God's support . . . But, if one considers things on a deeper plane, I think it was the war that made me an existential thinker . . . And in that way one could say it helped to make me approach more directly, with more immediacy, what I would then have called, and would no longer call, the true problem of religion.[124]

The Dolorist spirituality described earlier transformed the war in its entirety into an immense imitation of Christ. Catholic combatants, singly or as a group, saw themselves (or at least were seen by militant Christians) at the heart of the mystery, of the miracle: that it is out of death that life emerges. As the war multiplied the numbers of the dead, and the horror, the first reflex was one of despair. The man who was seeking God was thus placed in the most materially difficult conditions, which were, paradoxically, the most favourable conditions for the spiritual encounter to take place. God is recognized in suffering. Man is plunged first into the despair of not knowing God, or of thinking he has been abandoned by him. After days, even months of more or less violent internal struggle, the conversion itself takes place. Calm follows agitation, the soothing certainty of having found God succeeds the throes of the search. The individual who has just experienced the abyss and spiritual death lives again, is reborn. Conversion is a rebirth. Converts thus live an imitation of Christ in miniature: the sufferings of the crucifixion are followed by the joys of the resurrection.[125]

124. Gabriel Marcel, *En chemin vers quel éveil?*, Paris, Gallimard, 1971, p. 97.
125. Annette Becker, 'Lord and Tennent, the House of God in America/Le Seigneur et Tennent, la maison de Dieu en Amérique. Du réveil religieux à l'éveil politique dans les colonies anglaises d'Amérique au XVIIIème siècle', unpublished thesis, 1986. William James, *The Varieties of Religious Experience*, 1902.

And thus we have a set of nested mirrors: the war, the collective imitation of Christ, engendering spiritual newborns who imitate Christ as individuals.

The pre-war convert Dupouey expressed it in a letter to his wife: 'I find that our military effort has to be more energetic . . . This is expressed by saying that our capacity for suffering is still much greater than what has been demanded of us.'[126] We can understand how Ghéon, in the depths of horror, without God, can be converted through the example of the combatant Dupouey, his 'saint', his 'intercessor'.[127] The tears that he shed at the death of Dupouey or of others he had never even met were part of his despair, but show too that although he was near the bottom of the abyss, his rise would surely follow. 'My tears will not cease; my despair is limitless.'[128] The blood of the fighting men, like the tears shed over them, became physical symbols of the Imitation, as the convert and former soldier Louis Massignon saw it: 'Tears are the blood of the soul.'[129]

Thanks to Jacques Maritain's published notebooks, we are familiar with Pierre Villard's spiritual progress during the war. In the mind of his chosen correspondent, Jacques Maritain, Villard was a potential convert; but the burst of shellfire that killed him in 1918 prevented him from reaching the destination of belief.

The example of this stranger who one day simply wrote to Maritain seeking his religious help is interesting because it happened in the final year of the war. This is no soldier-enthusiast of 1914, this is a man who has had time to reflect. At times Villard was aware of his own exhaustion, although he continued to carry out his soldierly duty to perfection. 'I am worn out and weary . . . Never have I felt more firm, more resolute, more convinced I was right to join up. My only fear is of meeting my death before coming fully into the light.'[130]

Pierre Villard was seeking God, but unlike his guide Maritain and other converts described here, he was convinced that the war was an obstacle:

Military life has become for all of us soldiers a slow burial of our faculties. That is perhaps what is most profoundly sad about this war . . . These conditions of existence constitute an obstacle to all life, no matter how

126. Pierre-Dominique Dupouey, *Lettres et essais*, p. 183, 12 March 1915.

127. Ghéon, *L'Homme né de la guerre*, pp. 113–14.

128. *Ibid.*, p. 83.

129. Louis Massignon, *Parole donnée*, Paris, Julliard, 1962, p. 172.

130. Jacques Maritain, *Carnet de notes*, Paris, Desclée, 1965. The Villard–Maritain correspondence is published *in extenso*. Villard's letters of 4 and 6 July 1917, pp. 157–8.

incomplete: and all the more so to the Christian life . . . I do not want to fall into idealism. I have no taste for a Christianity cut off from reality.

To which Maritain replies: 'This "burial of all the faculties" caused by military fatigue could be compared, I think, in a soul like yours, to one of those "passive purifications", through the interior darkness and aridity of which the mystics speak. God is at work while the soul perceives in itself nothing but void and inertia.'[131] In two fine expressions, 'Lay down the whole past before God' and 'This life is not our work, but God's work in us',[132] the philosopher confirmed to Villard that far from separating him from his real self and his aspiration to be a true Christian, the war was bringing him closer to it. Maritain would not see the work of God finished in his pupil but, by leaving him his fortune, Villard enabled Maritain and his wife to buy the house in Meudon where they established Thomist study circles and annual retreats. The decision to make his religious intermediary his heir was also the testament of a convert, and a kind of posthumous final step on the path towards the new birth.

For the new births of Ghéon, René X and René Depuichault, death was necessary,[133] the death of man, of a 'saint' among saints – the soldiers of the Great War. This was the place assigned to them in the 'spiritual terrain of intercessions'.[134]

Ghéon assigned this role to the already dead Pierre-Dominique Dupouey, but he was also supported along his road to Damascus by his sister, and especially by Dupouey's wife Mireille, who continued her husband's 'work'. Other women, converts or devoted practitioners, used their wartime suffering to convince their nearest and dearest of the necessity of conversion at this particular moment. Isabelle Rivière, who had lost her brother Alain-Fournier, was convinced that he had returned to God before his death;[135] her husband Jacques Rivière was a prisoner,

131. *Ibid.*, 4 and 18 January 1918, pp. 167–9.
132. *Ibid.*, 4 November 1917, p. 164, and 18 January 1918, p. 169.
133. The two latter cases of conversion through the death of a deeply Catholic close friend at the front are recounted by Pierre Tailliez, *Récits d'un prêtre-soldat*, Paris, 1919, pp. 102, 269.
134. Massignon, *Parole donnée*, first chapter heading.
135. 'See how the last route finally opens out into the invisible trench where the salvation of death lies hidden': Isabelle Rivière, *Vie et passion d'Alain Fournier*, Monaco, Jaspard, 1963, p. 464. This was also the opinion of Michel Suffran, who devoted a volume to him in the collection *'conversions célèbres'*. He quotes an incident reported by Pastor Maury. Early in September 1914 a captain remarked to the pastor: 'Well, Maury, what is your God doing in all this?' A lieutenant hitherto unknown to him replied for him: 'I don't know where God is in this war, because one cannot explain the enigma of the world, but I know

and she hoped that the health of Jacques Copeau would allow him to reach the front: would not his enlistment in the war be the prelude to his conversion? 'With all my heart I wish that you could go so that you might have a chance to feel the great purification, the immense deliverance that war can bring. It cuts all ties with our petty, miserable, normal life, it leaves no communication save only that with pure sentiments, with death which is the wages of life.'[136]

In a less intellectual milieu than the heights of the NRF, Madeleine Sémer – like Jacques Rivière a 1913 convert – was a patriot engaged in a twin faith. She saw as a central aim of the war the conversion of her only son, who was called up in 1915. She had in effect brought him up without religion, and was now convinced that only his conversion at the front would simultaneously redeem her and assure him of eternal life. At his departure she gave him a cross and a medal of the Virgin: 'The cross, even for non-believers, is the symbol of the death of a just and pure man, a hero of sacrifice . . . The medal is an image of purity, sweetness and prayer.'[137] Maritain also sent a medal of the Virgin to Villard, and Mireille Dupouey one of St Anne d'Auray to Henri Ghéon.

Paul Sémer was converted at the front, and so, thanks to the war, Madeleine Sémer felt that she had given birth to her son 'twice over'. Similarly, the actress Eve Lavallière was converted in 1917. On the day of her first communion, the church was prepared for a religious service for a dead soldier. Her account mingles the blood of God that purifies her with the blood of the soldier.[138]

Non-combatants also served as intermediaries or gave comfort to Christians in their faith during the war, men who might be far from the war zones. Thus in 1916 Massignon learned of the violent death of Father Charles de Foucauld in the Sahara, while he himself was at the

---

perfectly well that I shall be hit when He decides, how He decides and where He decides' (Michel Suffran, *Alain-Fournier ou le mystère limpide*, Paris, Wesmael-Charlier, 1969, pp. 230–1). Henri Alain-Fournier was killed a few days later; for a long time those close to him tried to believe that he had been taken prisoner. The discovery of his body in November 1991 has brought to an end a campaign which is more concerned with death than history.

136. Copeau, *Journal*, Paris, Seghers, 1992, 17 November 1914, vol. I, p. 625 (letter from Isabelle Rivière copied out in full by Copeau). Isabelle Rivière was no more able to convince Copeau in 1914 than his friend Ghéon later. He wrote at the time of the publication of *L'Homme né de la guerre*: 'This is terrible to read. These outbursts cause me an indescribable unease. I am ashamed for him. And the worst thing is, that once the book is put down, one finds it uninteresting' (28 June 1919, vol. II, p. 38).

137. Dom Charles Poulet, *La Sainteté française contemporaine*, Paris, Beauchesne, chapter VII, 'Madeleine Sémer', p. 333.

138. Omer Englebert, *Vie et conversion d'Eve Lavallière*, Paris, Plon, 1936, pp. 142–3.

front:'By a strange exchange, he has been killed and I am protected . . .
Raised up above myself, I ascend, seized with holy joy, onto the parapet
of the snow-covered trench, he has found the way through, he has
arrived.'[139]

Finally, it was the great converts killed in the war – in its earliest weeks,
to maintain the integrity of their 'myth' – who arguably made the greatest
impact on their contemporaries, at least on those who were reading
them. Jacques Rivière said it forcefully:

> It would be absurd . . . to think that, because a little piece of metal went
> through their heads, it became impossible to have any contact with men like
> Péguy or Henri [Alain-Fournier]. They haven't been taken away from us. They
> are our dear souls. We still have much to receive from them . . . Never have I
> felt more strongly in me the action of Péguy and of Henri than since I lost
> them. The communion of the living with the dead. The communion of saints.[140]

This same certainty filled Maritain with regard to Ernest Psichari: 'In
truth he had not come to the end of his actions. His radiant influence
over souls took on an extraordinary intensity after his death . . . We know
that God loves the man who gives with joy . . . and that is how Psichari
gave his life.'[141]

Beyond the differences in age, religious belief and literary genius
which might divide Charles Péguy and Ernest Psichari, their almost
identical deaths within a few days of each other in August 1914, the
way in which their friends Massis, Maritain and Barrès took charge of
their memory and spread it throughout the literary world and the reading
public among the combatants, are wholly exemplary.

In the trenches, men read *L'Appel des armes* and *Le Voyage du
Centurion*. The young writer Psichari, completely unknown outside
his circle of a few friends, became the hero and herald of sacrifice for
France. The Psichari cult attained such heights that Copeau, trying to
remain level-headed, grumbled: 'Put that writer of slender talent in the

139. Massignon, *Parole donnée*, p. 69.
140. Rivière, *A la trace de Dieu*, 23 April 1915, p. 267. In January 1916 Alain-Fournier's
mother linked the two friends once more in a very moving message to Péguy's wife:
'Madame Fournier wishes to send Madame Charles Péguy and her dear children her warmest
wishes for the year which has just begun. She thanks her at the same time for the card
which she was kind enough to send during the holiday, a precious card which is a painful
reminder, which has brought back to her the happy time when her son left at the side of
his great friend Péguy, on pilgrimage to that fine cathedral and returned full of faith and
hope. Oh why did Notre Dame of Chartres not protect them?' (*Charles Péguy, Alain-
Fournier, Correspondance*, Paris, Fayard, 1990, p. 252).
141. Jacques Maritain, *Antimoderne*, p. 247.

same rank as Péguy? That's wrong, wrong, wrong, completely wrong!'[142]

Beyond internecine attacks between writers who wanted to claim the writings and deeds of Péguy and Psichari[143] for their particular sect, it is more important for us to follow the posthumous influence of these two men on other soldiers. Letters and reported accounts show that many intellectuals identified with the two writers, in particular with Psichari, who was the same age as most of them. What struck them was not so much the spiritual substitution – Renan's grandson making up for his grandfather's offence against God by his heroic death – as the death of a crusader, who thus became a model.

If Péguy and Psichari took on such importance when dead, it was because of their premonitions of death and their mystical preparations for their future. What remained of Péguy in the trenches, apart from those who were close to him, were some frequently repeated lines of poetry:

> Happy are those who die in a just war.
> Happy the ripened grain, the harvested wheat[144]

Like Joseph Lotte, who was himself strongly influenced by Péguy, and who understood the poem in January 1914, Péguy's readers during the war were convinced that 'what is happening is himself. And it is about being lost or saved. He never stands by the road to watch the soldiers going by: for the soldiers are himself . . . The whole body of work presents itself, so to speak, in the way a man lines up for the Last Judgment.'[145] Even Protestants quote 'the officer-poet' and these same lines of poetry.[146]

142. Copeau, *Journal*, 13 November 1914, vol. I, p. 622.

143. See in particular the Barrès–Maritain polemic of November 1914 in *L'Echo de Paris* and *La Croix*. Account in the *Journal* of Abbé Mugnier, 11 and 19 November 1914, Paris, Mercure de France, 1985.

144. *Eve*, 1913, Charles Péguy, *Œuvres poétiques complètes*, La Pléiade, p. 1028. See chapter 3 and the illustrations for the influence of this poem on the sculptors of war memorials, in particular on Maxime Réal del Sarte. Pie Duployé confirms this use of *Eve*: 'These hundred outstanding lines would alone be kept in anthologies and would very quickly enter the ceremonies of the Third Republic's great commemorations' (*La Religion de Péguy*, Paris, Klincksieck, 1965, p. 303). The original French is:

> Heureux ceux qui sont morts dans une juste guerre.
> Heureux les épis mûrs et les blés moissonnés . . .

145. Durel, (pseudonym of J. Lotte), *Bulletin des professeurs catholiques de l'Université*, 21 January 1914. Péguy, *Œuvres poétiques complètes*, p. 1576.

146. Taquet, *A la mémoire*, p. 8.

Reading *Le Voyage du centurion*[147] in the light of the war and the
death of Psichari/Maxence exerted a mysterious attraction on those who
felt that they were imitating Psichari and Maxence. What was literature
and what was reality for the men in the trenches? In Lieutenant Psichari's
words: 'He is the envoy of a people which knows the worth of the blood
of martyrs. He knows what it means to die for an idea. He has 20,000
crusaders behind him . . . He is the child of suffering.'[148] He who was
described in 1913 at the moment of his conversion by his friends the
Maritains 'as if in the very next instant he was about to take communion
or to die'[149] had suffered the fate of the generation sacrificed in the first
weeks of the war. He died resolutely, in the enthusiasm of communion
with his God and his country. Certain Catholic and nationalist groups
took up the images of Péguy and Psichari, using them for propaganda
purposes throughout the war – once public, faith and conversion became
grist for the mill of advertising.

Jacques Rivière's grief at the deaths of Péguy and Alain-Fournier rings
truer than Joseph Lotte's rhetoric in *Etudes*: 'On the tombs of the
Psicharis, the Lottes, the Péguys, let us swear to take up their unfinished
work . . . Dead men, awake! Sleepers, awake! . . . God will grant us the
victory.'[150] Rivière knew that death was 'something terrible'. Still he
believed; and, he said, death and the war had taught him to be a better
believer. In February 1916, the *Annales de Notre Dame de la Salette*
published an article on 'Ernest Psichari's Conversion and Notre-Dame
de la Salette'. Was it not tempting to plead for Our Lady of the mountain
in the name of the 'leader of the sacrificed generation'?[151] His conversion
had come after the dispatch of a postcard of La Salette by Jacques
Maritain, whose fictional hero, his own double, weeps at the evocation
of the Lady who weeps. The article goes even further: it reminds the
reader that the Catholic soldiers of the Great War, in order to convert, to
believe, to hold out, had need of consolation; in addition to their often
Dolorist and even punitively militant certainties, they needed the

147. Account of an initiation into the desert and conversion to the faith of a young soldier-
patriot, Maxence. The title, of course, echoes the faith of the centurion's meeting with
Christ (Matthew, VIII, 8–9).
148. Ernest Psichari, *Voyage du centurion*, published posthumously in 1914. Paris,
Edition d'aujourd'hui, 1919, p. 33.
149. Raïssa Maritain, *Les Grandes Amitiés*, vol. II, 'Les Aventures de la grâce', New
York, Editions de la maison française, 1944, p. 177.
150. *Etudes*, vol. 146, February 1916, p. 675.
151. Jacques Maritain, *Antimoderne*, p. 224.

consolation of the Virgin: 'the "Weeping Virgin" who had smiled at his conversion had come to seek his soul . . . to introduce him, reddened by sacrifice, into the place of eternal life'.[152]

152. *Annales de Notre Dame de la Salette*, 19 February 1916, p. 579.

2

'Which Saint Will Speak for Me in this Hell?': Intercession

Fighting men and families turned naturally to the intercessors most likely to sustain them. Almost all needed this depth of tenderness, proved in contrary fashion by Abbé Mugnier:

> Nothing is more irritating than to hear nuns, Catholics, saying: 'Prayers, we must have more prayers.' And this is how to beat the Germans! With that tireless praying that survives every failure of novenas, triduums, pilgrimages, apologias, consecrations, and so on. All that piety is irritating . . . We only pray to ask for something, we cannot see beyond that . . . Religion is nothing now but an overworked cult, nothing but masses, communions, Hail Marys, prayers, rosaries, the Blessed Sacraments, the Sacred Heart and the Holy Virgins. How do we find our way through this confusion to the pure and simple lines of the Gospels?[1]

Mugnier feared that such proliferating devotions revealed much more than the disinterested faith that should be their strength – that they risked setting the secondary before the essential, before faith. Undoubtedly many sought temporal comfort in the face of war, but it was pressure of current distress that challenged the Christian message at its very heart.

The Virgin Mary, whose many appearances marked the nineteenth century so deeply for the French, was the focus of more prayers than any other figure. Other popular intercessors were Thérèse of Lisieux, Saint Denis, Saint Martin, Saint Remy, Saint Genevieve, Saint Clotilde, and the blessed Joan of Arc.[2] Among those described by Abbé Coubé as 'our allies in heaven',[3] we must distinguish between intercessors called on to meet the needs of nationalistic and hagiographic propagandists

1. Abbé Mugnier, *Journal*, 25 June 1915 and 19 February 1917, Paris, Mercure de France, pp. 290 and 308.

2. Etienne Fouilloux, *Histoire du christianisme*, vol. XII, Paris, Desclée Fayard, pp. 190-9.

3. S. Coubé, *Nos Alliés du ciel*, Paris, Lethielleux, 1915, publication of his 1914 Advent speeches.

like Coubé, and others widely acknowledged as deeply and genuinely popular during the war.

Although such devotions – dedicated to the Virgin, Sister Thérèse of Lisieux or Joan of Arc – were strongly encouraged by the Church, some were so heavily favoured by the faithful that they appeared to overwhelm a delighted hierarchy that was nevertheless unaccustomed to such fervour. In contrast, other objects of devotion (the Sacred Heart of Jesus in particular) were more deliberately favoured by the clergy and propagandists within the French Church. Devotions springing from 'on high' or from 'below', multiple and burgeoning devotions created fears of excess and even superstition, while others hoped for a real religious awakening in France at war with promise of fruition to come.

> Prayers and medals accompanied soldiers to the front: I am convinced that prayers work because God loves prayers . . . As I leave you I beseech your prayers, for only in prayer can we find happiness, as we wait for better days to follow these terrible ones . . . Send me a little medal to remind me of you.[4]

> My dear brother, as I write, Maman is wrapping a parcel for you, with a little bottle of iodine in case you need it, to use with a firm bandage. You must wear the two medals, the St Anthony and the other one, because Maman is taking them off to give to you. Put them on, they will bring you luck.[5]

Jacques Maritain did the same for Pierre Villard: 'I am sending you a medal of the Holy Virgin, it would give me great happiness if you would wear it for me, not out of superstition but as a sign of our spiritual affection, and because the humblest material signs can be the occasion of a blessing or an act of God's grace.'[6]

Even ecumenism found a place in this enthusiasm for medals. English soldiers – few of them Catholic – asked the nuns of Albert, in the Somme, for 'medals, crucifixes, and even our pocket rosaries'.[7] Pierre Hirsch intensified such hopes of protection: 'Little holy medal . . . I entrust myself to you. You will go with me, on me, beside the medal I received from a Protestant lady when I left for the front, and the mezuzzah my father, an old soldier of the army of the Loire, gave me as he said goodbye and blessed me.'[8]

4. Correspondence of Abbé Salomon, archive quoted. Letter of 21 November 1915 and 17 February 1915.

5. Postcard from the sister of Joseph Foulquier, 1915, quoted in Rémy Cazals et al., *Années cruelles 1914–1918*, Carcassonne, Atelier du Gué, 1983, p. 69.

6. Jacques Maritain, *Carnets de notes*, Paris, Desclée, p. 159.

7. Charles Calippe, *La Guerre en Picardie*, Paris, Téqui, 1916, pp. 46 and 298.

8. Pierre Hirsch, *De Moïse à Jésus. Confession d'un juif*, Paris, 1933, p. 193.

Intercession

The Imitation of the Virgin

The Virgin Mary was the first focus of devotion. It is no surprise that 'The great consoler of the nineteenth century'[9] was a constant presence throughout the war. What finer symbol of enduring faith than the ex-voto crutches ('in gratitude for being healed') at La Salette, taken from the sanctuary walls for the war-wounded in the hospitals of the Grenoble diocese?[10] Discarded, no longer needed because of the miraculous 'weeping Virgin' but offered up in thanksgiving as public testimony to faith, the crutches regained their initial function with the added certitude of another miraculous healing.

In March 1918, as Paris suffered under bombardment from Big Bertha, Jacques and Raïssa Maritain left for Rome to plead with Benedict XV the cause of the visions on the mountain, intellectuals of the faith engaged in the same spiritual combat as the Dauphiné pilgrims who reached the summit of Trièves on foot. In April the Maritains had an audience with the pope to encourage his reading of the manuscript written by Maritain after 1915.

> *Jacques Maritain*:   The Virgin wept at La Salette, it is because of her tears.
> *Raïssa Maritain*:   Tears are a fitting response to the present state of the world.[11]

Militant, like J. K. Huysmans, Léon Bloy, Paul Claudel and Louis Massignon, on behalf of the Virgin of La Salette as 'regulator of penitence',[12] the Maritains insisted on the Virgin's overwhelming capacity for suffering. That was the cause of her popularity during the war. It was as the supreme mother, Virgin of the Seven Sorrows, who had always known and believed, that she was now implored and acknowledged.

The almost mythic final hours of the war for Charles Péguy were experienced as 'an immense pilgrimage at the end of which he would encounter the Virgin'.[13] He is held to have spent the whole night piling flowers at the feet of a statue of the Virgin. Similarly, the painter George Desvallières placed statuettes of Mary everywhere he could at the front, and the sculptor Maxime Réal del Sarte did the same with statuettes of

---

9. Philippe Boutry, *L'Histoire*, no. 50, November 1982, pp. 30–9.

10. *Annales de Notre-Dame de la Salette*, November 1914, p. 130.

11. Jacques Maritain, *Carnet de notes*, p. 124.

12. Jacques Marx, 'La Salette dans la littérature catholique des XIXe et XXe siècles', *Problèmes d'histoire des religions*, no. 2, 1991, pp. 95–121.

13. Halévy's expression was quoted by Raïssa Maritain in *Les Grandes Amitiés*, vol.1, New York, Editions de la maison française, 1941, p. 102.

Joan of Arc. Little private chapels to Notre Dame de Lourdes, Notre Dame de la Garde, Notre Dame des Victoires, Notre Dame de Fourvière, Notre Dame des Ormeaux, or Notre Dame de Bon Repos were created near the trenches or hollowed out of the soft chalk itself. Postcards of soldiers praying to 'Our Lady of the Trenches' or at 'the Church of Our Lady of the Trenches' were sent from the front or from home. Some had rough verses:

This Virgin was found	Cette vierge fut retrouvée
in a bombed-out church	Dans une église bombardée
in a severe baptism of fire.	Par un baptême de feu intense.
And the *poilus* call her	Et les poilus l'ont surnommée
Our Lady of the Trenches	Notre-Dame de la tranchée
For she keeps them going.	Car elle soutient leur patience.[14]

The pediment of a chapel in the Argonne bore a far from classical inscription: '*Reginae Victoriae, Pilosi milites aedificarunt hanc Ecclesiam*'.[15] Translating their affectionate nickname into Latin the better to honour the 'Queen of Victories' the 'pilosi milites' – hairy soldiers, the *poilus* – reveal in touching fashion the depth of the cult of the Virgin among the Catholic soldiers of the Great War.

In 1915, Colonel de Fossa was surprised to find almost a hundred messages to the Virgin on the altar of the little sanctuary at Noulette, at the foot of the battle-scarred hill of Lorette. The whole area was in danger of total destruction at any moment. The 'notes to the Holy Virgin', piously collected and sent to the bishop of Arras, Monsignor Julien, were published in facsimile in 1925 and provide a fascinating source for measuring the Mariolatry of soldiers at the front. Forty-five of the seventy-two messages thank Our Lady of Lourdes for protection up to that moment in 1915. Including invocations to 'the Holy Virgin', 'Holy Mary', 'Our Lady of Lorette' (eight) and to Our Lady of Deliverance (two), these seventy-two messages are addressed to the Virgin close to the hill of Lorette, which is logical. It may be that the Virgin of Lourdes was invoked most frequently because those men who noted their regiment were from the south-west, from Pau in particular. Perhaps they added the regimental number specifically to show that their homes were near the Massabiele grotto, in the hope that the Virgin they used to pray to, far from the war, would find a way to protect them in these 'accursed' times. Although some sophisticated notes were written by men accustomed to writing,

14. Collection, Historial de la Grande Guerre and Pas-de-Calais departmental archives.
15. 'For the queen of Victory, soldiers [*poilus*] built this church' (*L'Eglise de France pendant la guerre*, Paris, Perrin, 1919, p. 57).

most show hesitant or even phonetic spelling with occasional touches of Occitan dialect, recalling the language of Bernadette Soubirous herself: 'Souvenir avou sientte bonne Vierje marie Jusqua prèssant voum'avès conservé la vie je toujour confiance on vou pries pour nous qui avon recours avous'[16] [In memory of you blessed holy Virgin Mary Until now you have preserved my life I always have faith in you pray for us who turn to you].

Whenever the Virgin appeared in the nineteenth century she seemed to favour children, shepherds and shepherdesses. These messages, partly expressions of gratitude for protection up to that moment and partly cries of hope for a future visibly laden with tragedy for these young men, seem to echo the pattern. Twenty-nine of them ask to be able to see their 'little family' again, eight are thinking of their friends and brothers fighting in the same battles. All feel the horror of the times and are desperate for the protection of the Virgin. The war receives a qualifying adjective seventeen times: it is 'damned' (*maudite*) eight times, 'long and painful' (*longue et pénible)* three times, 'terrible' twice, and 'cruel': 'May the war end soon'. Only one letter speaks of '*la chère patrie*', 'the beloved country', and one of victory.

> Notre Dame de Lourde je madresse avou pour que vous me donnies la grasse derevenir un jour mon petit foiyee avec toute ma petite familles que je sui eloigniée. Preservé moie contres les maleur que jerisque chazue jour, et jevous ansuplie, faitte arêter le plus possible vitte ce Terible Carnage qui faet tant de Cadavre. Prier et levee lébras pour aréter tou ça je vous an serée reconnésant toute ma vie. Basses Pyrénées.[17]

> [Our Lady of Lourdes I turn to you so you can give me the grace of coming home some day my little home with my whole little family how far away I am. Preserve me against the disasters I risk every day, and I beg you, stop as fast as you can this terrible carnage that makes so many corpses. Pray and raise your arms to stop all this I will be grateful to you for the rest of my life. Basses Pyrénées.]

This evidence of the horror of war reappears among Father Salomon's correspondents. The writers were practising, even devout, Catholics, not atheist pacifists: 'What butchery', 'our country costs us dear', 'and one wonders when it will end and we will have the joy of going home to take up our lives set aside for this scourge'.[18]

---

16. *Lettres de Guerre à Notre-Dame trouvées dans l'oratoire du Parc de Noulette* (Pas-de-Calais), 4 July 1915. Letter no. 17. Original French spelling and punctuation shown.

17. *Ibid.* Letter no. 65.

18. Archives quoted. Here, letters from 1915 and 1916.

In 1918, the magazine *Etudes* recalled the importance of the simple prayer repeated millions of times during the war: 'Holy Mary, Mother of God, pray for us sinners now and in the hour of our death.'[19] This is appended to a card of Noulette, printed like a bulletin from the front, using the usual military language: 'This card is to be delivered to the regimental postman. It must bear no indication of its place of origin, nor any information relating to military operations.' The addressee in this case was 'Our Lady of Lourdes', and the 'part reserved for correspondence' reads as follows: 'June 8, 1915. My dear, dear mother, I am here to thank you for your divine grace which you have had for me, protecting me up to today, I beg you to watch over me and my comrades for the rest of this terrible war. (and my little family) Hail Mary . . . and at the hour of our death. Amen.'[20]

The Virgin was the most popular intercessor, being at one and the same time daughter of the Father, mother of the Son, and bride of the Holy Spirit. Throughout the nineteenth century – at places like la Rue du Bac (1830), La Salette (1846), Lourdes (1858) and Pontmain (1871), to mention only her most significant appearances – she showed particular favour to the French, whatever the tenor of her messages. The causes of Catherine Labouré and Bernadette Soubirous, who had died in an odour of sanctity, were introduced: the messengers of the Virgin would become saints.[21]

Every soldier of Catholic origin, even if non-practising or barely a believer before the war, could not help knowing all this. It only took a few words from the chaplain, a practising comrade or a militant of the *Rosaire vivant* for a man to pray to the Virgin, the supreme representative of the distant family. The *Annales de Notre-Dame de la Salette*, which in 1914 became the official organ of the *Association de Familles Chrétiennes*, bore this out confidently: 'In the aftermath of the war the Christian family will reap the fruit of these seeds of moral and social resurrection that are springing like a rich harvest from the great furrows of the trenches.'[22]

The religious hierarchy never lost sight of the future of the Church. Acts of faith were noted, published, advertised. Postcards of Mary were distributed everywhere, at home and at the front, pious images used as

19. Jean Dissard, 'La transfixion de Notre Dame', *Etudes*, vol. 155, 5 May 1918.
20. Letter no. 71.
21. *Histoire de la France religieuse*, vol. III, XVIIᵉ–XIXᵉ centuries, Paris, Seuil, 1991. Philippe Boutry, pp. 494–510. Bernadette Soubirous: cause introduced in 1913, beatification 14 June 1925, canonization 8 December 1933.
22. *Annales de Notre-Dame de la Salette*, 19 May 1915, p. 307.

vectors of an immense war correspondence, from missals offered at First Communions and the mailbags of civilian and military postmen. 'Blessed Virgin, protect our children . . . The Virgin Mary is with our valiant heroes who give their lives generously for Faith, Civilization, Justice.' Even when not used for correspondence, the cards still fulfilled their basic function as pious images. As written communication, the messages on the back often had little connection with the sentimental image of the Virgin on the front. They carry news, best wishes, hopes of coming home on leave. When the text is neutral, is it in order to strengthen the impact of the image, or because it is taken for granted? Was it impossible to send such explicit images without noticing them, without knowing what they signified? Perhaps some soldiers had nothing else to write on. The *Maison de la Bonne Presse* was well distributed at the front.

The *Rosaire vivant* is a powerful example of this osmosis between the genuine determination of the faithful to find true intercession, and the response of the institution.

The work of the *Rosaire vivant*, founded in the nineteenth century by Pauline Jaricot, re-established a form of devotion with distant medieval origins. For many years it was a Dominican monopoly, before becoming a liturgical feast based on the miracle of Lepanto on 7 October 1571. In several encyclicals on the Rosary Pope Leo XIII demonstrated his militant commitment in favour of this prayer.[23] God granted Mary a special place in the mystery of the redemption and 'The Rosary, this pattern of prayer, contains complete within it the entire cult of Mary.'[24]

If the original spirit of the Rosary was one of sacred joy in the Annunciation, the 'Hail Mary', it had quickly taken a more sorrowful turn. Moreover, the recitation of the Rosary had also become intertwined and decked out with the practice of indulgences. The *Rosaire vivant* claimed 100,000 subscribers during the war – obviously a low number in view of the millions of men involved, but a high number for such a demanding and highly structured activity. 'Each group of fifteen members constituted a Rosary, with a chief of the Rosary at its head. Each group of five members formed a "chapelet", with a chief of the chapelet at its head.'[25] Each subscriber received a monthly newsletter, *Petites fleurs du Rosaire*, with thoughts for time of war and especially a calendar of the month and a prayer, with several copies supplied for wider distribution. The calendar for March 1916 is typical of this trench literature:

23. *Adjutricem populi. Octobri Mense. Magnae Dei Matrix.*
24. Pope Leo XIII, *Octobri Mense.*
25. *Les Oblates de Marie immaculée pendant la guerre*, p. 215.

The Rosary prayer for salvation: I am still alive, I owe it to my good Mother . . . The danger was so great and the shells were exploding all around. All is well, we hope it will always be well with the protection of our Mother in Heaven.

The Rosary prayer of the trenches: In the woods we have murmured our prayers, our chants . . . under shelling and in the midst of the dead and dying. The Holy Virgin has protected us![26]

A form slipped inside the leaflet contradicts this optimism with its statistical coldness: 'Please fill in the following: Rosarians of my *Rosaire* killed in action . . . Missing . . . Wounded . . . Recommended for bravery . . .' This specialized 'Supplement to the *Rosaire vivant*' was seen only by subscribers, and was not to be shared like the prayers. Rosarians were expected to understand that the death of hero-saints was not really death.

Soldiers and their families could subscribe to the various publications produced by Marian sanctuaries: *Annales de Notre-Dame de la Salette* or the *Journal de la Grotte de Lourdes*. *Recommandations* ('Testimonials') and *Actions de grâce* ('giving thanks') circulated from the front to the home front and back again, by way of the sanctuaries of the Virgin, but without the hardships of pilgrimage. 'Two wounded soldiers, healed and returned to the front, thank Notre-Dame de la Salette for her motherly protection . . . My devotion to Notre-Dame de la Salette grows steadily, and I feel that my continuing survival is due to her intercession. Every night we dig trenches and we sometimes feel that we are digging our own graves.'[27]

Prayers to the Virgin at the front were matched by pilgrimages to various Marian sanctuaries by soldiers on leave or their families. The great diocesan pilgrimages to major sanctuaries were of necessity interrupted during the war, but, as in 1870, other pilgrimages proliferated.[28] In every part of France, prayers were offered to the Virgin closest to home, encouraging the increase in little local sanctuaries.

We separated after long embraces, and went directly to Saint Vincent's Church, and they showed me a chapel right at the back with a Virgin holding a branch. She was Our Lady of Good Help. A big tricolour flag hung at her head, against the wall, with plaques of marble all around her fixed in the wall or set on a big marble table, engraved with words of gratitude, and placed there by the relatives of soldiers at the front, their husbands or sons. My mother had bought

26. BDIC 8P229.
27. *Annales de Notre-Dame de la Salette*.
28. Michel Lagrée indicates this in particular in Brittany. Michel Lagrée, *Religion et cultures en Bretagne, 1850–1950*, Paris, Fayard, 1992, p. 305.

a photo of the Virgin, and she told me to place it among the flowers and the plaques. We said a Paternoster, and every time she came to town she went and knelt in front of this Virgin and prayed for me.[29]

Even Lourdes saw pilgrims primarily from the Pyrenees region, in addition to the war-wounded in its hospitals. Badly wounded men taken to Lourdes inevitably saw the choice of this town for their treatment as a good omen. So close to the grotto, so close to the Virgin, a miracle was more than probable, it was credible: after all, they had risked death a thousand times but escaped with no more than a wound.

In 1915 the Association of Notre-Dame de Salut organized a national pilgrimage to Lourdes, in spite of the war. The retreat speeches by Reverend Emmanuel Bailly were published promptly: 'What are you doing in Lourdes in this year of 1915? You have not come to present the Virgin merely with the sick and infirm . . . You have come to place at her feet our armies, our wounded, our losses; you have come to offer her the floods of tears and blood of all the victims of the war.'[30] The war aroused two religious attitudes: on the one hand, it was seen as a punishment of sin, while on the other it created an immense need for comfort in distress. Both attitudes were a source of spiritual progress, and were not contradictory. And although Father Bailly supported the punishment view, he knew, if he wanted to convince his listeners and readers, that faith in miracles is attained through the desire for consolation.

Overwhelmingly, prayers were addressed to the Virgin as protector, for succour and to give thanks for what was felt as a miraculous escape from death. Indeed, statistics prove that to have escaped death or serious wounding between 1914 and 1918 was such an extraordinary display of chance that it inevitably caused questioning amazement. At a superstitious level, a 'lucky star' was invoked; in the register of faith, it was a miracle. If Lourdes was hard to reach, the many imitation grottoes that appeared all over late nineteenth-century France could serve as substitutes.

Marble ex-voto plaques can still be seen today inside many churches, untouched since the Great War. The vast majority date from 1918 and 1919 as, sure that all danger was definitely over, the faithful came to thank the Virgin, often as the outcome of a vow pronounced during the

29. Account by Marius Hourtal, published in 1978. Quoted by Cazals, p. 56. (The church of St Vincent in Carcassonne still has the statues and ex-voto plaques.)

30. Emmanuel Bailly, *Retraite du pèlerinage national à Lourdes, 19–22 août 1915*, Paris, Maison de la Bonne Presse, 1915.

war. They can be found in sanctuaries dedicated to the Virgin, or in specially dedicated chapels in simple parish churches. Often statues of the other major intercessors of the war decorate the same chapel: Joan of Arc, Marguerite-Marie Alacoque, and especially Thérèse de Lisieux. 'Thank you, Notre Dame de la Peinière, for your protection during the war'; 'Thank you, 1917'; 'Thank you for bringing Papa back. In Gratitude, 12 July 1919' (Notre Dame de Pontmain); 'In Gratitude to Notre Dame de Valcluse, 1914–1918'; 'Gratitude to Notre Dame du Bon Port for grace obtained, August 14–July 17' (Antibes, Notre-Dame de la Garoupe); 'Eternal gratitude to Notre-Dame des Dunes who protected me, my family and my property during the terrible war 1914–1918. Dunkerque, 11 November 1918. V.E.'

The basilica of Fourvière in Lyons has the largest number of ex-votos engraved during the war that I am aware of. This does not mean there were not just as many in other sanctuaries, but that they were often removed and placed in storage in the course of later restoration work.

At Fourvière, the crypt walls are entirely covered with these rectangles of marble engraved in gold, with dates running from the end of the nineteenth century up to the 1980s. The panels of the choir consist almost completely of ex-votos dating from the Second World War. In the nave, of fourteen walls covered with ex-votos, nine are devoted to the period from August 1914 to 1920: and so the great majority of these plaques, several hundreds in all, relate to the Great War, and turn the basilica of Fourvière into a reliquary of the suffering and hopes of the soldiers and their families.

Both before and after the war, Mary was thanked for a cure, or for avoiding accidental death. During the war and immediately after it, gratitude was expressed exclusively for having escaped from death. 'Gratitude to Mary, 2 August 1914–11 November 1918'; 'Thanks to Mary for having protected our three sons during the war 1914–1918'; 'Officer grateful to Notre-Dame de Fourvière'.

Although most messages thank Mary, some have chosen the name of Our Lady of Fourvière specifically, just as in Antibes some address Our Lady of Bon Port, or some in Dunkirk address Our Lady of the Dunes. The vows behind these plaques were intended to reach the Mother of Christ, but some proclaim allegiance to a local cult, either because the donors come from the region, or because the specific message of the Virgin – even the church building itself – was better suited to their spirituality. Indeed, the basilica of Fourvière was itself constructed as an ex-voto, in recognition of the Virgin's protection of Lyons during the Franco-Prussian War and invasion of 1870–1. Commissioning a marble plaque to decorate the crypt of an ex-voto building with an ex-voto text formed part of a process of connection with Mary, the Church, the city of Lyons and with the historical memory of the nineteenth century and the nation leading up to the First World War.

In this interplay between the war – identifiable by its dates and sometimes the name of a battle or a regiment – and death, faith and nation, certain arrangements of ex-votos are particularly significant. In the centre of a panel, one plaque materially identical to all the others reads: 'E.C. who died for his country'. It is the very life of their relative or friend that has been offered here by those who had this message installed. Plaques of gratitude to Mary have been arranged all around it; they too appear to be implicated in the offering of this death in the war, so that it helps to mediate in favour of intercession. Similarly, in Antibes, at the centre of 'ordinary' ex-votos, there is a sample of the honorary diploma sent by the authorities to every family with a relative who 'died for France'. Rude's patriotic bas-relief is thus twice removed from its original use: the sculpture, chosen by the authorities of the Republic, was first used to embellish the diploma of honour for those who were killed in the eponymous battle. As a metonym, it represents the *Arc de triomphe*, the victory of republican courage over death. (The diploma was of course created before the decision to bury the Unknown Soldier beneath the arch.)

What was the intention of the parents of Joseph Bollier, what did they wish to say to Mary, when they presented this precious document which should have taken pride of place at home beside the photograph of their dead son? They transformed this official paper into a relic for everyone to see; and since they could not thank the Virgin for having saved their son, they could still be confident that they had 'imitated' her. Unlike the majority of these ex-votos – plaques that remain anonymous or identifiable only by initials – the name of the dead man offered to the Virgin is fully and elegantly inscribed on the diploma; the gift is personalized, as are the ex-votos with portraits. The most spectacular ex-votos are in fact part of an artistic legacy, of the nineteenth century, including of course the Franco-Prussian War of 1870–1. They are particularly prevalent in the south of France, at Notre-Dame de Laghet near Nice, Notre-Dame du Bon Port in Antibes, Notre-Dame de la Garde in Marseilles, and at Notre-Dame du Château at Allauch. The pictures, painted or embroidered, were hung during the war in response to a particular divine favour granted, and especially, like the marble plaques, just after the end of the war. The year 1918 was not seen as the moment of victory, but as the incontrovertible certainty of grace received, of

Figure 7. Ex-voto to the Virgin, Notre-Dame de Laghet (Alpes Maritimes): 'Thanks to Notre-Dame de Laghet for the grace received for our dear sons from 1914 to 1920.'

Figure 8. Ex-voto at Notre-Dame de Laghet. While the husband fights at Verdun, his wife prays, both under the protection of the Virgin (drawing by the soldier himself).

having been spared. Soldiers and their families vow 'eternal gratitude' to the Virgin who brought them safely home. One mother embroidered 'Thanks to Notre-Dame de Laghet for favours received for our dear sons, 1914 to 1920'. She added various ornamental embroideries and attached a Sacred Heart in stamped metal and a photograph of each of her two sons.

All the pictures, painted or embroidered, include some words of gratitude to Our Lady, as if, in this world of only recent literacy (proved by mistakes in spelling or grammar, in contrast with the faultless marble ex-votos, the work of professional engravers), the image alone was not strong enough to express the full feelings of gratitude.

The double register, of earth and heaven, has been well analysed in a study of Provence of the eighteenth and nineteenth centuries by Bernard Cousin.[31] The Virgin looks down from the top part of the picture, but the war has invaded everything. For example, there is a picture at Notre-Dame de Laghet where flames and cannon-fire appear to rise to meet the rays emanating from the Virgin. These ex-votos are saying that even the most industrialized of wars leaves a space for the miraculous: but this must be confirmed in writing, in the cry of gratitude which overlays the image and restores faith in miracles to its prime position.

The grateful soldiers occupy an appreciable part of these creations, usually in three ways: as main subject of the ex-voto, they are represented in combat, at the very moment of the miraculous event; their name is almost always indicated as a 'signature' of the thanksgiving; and finally a photograph is added, attached to the frame. The photographic evidence reinforces the determination to be accurate, clearly shown in the details of the design and the very individualistic feeling of the offering. This particular individual received a special mark of grace, and he is bearing witness. In collective danger, war, he personally has been saved, and the Virgin has to know that he knows it.

The entire process is explained in a letter of recommendation of 1916:

Permit the mother of an ordinary soldier of 24 to recommend him to your prayers to Notre-Dame de la Salette . . . I attach his photograph; the weeping virgin will recognize him for She has already seen him praying six years ago, up there . . . He has already been protected several times. He wears a medal of the Holy Virgin and an image of the Sacred Heart . . . Oh! may Our Lady of

31. Bernard Cousin, *Ex-voto de Provence. Images de la religion populaire et de la vie d'autrefois*, Paris, Desclée de Brouwer, 1981; *Id.*, *Le Miracle et le quotidien. Les ex-voto provençaux, images d'une société*, Aix, 1983; Catalogue de l'exposition *Ex-voto du terroir marseillais*, archives communales, Marseilles, Imprimerie municipale, 1978. I am deeply grateful to M. Cousin for sending me this catalogue and enabling me to find new examples.

La Salette preserve our son for us . . . and may he be able to return again to this blessed mountain to thank her and take back his photo which he will exchange for a little ex-voto, not a big one, for we are poor.[32]

These ex-votos provide settings for the miracle, they are dramatized prayers and hymns to life from men and women who had recently endured mass death. This had already happened with the ex-votos installed after the war of 1870. One stands out as different from the individual practice described above: the ninety men of Allauch who were mobilized in 1870 all returned unharmed, and collectively thanked the Virgin. They commissioned this picture, and the painter inscribed all their names on it.[33] Although I am not aware of any such collective ex-votos for the Great War, the reason is not far to seek: it was impossible for any group of ninety men in the front line to return unharmed.

At Notre-Dame de la Peinière, in the diocese of Rennes,[34] 'the observer in Bréguet aircraft no. 2752, who miraculously escaped death when the pilot was killed', created a picture in which the art historian interested in coincidences would see a collage closer to the New Realism of the 1960s than the beginnings of Cubism. Lieutenant Verten de la Mermandière set a captioned photograph of the accident and the scattered remains of the aircraft at the centre, surrounded by symmetrically arranged pieces of the aeroplane. The title of the work, 'Ex-voto of gratitude', and the word 'miraculously' are the only religious elements of this montage. Text, photograph and aeroplane debris have been carefully arranged and framed in order to be hung in the sanctuary. It would be a magnificent illustration for Jacques d'Arnoux's *Paroles d'un revenant*. The lieutenant, shot down at Chemin des Dames in 1917 – miraculously saved but grievously wounded – then battled with pain for seven years before he was finally able to walk again.[35]

This offering in recognition of a miracle can be compared to many other votive gifts hung in churches: helmets pierced with bullet holes, or the military medals found everywhere in France.[36] The faithful render up to the Virgin the human proofs of their courage. They show her that they are not fools; that they know they really owe her everything, because her intervention has made their salvation visible.

---

32. *Annales de Notre-Dame de la Salette*, 16 January 1916, p. 558.
33. *Ex-voto du terroir marseillais*, p. 125.
34. On this sanctuary, see Lagrée, *Religion et cultures en Bretagne*, p. 306.
35. Jacques d'Arnoux, *Paroles d'un revenant*, Paris, Plon, 1925.
36. *Ex-voto du terroir marseillais*, pp. 133–4.

Our Allies in Heaven

To give thanks to the Virgin or the saints is also to attribute the victory to them. Gifts of medals, ex-votos of gratitude, 'Thanks to the Virgin' or 'Thanks to Saint Valéry, 1914–1918' are a visible participation in a politico-religious view of intercession.

This produced the certainty that the victory of the Marne in 1914 was a miracle of the Virgin, as all Catholic observers noted that 8 September was the feast-day of the Virgin's nativity. A whole body of literature was created on the basis of this coincidence of date and the apparently incomprehensible halt in the German advance. It was driven in part by the declarations of generals, the ceremonies presided over by Cardinal Amette in Paris, and by the need both at the front and at home to find some meaning in the rapid advance of the Germans, and then the sudden reversal of the situation.

> In the great battle of the Marne between the Feast of the Nativity and that of the Holy Name of Mary we had on our left St-Geneviève, in the centre St Rémi and on our right Joan of Arc ... The Great Battle, like the fires of Purgatory. The whole of France in this long furrow, awaiting the day of the Resurrection.[37]

This determination to add a spiritual element to the military halting of the Germans was similar to displays that followed the vision of Mary at Pontmain during the first Franco-German war.

Indeed, the Pontmain vision, on 17 January 1871 at the height of the Prussian advance westwards across France, had been perceived as a miracle:

> Mary brought to her rebellious daughter
> The pardon of Jesus, which at Pontmain forced
> The German conquerers to flee, back on their tracks ...[38]

Scholarly works even quoted the commander of the Prussian troops: 'It's over, we won't get any further. Over there, in Brittany, an invisible Madonna is barring our way.'[39] This appearance of the Virgin at the place indicated on the military map, as well as the use of the enemy's words,

37. Paul Claudel, *Journal*, vol. I, 1904–1932, Paris, La Pléiade, 1968, October 1914, pp. 298–9.

38. Joseph Odelin, *Du théâtre à L'Evangile, les étapes d'une conversion, 1850–1917*, Paris, Beauchesne, 1919, p. 240.

39. Bernard Saint-John, *L'Epopée mariale au XIXᵉ siècle*, p. 330. Von Kluck himself, noting in his memories his great surprise at the resurgence of the French troops on the Marne, was to repeat the arguments in favour of the miracle again after the war.

finds its parallel in 1914. Between 1871 and 1914, a whole Marian literature had been preparing minds for such things.

Although Léon Bloy often fulminated in his *Journal* over the neglect of this miracle, an abundant literature on the subject appeared throughout 1915, culminating in the anniversary of the battle in September.[40]

On 8 September 1914, the priest Jean Quercy wrote in his journal (published in 1915):

> What troubled the minds of the Kaiser and his General Von Kluck? Was it gentle Geneviève who stopped this new Attila? Was it Joan of Arc, angry at seeing him violate Compiègne and Reims? Was it Our Lady who wanted to expel him from the land where her sanctuaries flourish? . . . I await strategic explanations for the victory; but I certainly have the right to have our supernatural allies hovering over the battlefields of the Marne. The best military critics recognize that every victory has its mystery; that is God's element.[41]

This text is an echo of the sermon of Mgr Gibier, Bishop of Versailles, on 5 September 1915 in the cathedral of Meaux. Jean Quercy arrogates to himself 'the right' to believe in miracles despite anticlericals, nonbelievers or those of faint belief who saw religious demonstrations over the victory of the Marne as unpatriotic. Were the soldiers and their generals not capable of winning? Did they require external intervention, however miraculous? The fight against pre-war anticlericals, buoyed up by 'infamous rumour', found a new source of inspiration.

In 1916, Abbé Coubé wrote in the preface to a missal of the Marne miracle: 'To awaken and perpetuate our gratitude to God for the great favour of the Marne victory, such is the aim of this prayer-book and its pious illustrations.'[42] The text was a repetition of what had become commonplace in only two years: there are absolute miracles beyond all human comprehension, and relative miracles, where God chooses a side and then permits an unforeseen outcome, as in the miracle of the Marne. It was a victory where 'God helps those who help themselves.'[43] The courage of the French soldiers brought God's intervention, putting him squarely on their side and thus ensuring victory. Abbé Coubé was

40. Victor Giraud, *Le Miracle français*, Paris, Hachette, 1915.

41. Jean Quercy, *Journal d'un curé de campagne*, Paris, Beauchesne, 1915, p. 107.

42. *Missel du miracle de la Marne*, with 16 engravings by Joseph Girard, p. 16 (Historial de la Grande Guerre, Péronne, Somme). The missal is reproduced in Annette Becker, *Croire*, Paris, CRDP Editions, 1996, p. 45.

43. Capitaine Ferdinand Belmont, *Lettres d'un officier de chasseurs alpins (2 août 1914–décembre 1915)*, Paris, Plon, 1916, p. 279, 6 November 1915.

repeating the argument of members of the Church hierarchy, such as Mgr. Gibier, Bishop of Versailles, or Mgr. Marbeau, the Bishop of Meaux.

This debate over the miracle also appears in many letters. The Miracle of the Marne was seen as proof of the Virgin's intervention on behalf of France, a continuation of her many French appearances in the nineteenth century. The December 1914 issue of *Annales de Notre-Dame de la Salette* debates the matter:

> Could it be that Providence arranges these connections in order to sustain our faith and confidence? Here are a few that we are reporting, with appropriate reservations: it was on 8 September that the enemy began to withdraw. It was on 19 September (anniversary of the 1846 appearance at La Salette) that communiqués announced for the first time that the enemy was leaving the department of the Aisne. May the good Mother our Queen continue her historic interventions in favour of her 'land of France'.[44]

Not only does the 'coincidence' prove the miracle of the Virgin, but it serves as a reminder of her appearance in 1846, in Dauphiné, in France. The Miracle of the Marne even proves, against the grain, the sayings of Mélanie, somewhat disdained and even disbelieved by some of the hierarchy and the faithful. In certain Catholics, militancy is revealed once again as inseparable from faith.

The illustrations of the Missal of the Miracle of the Marne are particularly interesting in this respect. In sixteen engravings, 4 centimetres by 6, set continuously above the text and repeated every 16 pages, Joseph Girard gives a résumé of Catholic thought on the miracle of the Marne, set in the whole context of the war from the moment of mobilization. The fine quality of the original drawing, the engraving, the page design and the production are as striking as the message contained in these drawings. Form and content have been carefully studied and linked. When one is aware of the poor technical and artistic quality of many contemporary productions – books printed too quickly with too few means – the elegance of this work takes on the character of a miracle.

It shows soldiers determined to set off for the war, then retreating, with 'the enemy in sight of Paris'. In the distance, men in pointed helmets can already make out the Eiffel Tower, symbol of French modernity, like the electric wires crossing the entire small village in the engraving of the mobilization, a very improbable reality in the France of 1914. But the enemies perceive most especially the towers of Notre-Dame and the silhouette of Sacré-Cœur. Engravings that might seem strictly military and

---

44. *Annales de Notre-Dame de la Salette*, December 1914, pp. 173-4.

descriptive are discreetly filled with symbols which go on to be developed throughout the other pictures. The book opens and closes with Christ showing his sacred heart, and St Geneviève protecting the city of Paris, symbolized by its two sanctuaries, Notre-Dame and Sacré-Cœur. Abbé Coubé recalls that St Geneviève had 'worked' with St Clotilde for the conversion of Clovis, taking the sequence logically to the image of Reims, 'the martyred cathedral', in flames. But now the men in the foreground are no longer soldiers caught in the throes and disasters of war. 'The Adoration of the Sacred Heart' of 4 September and the 'Triduum of 6, 7 and 8 September' were acts of fervour that precipitated divine intervention. The engravings thus function on a double register, earth and heaven. A crowd of saints watches over the cathedral of Reims, which will not be completely destroyed; armies of knightly saints ride across the sky over the French cannons. Christ on the cross illuminates the battlefield, his sacrifice taking place in the sky above the heads of soldiers being disembowelled by bayonets, while military chaplains say mass in the trenches and bury the heroes who have now become saints. Side by side, 'France in Montmartre' and 'France at the Vatican' give thanks to the Sacred Heart and to the pope for the miracle. The engraver has skilfully drawn the two domes of Sacré-Cœur and St Peter's in Rome so as to exaggerate their resemblance; to architects or art-lovers, this may be a lack of honesty, but the objective is not concerned with aesthetics. The engravings show the heart of Catholic Paris joining the heart of Christianity by way of the Miracle of the Marne. The episode becomes a new feat of God on behalf of the French and lets them hope for a renewal of relations between France and the Holy See. Under the title *Le Pape, la guerre et la paix*, Charles Maurras published in 1917 his 139 major articles written since the beginning of the war. 'The most valiant, most eloquent, most decisive defender of the Catholic cause'[45] could have illustrated his book with the work of the engraver of the Missal.

Unfortunately we do not know how many copies were printed of this missal, a masterpiece of luxurious propaganda; but, going well beyond the militaristic 'eyewash' of Catholic activists close to *Action française*, it helps to explain the blend of beliefs that helped to sustain the soldiers of the Great War. Faith in their country, a basic ingredient of the struggle, was shored up by a faith composed of many threads, but which can be called religious. This vaunted, often exaggerated, and often misunderstood fervour certainly existed, and the victory of the Marne was to some

45. Eugen Weber, *Action française*, Stanford, Stanford University Press, 1962.

extent the fundamental link in the sequence of miracles experienced both collectively and individually by the French during the Great War. Whether despite or because of propaganda, faith is no joking matter in questions of life and death – of oneself, one's country or one's civilization. 'Never since the time of Joan of Arc has it been clearer that the supernatural governs the world.'[46]

Many postcards repeated the message. Christ and other 'heavenly allies' – St Michael, Joan of Arc, St Geneviève – pray: 'Protect them, Lord, for our army to be victorious, for the greatness of our future, for the glory of our nation.' Soldiers' letters and prayers follow exactly the same pattern: 'I went to pray to Our Lady of Hope, our local Madonna. The Grace of God is almost the only feeling I am concerned with.'[47]

After the Virgin, Joan of Arc and Thérèse of Lisieux were the two most popular intercessors of the war. Neither had yet been canonized,[48] but throughout the war both were already addressed as saints, as shown by the hundreds of ex-votos displayed in the chapel of Carmel de Lisieux: 'Gratitude to St Thérèse of the Infant Jesus who protected and saved me at Verdun on 26 July 1916. Adrien B., soldier.'

Perhaps, like Marguerite-Marie Alacoque, these two girl-heroines of the faith – one from the remote fifteenth century, the other recently dead – owed their canonization in the 1920s to their popularity during the war. In effect, the two campaigns, set in motion in the nineteenth century, were strengthened from their roots by piety in the trenches and on the home front.

Joan, like the Virgin, was the bringer of victory; Thérèse, like the Virgin, offered protection and consolation. As if they had allied themselves with Mary in her varying functions, the two future saints offered the certainty of miracles, collective or individual; they presided over conversions. Belief in the reversibility of suffering lay at the roots of this fervour. From the dramatic event of the Crucifixion, the martyrdom at Rouen, or the long dialogue with the unseen in a death at twenty-four, came the lesson that the greatest sorrow gives birth to the highest bliss. The great mass of the soldiers of 1914 shared the youth of Joan and Thérèse.

In an Artois church transformed into a military hospital, the soldiers lying on the floor of the nave could see only the three statues standing

46. *Journal de la Grotte de Lourdes*, 10 January 1915.

47. *Correspondance* of Abbé Salomon, 24 February 1917.

48. Joan of Arc: her cause was presented in 1894, she was beatified in 1909, canonized in 1920. Thérèse's cause was presented in 1914, she was beatified in 1923 and canonized in 1925.

Figure 9. Soldiers in a church converted into a field hospital. Joan of Arc has been put above the altar. (Collection Frédéric Gugelot.)

on what had been the altar: the Virgin flanked by Joan and Thérèse. The cult of Thérèse certainly preceded her promotion to sainthood. It was inevitable that, once recovered, these men would go on to thank the three mediators, or at least the one which each found particularly dear: the Virgin, for whom all things are possible; Joan of Arc, whose faith and patriotism are inseparable; Thérèse, with her infinite compassion. Even without being wounded, thousands of soldiers sought out churches, which might be partly ruined, but whose solidly built walls could still offer shelter. In the midst of such ravages, if one statue were preserved, how not to read a miracle into it?

The 'statuemania' of the nineteenth century had not only brought republican heroes to public squares. The most popular saints of the nineteenth century had been sculptured, installed by the thousand in the humblest parish churches, and among them, ahead of all others, were the mediator-women. As women, they had principally attracted the prayers of women, in the same way that pious books had been mainly read by women.[49] These books and sculptures were the work of men, for a public that was mainly female. At the front, a world of men was now discovering them and soldiers' correspondence often referred to these spiritual encounters of the war. Their letters noted them for their wives and parents, who before the war were seen by the men as more pious than themselves, and the sharing of prayers and devotions thus formed a fundamental link between trench and home front. Sacred medals and prayer-books were exchanged, as well as postcards designed as pious images. 'O blessed Joan, intercede with almighty God, that He may protect our armies and those of our allies. Pray that he may spare the lives of those we love and who defend us, that he grant them the courage to suffer and the strength to conquer the barbarians.'[50] No less than this could be expected, from the saint described by Abbé Coubé as 'the most French saint in heaven . . . Her patriotic role is not ended; war

49. Claude Savart, *Les Catholiques en France au XIXe siècle, le témoignage du livre religieux*, Paris, Beauchesne, 1985, p. 673; C. Savart, 'A la recherche de l'art', known as Saint-Sulpice, *Revue d'Histoire de la spiritualité*, 1976, no. 53, pp. 265–82. In this pioneering article, Claude Savart attempts a detailed account of the statues in some twenty churches of the Haute-Marne between 1860 and 1930. His very small sample (119 statues) nevertheless illustrates what is very evident for the war period. The 36 different subjects include 27 representations of the Virgin, 17 of Christ (including 12 of the Sacred Heart of Jesus), 10 of Joan of Arc and 14 of Thérèse of Lisieux. (He did not attempt a tally of calvaries and crucifixes.) Only St Antony of Padua, with ten statues, approached this popularity among purchasers, sculptors or the faithful.

50. Postcard, collection Historial de la Grande Guerre.

is her element; she is the invisible generalissimo of 1915.'[51] The war gave Joan of Arc a true 'rallying function' for the whole French nation, through the *Union sacrée* and anti-German hatred. Charles Calippe described a girls' boarding-school occupied by the Germans in Roye, in the Somme: 'They shattered a magnificent statue of Joan of Arc who, from her finger pointing to heaven to her pure gaze, no doubt appeared too menacing to these pioneers of a *Kultur* that every page of the Gospels condemns.'[52]

Many American soldiers, Catholic or not, were fascinated by the myth of Joan. In tours organized for them before their repatriation in 1919, the visit to Domrémy was almost as important as the visit to Paris, as proved by collections of postcards taken back to the United States from France, showing the cathedral of Reims in ruins or the château of Versailles. These tourists and collectors were primarily American soldiers, with a very clear ideology: they were bringing home images of everything they had helped to protect from German destruction. They had participated in saving French civilization, of which Joan of Arc was one of the most powerful symbols: 'Most of us had heard of her in school, but we would never have imagined visiting her native village. She had led a crusade for freedom, and we knew we were doing the same thing.'[53]

A trace of this kind of fervour can be found in the correspondence of Louise de Bettignies, a young woman from Lille who was arrested and condemned to death by the Germans for working for the Resistance in the north of occupied France. From the fortress of Siegburg where she awaited execution or clemency, the heroine who risked her life in missions for the Intelligence Service did not forget her desire to enter the Carmelite sisterhood, and the recent example of Thérèse: 'I discovered that this time I was spending in prison was an excellent novitiate . . . Was it not the moment to live out the prayer of oblation of

51. Coubé, *Nos Alliés du ciel*, p. 193.

52. Charles Calippe, *La Somme sous l'occupation allemande*, Paris, Téqui, 1918, p. 209. For a recent analysis of Joan of Arc, see Gerd Krumeich, *Jeanne d'Arc à travers l'histoire*, Paris, Albin Michel, 1993, and Michel Winock, 'Jeanne d'Arc', in P. Nora (ed.), *Les Lieux de mémoire* 'Les France', 3, 'de l'archive à l'emblème', Paris, Gallimard, 1993.

53. Clarence L. Maham, 'Hoosier Doughboy', unpublished memoir, First Division, Carlisle Barracks. Quoted by Mark Meigs, *Optimism at Armageddon, Voices of American Participants in the First World War*, McMillan Press, London, 1997. Although, as seen in a letter from Harry Guryn to his mother, not all soldiers were equally thrilled by their visit to Domrémy, the influence of Joan of Arc on the life of the American soldier and in particular on his sacrosanct game of baseball, was unmistakable: 'I had the chance to visit Joan of Arc's home village, but I preferred to play baseball, and naturally we lost. It's the first time that we lost.' Quoted in Frank Freidel, *Over there: The Story of America's First Great Overseas Crusade*, Boston, Little Brown, 1990, p. 194.

Little Sister Thérèse? This dear sister keeps me company, like the memory of Mother Isabelle. Add Christ to the list, and you will know my cell-mates.'[54]

Thanks to the Carmelites of Lisieux who were editing *Pluie de roses* (their account of Thérèse's interventions, to be added to the dossier on beatification then being considered in Rome)[55] we can read most of the letters addressed to Thérèse during the war.[56] Not all have been published, and unfortunately we do not know how many were received. The preface makes it clear that the editors chose to publish 'only one or two interventions of the same type, for one cannot keep count of all the bullets stopped by a relic, a medal, an image or a leaflet of Sister Thérèse. Several of these "shields" have been sent to the Carmel as evidence, and one can see on them the ragged traces of projectiles.'[57]

The letters are printed in chronological order. They become more numerous from 1916, the year of the great battles of Verdun and the Somme, but this may reflect an editorial decision. Most were sent from the front, from hospitals, but civilians also reported acts of protection. There are letters from all parts of France and the colonies, as well as from foreigners, Italians or Englishmen – surprising in view of the low percentage of British Catholics. (The Irish are quoted separately.) Clearly, this publication does not lend itself to a serious quantitative study, but it offers the contents of 223 letters for analysis. It also adds the texts of ex-votos placed on the walls of the chapel of Carmel during the war and still visible there today.

The cover of the book sums up the essence of the contents in a pious image, divided into three levels. In the background several burning churches are shown against the sky, the most recognizable being the cathedral of Reims. In the centre, the men of a 'Batterie Sœur Thérèse' are resting after the attack, one of them reading, unmistakably and fervently, *L'Histoire d'une âme*, the posthumously published autobiography of the Lisieux Carmelite sister, of which 800,000 abridged copies were printed in 1915. Thérèse stands in the foreground before a calvary cut in two during the battle, but on which one can still read the words 'spes unica' (our only hope). Her gaze and her raised hands

54. Quoted by Antoine Redier, *La Guerre des femmes. Histoire de Louise de Bettignies et de ses compagnes*. Paris, Editions de la vraie France, 1924, pp. 255-6.
55. The speed of the process is worth noting: it was undertaken early in 1914, only seventeen years after the death of Thérèse.
56. *Pluie de Roses. Interventions de Sœur Thérèse de l'Enfant-Jésus pendant la guerre*, Bayeux, 'Pour le Carmel de Lisieux', 1920.
57. *Ibid.*, p. viii.

summon luminous rays and a shower of roses which descend from the sky to illuminate and transform the battlefield.

The engraver has captured perfectly the atmosphere of fervour surrounding Thérèse and created by her. It emanates from the letters where she is described as 'the little sister of the trenches', 'the favourite war-godmother of the fighting men', 'the *poilu*'s saint', 'the soldier's shield', 'the angel of battles'. The engraving was reproduced as a postcard, and can be found in great numbers among image collections of the First World War. On the back is printed the famous quotation of Thérèse: 'I want to use my heaven doing good on earth. After my death I will cause a rain of roses to fall.' Unlike other postcards sent during the war, where we have already noted the frequent lack of relationship between the recto and the text on the back, those that show Thérèse praying for the soldiers carry written messages clearly indicating why the card was chosen. Some on pilgrimage to Lisieux mention it, others echo the message printed on the card: 'Happy to know you are better, I thank the good Lord, through the intercession of the young nun whom we have prayed to on your behalf.'[58]

It is not surprising that Thérèse – in her youth, in the simplicity of her dialogue with Christ, in the radiance of what seems to be the power of her death – should have been so important to the Catholic soldiers of the Great War and their loved ones: 'Of course we have Joan of Arc, but the little sister is much closer to us.' This soldier is unconsciously analysing Thérèse's creative effect. Although in her determination to give her life to Christ by way of Carmel she seemed less obviously destined to become a saint of the trenches than the patriotic Joan, still her emphasis on family, on constancy and the need for suffering could not fail to touch the young men of her generation, unprepared for these years of suffering that they were undergoing. Not only do they thank her for her protection from wounds and death, in letters which are so many ex-votos often accompanied by medals or pious objects carved for display at the Lisieux Carmel, but many of these texts also describe conversions caused by the appearance of the 'little sister' in their lives. She was lending a sort of meaning to their war by making them into Christians.

> I had left the Church after my first communion. Still, when I departed for the front, I accepted a relic and an image of the Little Sister, and each time I found myself in danger in battle, I instinctively called on her for help, noticing that every time she was protecting me . . . It was at a very hard moment, for the guns were roaring at each other full blast. I was thinking with great sorrow

58. Collection Historial de la Grande Guerre.

of my little family and I said to Sister Thérèse: 'My sister Thérèse, bring me back, I beg you, to my wife and my children, and I promise you I'll go to your tomb . . .' Scarcely had I uttered this prayer than I saw a cloud open above me and the face of the saint stood out against the blue sky. I thought I was the victim of an hallucination. I rubbed my eyes over and over, but I could not doubt what I saw, for her face got clearer and more resplendent as I gazed . . . Since that time, I have no longer felt alone. I also felt the strongest hope of seeing my family again and I kept alive the unshakable resolution of returning to the God of my childhood.[59]

The Sacred Heart of Jesus

'God is with us! The Sacred Heart, the Holy Virgin and Saint Michael will take into account all these our sufferings, for the remission of so many of our sins.'[60] The devotion to the Sacred Heart of Jesus provides another way of assessing and differentiating clearly between proselytism from above during the war, and the expectations of the faithful. Intimately identified by its adherents with France itself from its earliest days, the cult of the Sacred Heart was already well established by 1914. From the visions of Marguerite-Marie Alacoque at Paray-le-Monial under Louis XIV to the Chouans in the 1790s and the charge of General de Sonis and his Pontifical Zouaves in the battle of Loigny in December 1870,[61] the notion had developed of inscribing the Sacred Heart on the king's flag and later on the flag of the Republic. France, the eldest daughter of the Church, felt compelled to show the world a model: the consecration of an entire nation to the Sacred Heart. In Paris, the basilica of the Sacred Heart (Sacré-Cœur) was built between 1876 and 1910, after its official consecration voted by the National Assembly in 1873; now it stood high over Montmartre, open night and day to the devotions of the faithful.[62]

59. *Pluie de Roses*, p. 4.

60. Etienne Derville, *Correspondance et notes*, Tourcoing, 1921, September 1915, p. 165.

61. Michel Lagrée notes that one-third of the 3,000 French troops were Breton. His description matches closely that of the Catholic soldiers we are discussing here: 'There is a type with a specific "vocation", reminiscent – deliberately – of the medieval crusade, but also of the militant warrior for which the modern era, since the French Revolution, supplies many examples' (Lagrée, *Religion et cultures en Bretagne*, p. 158).

62. Close to the vast figure of Christ in the mosaic of the dome, Marguerite-Marie Alacoque and General de Sonis appear among the fervent admirers of the Sacred Heart. See Jacques Benoît, 'Le Sacré-Cœur de Montmartre, spiritualité, art et politique, 1870–1923', Ph.D. thesis published under the title *Le Sacré-Cœur de Montmartre de 1870 à nos jours*, Paris, Les Editions ouvrières, 1992.

Christ's message to Marguerite-Marie, delivered in his appearance of 1675, contained both a threat and a message of infinite love for mankind: unrecognized love demands atonement. The Paray message has its origin in a dialectic between love and fear, between the unknown gift and punishment. In 1689, the message with its universal tenor was 'nationalized': the Sacred Heart will reign over France on condition that Louis XIV has its symbol embroidered on his standards. The entire devotion to the Sacred Heart would henceforward rest on this hope of a contract between the Sacred Heart and Louis XIV, to be transformed in the nineteenth century into hope for a contract between the Sacred Heart and the French authorities, whom the partisans of the Sacred Heart would strongly prefer to be monarchical. Despite Marguerite-Marie's beatification in 1864 and the continuing flood of pilgrims into Paray-le-Monial, the longed-for contract remained a pious hope. Neither Louis XIV nor his successors as Heads of State ever followed the comminatory visions of the Visitant. But the great crisis of 1870–1, which for French Catholics combined the disasters of defeat, the Paris Commune and the fate of the Pope, reminded them that sin was the cause of it all; could the Sacred Heart be the cure? The proliferation of pilgrimages to Paray in the years 1870 to 1880, and the constant repetition of the National Vow: 'Pity, oh God! It is for our country . . . Save Rome and France / By your Sacred Heart'[63] revealed the remarkable growth of this devotion. The dioceses of the south-east, close to Paray, were well represented, with many pilgrims from the west as well.

During the Great War, 'an original trinity was established between religion, patriotism and populationism'.[64] Because the family was central to devotion to the Sacred Heart it easily met the main concerns of the soldiers of the Great War, and their letters reflect this representation. Pierre Tisserant evokes this familial devotion:

Poor little Maman, I can still see you on pilgrimage to Notre-Dame des Victoires[65] and to Sacré-Cœur, and I especially see you praying steadily all night for me. I must be well-protected by this network of prayers, but on the other

63. Philippe Boutry and Michel Cinquin, *Deux pèlerinages au xixᵉ siècle, Ars et Paray-le-Monial*, Paris, Beauchesne, 1980, p. 291.

64. *Ibid.*, p. 272.

65. In 1836 Abbé Dufriche-Desgenette, curé of Notre-Dame des Victoires, created an 'Arch-brotherhood of the Very Holy and Immaculate Heart of the Virgin for the conversion of sinners'. Notre-Dame des Victoires had great success in the nineteenth century. In 1843 almost one French parish in ten was affiliated to it. F. Lebrun (ed.), *Histoire des Catholiques en France*, Paris, Privat/Pluriel, 1980, p. 379.

hand you should not worry so much, especially since I am in a relatively calm sector . . . I thank all three of you for the trouble you took to go to Sacré-Cœur during the period of action I am going through.[66]

Convalescing in hospital after his aeroplane was shot down, Jacques d'Arnoux was visited by his father : 'The Sacred Heart saved you on the first Friday of the month, at the moment in the Holy Mass when the whole family was taking communion.'[67]

A French officer killed at Lorette carried two portraits in his pocket, perhaps of his wife and himself before the war, and a medal of the Sacred Heart. On one side, Christ shows his bleeding heart. On the back, we see Marguerite-Marie praying to the same Christ, and his exclamation: 'Here is the heart that so loved mankind.'[68]

Unfortunately, there is no way of knowing how many of the hundreds of thousands of medals struck during the war were actually worn, either at the front or at home. The advertisements in each number of the *Messager du Cœur de Jésus* showed that the 'merchants in the temple' were ready: '15 centimes apiece, 1 franc per dozen, 6 francs per hundred, 50 francs per thousand'. They were available in paper or celluloid.

Can one believe Louis Perroy, historian of devotion to the Sacred Heart for *Les Etudes*? 'Will it be said that what was not achievable under Louis XIV can be achieved in our century without principles or faith? . . . Who could have believed that the war of 1914 would see our soldiers wearing nearly a million battle-flags of the Sacred Heart? A hundred thousand soldiers and officers have joined the "Guard of the Sacred Heart".'[69]

By linking devotion to the Sacred Heart closely to devotion to the Passion, the revelations at Paray appealed unerringly to soldiers who were regular churchgoers, whose *dolorisme* we have looked at, and their certainty of imitating Christ. To follow the path of medals from Paray-le-Monial to the various believers is to gain the impression that the Sacred

66. Pierre Tisserant, *Lettres, 1914–1917*, p. 181, 5 December 1916, p. 234, 25 April 1917.
67. D'Arnoux, *Paroles d'un revenant*, p. 138.
68. Archives départementales du Pas-de-Calais, Fonds Lorette, 42 J 173.
69. *Etudes*, vol. 154, 1917, p. 470.
70. The same can be observed in the Second World War. At Notre-Dame de la Garde an ex-voto consists of a pennant of the Sacred Heart cut in four then joined on a cloth with four medals of the Immaculate Conception. The text reads: 'July 1946. This pennant was carried by the late J. Servolin in the war of 1914–18. Kept carefully in our family cradle. I shared it between my four grandchildren during the war of 1939. They were protected by the Sacred Heart and the holy Virgin. I offer it now in gratitude to Notre-Dame de la Garde. M.S.' *Ex-Voto du terroir marseillais*, p. 134.

Heart itself is going on pilgrimage, uniting along its way the scattered members of families separated by the war.[70] On 11 February 1917, the commandant of the Fort de Vaux wrote his act of consecration of the fort to the Sacred Heart of Jesus:

> In the midst of the terrible trials our country is undergoing, I come, Lord, to respond, insofar as it is in my power, to the ardent desire of your Heart . . . I dedicate this fort to you, so that from now on you may keep it under your all-powerful protection, and so that you may spread in abundance the blessings you promise to places where the image of your Sacred Heart is displayed and held in honour . . . Yours are our hearts; may they love you above all else . . . may they realize that this sacred union germinating in wartime must continue in the peace to follow; that this sacred union sealed by so many bloody sacrifices, must end in the highest conception of duty towards our country . . . Yours is our fatigue, our anguish and, if necessary, our blood. We offer it to you for the expiation of our sins, for the expiation of France . . . O Mary, queen of France and our mother, save us. Saint Michael, preserve us for the victory. Blessed Joan of Arc, pray for us. Amen.[71]

'The monthly echo of the Sanctuaries of the Sacred Heart', *Le Pèlerin de Paray-le-Monial*, introduced a new column, 'The Sacred Heart at the Front', and published its 'Intentions' on the first page. This example from March 1916 is significant:

> The end of the war and the honourable peace desired by France and her allies. All families particularly tried by the war. All French and allied soldiers. Priests, monks and seminarians mobilized. French prisoners. Spiritual and temporal interests of a very large number of families. Fifty widows and their children. Twenty vocations. The future of eighty girls. The conversion of thirty hardened sinners. The perseverance of three converts. Four difficult reconciliations. The curing of twenty-seven sick. Fifty priests and their works.

Here we have a cross-section of French society which came on pilgrimage to Paray before the war, and whose militant purity must be preserved in wartime circumstances. The emphasis on families, soldiers, widows was not fortuitous: throughout the entire war the consecration of families was the object of prayer.

In 1907, the Peruvian Very Reverend Father Matheo Crawley-Boevey was suddenly cured in Paray where he happened to be on pilgrimage. He decided to dedicate his life to the enthronement of the image of the Sacred Heart throughout the entire world, family by family. Three million families are said to have enthroned the Sacred Heart in 1915. 'Nothing

71. Geoffroy de Grandmaison, pp. 290–1.

is more likely to succeed at the present time than your undertaking.'[72] During the ceremonies of the Sacred Heart in Paris, tracts were distributed, like this one for the refugees of the Somme: 'Our family dedicates itself to the Divine Heart of Jesus to prove our love to him, place ourselves under his protection and hasten the coming of his reign in our country . . . Signature of parents; of children.'[73] The consecration of families cannot be conceived without *dolorisme*, as the prayer of Father Crawley-Boevey demonstrates:

> For to live without loving you,
> And to love you without suffering, O Jesus, is to die.

The parallel between the red cross of the hospitals and the Heart of Jesus was drawn constantly, as the red cross dedicated to wounds of the body found its spiritual parallel: 'the wounds of the soul will also have their red cross and their divine cure: enthronement'.[74] This inevitably irritated the caustic Abbé Mugnier: 'The Sacred Heart! This red heart withdrawn from the human body. A devotion made for a century of operations, for an era of surgeons . . .!'[75]

During the war, the Sacred Heart thus regained the full power of its message of redemption. In this case it was not the Jesus of childhood, the Jesus of the holy family, or Christ on the cross. 'Does not the Sacred Heart tend to occupy, metaphorically, the vacant place of the father? . . . the cult appears virile, in its defence of the faith and the country.'[76] The insistence on enthronement in families gave this devotion a double status which in essence returns to the original double message of love and fear. This is how it was expressed during the war by the new convert Max Jacob, the poet of 'The nocturnal adoration at the Sacred Heart of Montmartre':

> . . . The eternal light goes through his belly, it is the Sacred Heart of Jesus. The light of the Father cleaves the Son in order to cleave me too, and this

72. Benedict XV, apostolic benediction, 27 April 1915. Quoted in the book by Matheo Crawley-Boevey, *Visites et séjours à l'Abbaye de Sept-Fons*, August 1917, February 1918. The copy in the Bibliothèque nationale is identified: 6th edition, 145th thousand. Dom J. B. Chautard, abbé at the Trappist monastery of Sept-Fons, was the author of *L'Ame de tout apostolat*, one of the books for spiritual reading and meditation most widely seen in the trenches; A. Hamon, *Histoire de la dévotion au Sacré-Cœur*, vol. 5, *Royal triomphe*, Paris, Beauchesne, 1939, pp. 295–8.

73. Archives nationales, F7 13213; M/3408, 23 June 1915.

74. Hamon, *Histoire*, p. 301.

75. Abbé Mugnier, *Journal*, 17 September 1915, p. 292.

76. Etienne Fouilloux in *Histoire du christianisme*, vol. XII, pp. 190, 194.

passage is the Holy Spirit.
Oh God! You have wounded me with love . . .[77]

Thousands of 'war-wounded', to paraphrase a text so luminous and fervent, were ready to believe this message. *Le Prêtre aux armées* published 'short prayers' for them, 'Jesus, sweet and humble of heart, make my heart like yours. Heart of Jesus, I trust you. Sweet Heart of Mary, be my salvation. Mary our hope, have pity on us. Jesus, Mary!' Each of these invocations earned 300 days of indulgence. The words, published on detachable sheets for distribution at the front, were accompanied by vignettes of Christ with his arms outstretched towards the worshipper, drawing him into grasping his heart.

As in devotion to the Rosary, where all of France was able to commune in love of the Virgin, devotion to the Sacred Heart connected the personal, internal piety of the faithful and their loved ones to that of the nation. France, France at war, consisted of every individual and every family. This was the second part of the message of Paray and the accompanying devotion. The worshippers of the Sacred Heart recognized that everything has meaning: war has broken out, the war goes on, France will win the war. But why is it so long and so hard? Christ loves but Christ punishes.

In the eyes of the ecclesiastical hierarchy there was only one appropriate way to respond to the burdensome message of the heart, to consecrate first French dioceses and then the whole country. One after another the French bishops published the texts of their consecration. As the former chaplain of the basilica of the Sacred Heart at Paray-le-Monial, the Bishop of Besançon, Monsignor Gauthey, was particularly active in this enterprise. The diocese was consecrated by 1914, then a church dedicated to the Sacred Heart was built on the Brésille plateau above Besançon.[78]

Claire Ferchaud, the young girl from Poitou, undoubtedly went furthest during the war in her obsession for the Sacred Heart, even managing, in her fervour, to offend the official heads of the cult. Originally from the west, cradled in the Chouan tradition – strongly Catholic, counter-Revolution and Royalist – she none the less contacted President Poincaré several times in 1917 and was eventually received by him. She wrote to him on 16 January 1917:

77. Max Jacob, *La Défense de Tartuffe*, Paris, Gallimard, 1964, p. 177 (first published 1919).
78. It was opened for worship in 1923. Louis Mairry, *Le Département du Doubs sous la IIIe République*. Besançon Cêtre, 1992, p. 276.

M. le Président, a humble girl from Poitou has just received a mission from heaven that makes her timid nature tremble . . . It is from the divine mouth of God in heaven that I was directed to transmit to you the express desire of Jesus . . . The war is a punishment from heaven. God no longer has his rightful place in France . . . Secondly – and this is the goal of my mission – Jesus wants to save France and the Allies, and it is through you, M. le Président, that Heaven wants to act . . . Centuries ago, the Sacred Heart told the Blessed Marguerite-Marie: 'I want my Heart to be painted on the national flag, and I will make them victorious over all their enemies.' God seems to have said those words for our present times . . . Jesus showed me his heart broken by the infidelity of man. A great wound divides his Heart. And of this deep wound, Jesus said: 'It is France that made it.' But . . . he advances toward us, M. le Président, offering his mercy. Over and over, Jesus made me see M. le Président, whose soul was being strongly affected by Grace . . . I seemed to see God addressing these words to you: 'Raymond, why persecutest thou me?'

Here are the sacred words I heard from the very mouth of Our Lord: 'Go and tell the leader who governs France to go to the basilica of the Sacred Heart in Montmartre along with the kings of the allied nations . . . they will give the official order that the Sacred Heart be painted on all the flags of every regiment. Every soldier is to wear this insignia of salvation.' . . . Those are God's orders. If you refuse . . . you will soon be turned out of your high office. Great mischance threatens you. France along with her head of state will be crushed. The fire of heaven will reduce her to ashes . . . Ah, I tremble! Poor France! We will have nothing left of her but the memory.

Claire of the Crucified Jesus[79]

To support her words, Claire travelled to Paris to pray at Sacré-Cœur, not without effect on the Paris hierarchy.[80]

Cardinal Amette allowed her to spend an entire night praying in Sacré-Cœur, although he writes: 'I am willing to believe that this girl is sincere, but she may be an eccentric or under the power of suggestion.'[81]

Claire therefore spent the night of 15 March 1917 in Sacré-Cœur, during which time

Jesus gave her his last counsel for France . . . The French people are a hair's breadth away from destruction. The traitor lives at the heart of France. It is Freemasonry which, to gain the eternal perdition of the country, and in accord with Germany, has engendered this war . . . Without me France would be

79. Claire Ferchaud, *Notes autobiographiques, 1896–1972*, Paris, Téqui, 1974, vol. II, pp. 13-15.

80. See Benoît, 'Le Sacré-Cœur de Montmartre', p. 805.

81. Ferchaud, *Notes autobiographiques*, Letter from Cardinal Amette to Canon Créin, Superior of Montmartre, 12 March 1917, vol. II, p. 22.

lost . . . But I ask the brave little soldiers of France, all the way up to the generals, to fly the flag of the Sacred Heart, in spite of the formal prohibition that will ensue . . . how lovely France will be one day![82]

On 21 March, accompanied by the Marquis de Baudry d'Asson, the Vendée deputy, Claire finally met Poincaré for a few minutes, and confided Christ's message to him. She was sure that she had moved him, even convinced him, but Poincaré made no mention of the visit in his memoirs. On 21 March 1917, the meeting of the new ministry was his only concern: 'I insist on the necessity of a firm government, utterly intent on pursuing the war to a victory that will assure us of the necessary reparations and guarantees.'[83]

Poincaré was France's political leader, but the opinions of Claire Ferchaud were also leading the nation. The presence of the conservative deputy from the Vendée at her side is unnecessary to recognize in her 'visions' the most reactionary, anti-revolutionary discourse of the Catholic Church. Although Poincaré was given the title of President, Claire never mentioned the word 'Republic'. She preferred the word 'head', which allowed a certain ambiguity. The habitual theme so well known to readers of *Action française* resurfaces: the Masonic plot against eternal and Catholic France.[84] This plot had led to war, and would certainly lead to defeat without the intervention of the Sacred Heart via the girl's visions. It is understandable that Cardinal Amette – himself a fine politician, deeply aware of what the Church had to gain from a cooperative attitude during the war – did not care to get too involved with the most extremist and often rumour-spreading fringe of the Catholics, which represented only a small percentage of the faithful.

At the same time, the reports from *préfets* to the Intelligence Bureau were more worried about strikes and protests from the left and the workers' movement. Of eighty-three reports in June 1917, only one, from Pyrénées-Orientales, stressed the risks of 'clerical propaganda': 'The readers of *Action française* are relatively numerous here. There are men in this party whose exaltation could be dangerous, if it happened – which is not being predicted for the moment – if serious discontent should

82. *Ibid.*, Letter from Claire to the Abbé de Loublande, p. 23.

83. Raymond Poincaré, *Au service de la France*, vol. IX, 'L'année trouble', 21 March 1917, Paris, Plon, p. 80.

84. Even before 1917 soldiers were complaining in their letters of restrictions on religious practice at the front: 'It is true that with the leaders that we have, who are mostly Freemasons, there is nothing to be done and most of the regiment are hostile to religion. It is a very sad regiment' (Letter to Abbé Salomon, archives quoted, 5 September 1915).

arise among the population. It is probably among them that leaders and agitators would be found.'[85]

So Claire Ferchaud had few supporters, although they were vehement, convinced that her voices were those of a new Joan of Arc. The war was one of 'good and evil, the holy war. But only mystics know the intimacy of the secret hidden in that last word.'[86] Canon Poulain celebrated 'religious thrills . . . The flag of the Sacred Heart, unleashing the victory, will bring good fortune.'[87]

Although Cardinal Amette and the French bishops consecrated some of their churches, even entire dioceses, to the Sacred Heart, asking pardon for sins committed and calling for victory, Christ's most political message to Louis XIV was not necessarily taken into account. Cardinal Billot himself, although close to *Action française*, pointed out to Rome that very few pages dedicated to the visions of Marguerite-Marie Alacoque concern the message to Louis XIV, and that it was moreover not known whether Louis himself knew anything about it.[88] It remained for the activists to redouble the pilgrimages to Paray, and the petitions for the addition of the Sacred Heart to the tricolour and the recognition of the right to wear its insignia on uniforms at the front. Starting in 1915, the republican majority among the soldiers complained and asked to be allowed to wear the republican symbol on their caps, the figure of Marianne.[89]

Claire Ferchaud, manipulated to an unknown degree by her bishop Mgr Humbrecht, continued to press for the wearing of the Sacred Heart. To this end she wrote to fifteen generals on 7 May 1917. Paul Painlevé, the minister of war, reacted to her campaign, and General Pétain was required to remind officers 'that they must abstain from any act of a religious nature, constituting a flagrant violation of the freedom of conscience of their men and of the religious neutrality of the French State'.[90]

Once again in this survey, the expectations and responses of the faithful and the more or less openly acknowledged political aims of some

85. SHAT, Vincennes, carton 16 N 1538. Report of 16 June 1917.
86. Joseph Serre, *Les Deux Règnes, l'avenir de la France et du monde par un mystique lyonnais*, Lyon, 1917, p. 2.
87. Edouard Poulain, *Pour le drapeau du Sacré-Cœur, pour le salut de la France*, Chez l'auteur à Beauchine (Deux Sèvres), 1918, p. 94.
88. Jacques Fontana, *Les Catholiques français pendant la Grande Guerre*, Paris, Cerf, 1990, pp. 236–8.
89. Letter dated 7 August 1915 to the préfet of the Gironde, quoted in Maurice Agulhon, 'Marianne et la Grande Guerre', *Guerre et Cultures*, pp. 373–85.
90. Grand Quartier Général, 6 August 1917, no. 5796.

clergy coincided and were mutually supportive. In the Doubs, the petition was massively endorsed. In l'Isle sur Doubs, for example, 1,200 of the 2,600 inhabitants signed it, especially women, children and Alsatian refugees. The *préfet* of the department, a republican hostile to the Sacred Heart, could impose a few fines for contravention of his orders prohibiting the wearing in public of national insignia attached to other symbols; but he could do little in the face of thousands of rule-breakers on the home front, and even less at the front itself.[91]

In some towns, pedestrians were arrested and charged with minor infractions. A brochure records a trial in 1915 at La Roche-sur-Foron (Haute-Savoie). The defendants managed to prove that their insignia, including yellow in addition to the national colours, were not illegal; they were exonerated, but not without two priests pleading their cause:

> Your Honour, I do not complain of appearing before you, but I would prefer to appear before the men of the trenches . . . praying to the Sacred Heart of Jesus to support them. I believe my cause would be won . . . What is being condemned in me is not guilt or sedition, it is the Catholic in me . . . It is not a bad thing to proclaim the Sacred Union, but it is better to practice it, or at least not to destroy it.[92]

At the front and behind the lines, witnesses were indignant that the judicial authorities had nothing better to do: 'Strange and edifying things are happening now. The wearing of religious insignia has been judged incompatible with the needs of national defence . . . We shall remember the concerns that were so important to certain Frenchmen during the most terrible war the world has ever known.'[93]

Beyond these polemics, which can perhaps appear trivial, at Paray itself it is striking to note that although organized diocesan pilgrimages faded because of the war, the number of communicants did not diminish. Indeed, for the rest of the war they settled at around 80,000 at the Visitation. But subscriptions to *L'Heure sainte* dropped from 4,909 in 1913 to 1,600 and 1,550 in 1915 and 1916 respectively, which perhaps explains why publication of the figures ceased in *Le Pèlerin de Paray-le-Monial*.

The numerous communicants included of course the soldiers and wounded of the military hospital established in the living quarters of

---

91. Mairry, *Le Département du Doubs*, p. 276.

92. *Le Triomphe du Bon sens au tribunal de La Roche sur Foron, le 24 septembre 1915*, Le port des emblèmes du Sacré-Cœur, Chambéry, 1915, pp. 18 and 27.

93. Marc Boasson, *Au soir d'un monde, lettres de guerre, 1915–1918*, Paris, Plon, 1926. (Introduction by Gabriel Marcel), 5 August 1915, p. 37.

the Sacred Heart. The town had become a military emplacement, and it now saw its new function as the double message of patriotic exhortation and religious consolation. 'Fourteen hundred young men called to the colours will be lodging here . . . We are sure the people of Paray will warmly welcome these pilgrims of a new type. Such is the closeness between patriotism and religion.'[94]

Some important events marked the Paray conflict. In January 1917, the canonization process of the blessed Marguerite-Marie began anew. Given the coincidence of dates, this fact may have favoured the visions of Claire Ferchaud. Mgr Berthoin, Bishop of Autun, asked his faithful for prayers to advance the cause of the canonization, 'for the success of this great matter, so closely connected to the reign of the Sacred Heart over France and the world'.[95]

While Rome was examining cases of miraculous healing attributed to Marguerite-Marie, would not a patriotic miracle be crowning proof of the exceptional sanctity of the French Visitandine, a proof that would redound to the glory of all French Catholics?

On 25 and 26 March 1917, the entire world had to be convinced. French, British, Belgian, Italian, Japanese, Polish, Romanian, Russian and Serbian flags were blessed before the reliquary of Marguerite-Marie, in the presence of Mgr Berthoin and the Archbishop of Westminster, Cardinal Bourne. The hope for a 'future reconstitution of Christianity'[96] was strongly expressed. A canticle was chosen that recalled strongly the experiences of 1870. Each country had the right to its own verses, and there was even one added for the United States on April 4.

> God of mercy,
> God the Saviour,
> Show thy power
> In the name of the Sacred Heart.
>
> Pity, my God! Through sacred sorrow,
> France in tears is on her knees.
> With honour and glory, brighten her sword,
> Her loving heart turns toward you . . .
>
> Pity, my God! Protect America.
> She has struck with justice
> The cruelty of a cynical enemy.
> May she finish him in triumphant blows.

94. *Le Pèlerin de Paray-le-Monial*, April 1916, p. 81.
95. *Ibid.*, January 1917, p. 325.
96. *Ibid.*, conclusion.

To popularize these 'Gesta Dei per Francos' that might be missed by those who did not read *Le Pèlerin de Paray-le-Monial*, two postcards were published in great numbers. On the first, a crowd of Parisians kneels before the basilica of Montmartre. Over their heads floats the tricolour flag with its white stripe largely covered by the Sacred Heart, 'in hoc signo vinces'.[97] A correspondent notes: 'I am at the feet of Jesus, deeply moved by this admirable faith.' On the other card, French soldiers launch an attack, with allied generals leading their men in the same movement, towards Christ and victory. 'By the three Hail-Marys, the Heart of Jesus will reign.' In the sky, among the aeroplanes and Zeppelins, float the figures of Christ, the Montmartre basilica, and the blessed Joan of Arc who is flying with the banner of the Heart of Jesus in her arms. A correspondent has pasted in the corner of one card a Heart of Jesus giving the right to 200 days of indulgence.

Faith or 'Superstition'? Belief

In 1917, several articles in the *Revue du clergé français* and in *Etudes*[98] warned their readers against the 'superstitions' that appeared to be flourishing in the war: 'The image of the Sacred Heart is not an amulet with magic powers. By temporal grace, by miraculous safeguards, God can and will draw your attention to a means of salvation . . . but nothing pleases God so much as the *purity* of our faith and the disinterested nature of our love.'[99]

The propagators of the cult of the Sacred Heart themselves, outstripped by the success of their own works, were forced to reflect on the fetishistic aspects of the devotions. Were not the banners and medals of the Sacred Heart seen as saving instruments in themselves, separate from any realization of the message of Christ at Paray or of Christianity in general? 'We are still awaiting the temporal triumph of the Messiah and his faithful, some magic millenarianism where prestigious dramatic effects will have so deeply transformed existence that it will retain nothing of its nature as a testing-ground.'[100] Claire Ferchaud and her supporters were probably the major targets for this doctrinal attack, but could soldiers and their families be forbidden to believe as they wished and were able?

97. 'By this sign you will overcome'.
98. Following Italian publications on this topic. Agostino Gemelli, 'Folklore di guerra' and 'Le supestitioni dei'soldati in guerra', *Vita e Pensiero*, 1917.
99. H. Judéaux, 'La dévotion au Sacré-Cœur, orthodoxie et révélations privées'. (Address on 29 June 1917 at Paray-le-Monial.) *Etudes*, no. 152, 5 July 1917, pp. 175–91 (p. 185).
100. *Ibid.*, p. 186.

Comets, meteorites, planetary conjunctions and the flight of birds were all interpreted as signs of the war's end, sometimes as signs of victory. Flaming swords and tricolour stars were seen in the sky by French soldiers, like the British soldiers' fictional Angel of Mons. Prophecies multiplied. The prophecy of Messina in particular, seeming to come from Italy, was taken up in France. Apollinaire, always interested by street notices, copied one down in full for an article: 'Jesus Christ risen in person (in flesh and bone), came down again to earth on 9 December 1917 . . . he will preach the truth for the salvation of the world, the destruction of the Teuton, and he will fight the Antichrist Wilhelm II'.[101]

The blend of traditional rural origins – the vast majority of French soldiers were country people – of more or less Christianized ancestral beliefs, of recipes for avoiding wounds, even death, and of prayers appropriate to the circumstances, came together in the accounts of French and Italian priests, anthropologists and classical historians trying to understand what they saw at the front in the light of their research.[102]

Detailed questionnaires were circulated by researchers during the war. For Italians, Father Gemelli used a Swiss questionnaire also utilized in France.[103]

The first superstitious practices noted by the different authors were prayers, sometimes pre-dating the war and revived during the conflict:

Prayer to protect against firearms. As a counter-charm, recite this prayer three times in succession every morning before breakfast, wear it and you will be preserved from all peril and danger of death, and you will always overcome your enemies.

Prayer. Eccé, Crucem, domini, fugité, partès, adversé, vicis, l'eodé, Tribu, Juda, make the sign of the cross, radix, clavo.[104]

---

101. Guillaume Apollinaire, 'Il est ressuscité', Echo for *Le Mercure de France*, 16 January 1918. Reproduced in *Œuvres en prose*, Paris, La Pléiade, vol. II, p. 1358.

102. The *Revue des études anciennes*, vol. 17, 1915, pp. 73-4, contained the summary of a lesson by Camille Jullian at the Collège de France on 'the folklore of the war'.

103. '3. Do we know of strange practices before, during and after battle . . .?
    4. By what means do we believe we can preserve our lives? Objects that have been blessed . . .
    6. Are there inoffensive or superstitious means to achieve the aim without fail?
    7. What are the omens announcing the war . . .'; W. Deonna, 'La recrudescence des superstitions en temps de guerre et les statues à clous', *L'Anthropologie*, 1916, pp. 243-67.

104. Lucien Roure, 'Superstitions du front de guerre', *Etudes*, vol. 153, 1917, pp. 710-11.

This incomprehensible text is probably borrowed from the Apocalypse: 'Here is the cross of the Lord; flee, enemy cohorts. He has vanquished the lion of the tribe of Judah, the cast-off son of David' (Apocalypse, V,5).

On the back of a reproduction of the statue of Notre-Dame de Lourdes can be read:

> Children of France! Accept this image of the statue of the Holy Virgin . . . She will bring you back to your homes. Recite three Hail Marys every day to obtain the salvation of France and the triumph of the Sacred Heart through Our Lady of Tears. The Holy Virgin prays that her children who come home safe and sound from this war may send their witness to the address below for her Glorification.[105]

Although the text of the prayers was not heterodox in itself, the infallibility claimed for the formulas, with threats added in certain cases, certainly brought them into the Catholic definition of superstition: 'Excessive attachment to religious beliefs or practices that are of little purpose, if not downright false.'[106]

It is precisely the primary utility of these 'precious prayers' that explains their growth and spread during the war. 'Chain-Prayers' circulated in the same way:

> Novena. O Jesus, I have come to beg your help. Heart of Jesus, save France. Protect us from German bullets, Joan of Arc, save us. Saint Michael, pray for us. This prayer was sent to me and must be circulated throughout the front. It is said that those who write it will be preserved from all calamities and those who neglect it will have bad luck. Send it to nine different people one each day and on the ninth day you will receive great joy. Do not sign it, only give the date you received it. Do not break the chain, have faith. 9/8/15.[107]

These 'Chain-Prayers' and 'Prayers in the Form of Novenas' were already circulating before the war, and had been condemned by certain bishops; did not every formula of prayer require the imprimatur of the Church before being circulated among the faithful?

As we have seen, accounts from soldiers cared for as insane during the war give a different understanding of phenomena difficult to apprehend. An account by the psychiatrist G. Dumas describes one of his patients:

---

105. *Ibid.*, p. 710.
106. *Dictionnaire de Théologie Catholique*, vol. XIV, 1941, p. 2987.
107. Quoted by Roure, 'Superstitions'.

He communicates with the beyond . . . At Les Eparges, he saw wild geese pass in the sky; they began to cry, and these cries meant: 'you are protected'. Another time he saw the Son of God come sliding down from His cross and making a sign of friendship. A few days later, as he lowered his head at the sound of shellfire, he saw the Virgin making a gesture of protection. Every night in bed he hears the voice of God the Father with whom he holds long conversations. He demonstrates other forms of intellectual deterioration and emotional indifference.[108]

Whatever the illness of this soldier, he presented terror of the war in its raw state, and a need for protection mingled with memories of agricultural or even historical ritual (the geese), along with fragments of Catholicism.

Among American soldiers there were very few who did not go into battle with a Bible in their pocket, particularly since they were supplied free of charge by various Protestant or Catholic charitable organizations. Some soldiers read them, but most did not feel the need to do so. The presence of the sacred book on their bodies, the physical contact with the object rather than the spiritual contact with its contents, was what gave reassurance. The entire Bible was thus utilized as an amulet. A division chaplain shows no surprise:

I had to search the dead bodies for their little possessions. The doctor and I were amazed to find that nearly every man had a Bible or cross on him. 'They do seem religious, -he said- these boys; I should never have thought they would have such things.' Perhaps they carried them as a charm, a sort of magic, perhaps because they felt more than they know that 'such things' contained the secret of life and death and immortality, perhaps because they had a deep love for them. None can say.[109]

Among French soldiers, good-luck charms of a more or less heterodox nature were added to the use of religious texts as amulets. In the thirteenth century, St Thomas Aquinas, following the lead of St John Chrysostom, was already condemning the wearing of prayers around the neck. Was this custom an appeal to magic, or was it an observance genuinely believed to be Catholic, even as the soldiers devalued it? Soldiers of the Great War were known to put slips of paper into three different pockets, bearing the names of Caspar, Melchior and Balthazar. Objects of wood or metal were kept or transformed into rings with crosses engraved on them. The young American Alan Seeger, who had

---

108. Georges Dumas, *Troubles mentaux et troubles nerveux de guerre*, Paris, Alcan, 1919, p. 19.
109. Maurice Ponsonby in *The Committee on the War and the Religious Outlook. Religion among American Men*, New York, Association Press, 1920, p. 89.

joined the Foreign Legion and worked alongside Algerian marksmen, describes in one of his poems how he had a ring made from a shell splinter that killed one of his comrades. On the ring, at his request a marksman had engraved the word 'Mektoub' in Arabic. He was pleased to be taking up what he took to be the fatalism of Islam: is not the day of his death already written 'in the book of Destiny whose leaves are made of Time?'[110] Many American soldiers were certain that the shell destined to kill them had been made especially for them. One often finds words to this effect: 'If my number isn't on this shell, it won't get me.'[111]

Nails or horseshoes were hung on trench walls next to the crucifix. This mixture of piety and superstition, although not exclusive to the Great War – archaeologists remind us of the importance of such objects in Antiquity – seems to have been highly developed at the front. Léon Bloy himself was drawn into it when he sent a piece of clothing supposed to have belonged to Mélanie, the shepherdess of La Salette, to his various friends at the front:

> Do you remember, my dear friend, that poor mason, Mélanie's brother, who shared a piece of his sister's clothing with us at Corps? I have great confidence in this relic. I have given pieces to some friends who are in danger like you, and I hope they will be protected, I firmly hope so. Perhaps you don't have the object in your possession. In that case, I enclose with this letter a little bit of my own piece, begging you to sew it firmly onto some piece of your own clothing that you never take off.[112]

110.   . . . When, not to hear, some try to talk,
        And some to clean their guns, or sing,
        And some dig deeper in the chalk –
        I look upon my ring:
        And nerves relax that were more tense,
        And Death comes whistling down unheard,
        As I consider all the sense
        Held in that mystic world . . .

Alan Seeger, 'Maktoob', *Poems*, London, Constable, 1917, p. 143. Alan Seeger was killed on 1 July 1916 at Belloy-en-Santerre.

111. A scene in the famous film by Howard Hawks, *Sergeant York*, shows the death of a soldier. His friends are sure that 'the shell was made for him'. The real Alvin York had helped in the making of the film of his life – from his conversion to the Argonne front – starring Gary Cooper in 1941. If the aim of the film was indeed to persuade Americans to enlist in the Second World War, a certain number of details, including that of the shell, enable the film to exceed its propaganda aspect to become a masterpiece of civil religion in the United States.

112. Léon Bloy, *Lettres à Raoux*, 1936. Letter of Easter Tuesday 1915, p. 247. The fervently Catholic Captain Raoux was killed at Verdun in February 1916.

Figure 10. Drawing by the Australian artist Will Dyson, *Fatalist* (1917). (Australian War Memorial, ART 02224.)

For Protestants, crosses, medals, images and relics were naturally seen as vain observances, and linked Catholicism to certain forms of fetishism. The German enemies were mainly perceived to be Lutherans, as we have seen, and it was therefore tempting to accuse these 'barbarians' of 'evils' from which not even Catholics were exempt. In France the superstitious use of nails sometimes went so far as striking one into a statue of a saint, for example St Anne of Auray. Perhaps this is a way of prolonging a prayer by making it material, by putting prayer/pin, or nail, into contact with the statue of the intercessor, in a practice that claimed to be the opposite of sorcery. During the war a certain number of wooden statues[113] were constructed in Germany into which visitors or pilgrims were invited to set nails. The most spectacular was in Berlin, in 1915, where a statue of Hindenburg 12 metres tall was erected beside the Column of Victory. From the moment of its inauguration people drove nails into it, officially controlled by a sales office whose receipts were meant to support the war. At the news of the fall of Douaumont, the Crown Princess drove in a nail of gold, and each of her four children a silver nail. 'Is German *Kultur* regressing to African fetishism?'[114] In a serious academic lecture to the French Scientific Association, Dr Bérillon asked this kind of question of himself, and associated the pointed helmet and *kalpach* of the Hussars of Death to the 2 million nails driven into Hindenburg's statue. Such practices were no longer encountered except 'among the half-savage tribes of Central Africa and the Congo', associated with other 'mental attitudes that are all related to deficient cerebral control, proof of very clear inferiority, psychological as well as moral'.[115]

Even if the French had not yet reached this ultimate stage of barbarism, Charles Calippe rose up in rage against all the 'protective devices against certain mishaps', simultaneously explaining the spread of these devotions

113. For a listing of these statues and an anthropological view, Deonna, 'La recrudescence des superstitions'.

114. Roure, 'Superstitions', p. 725. It is interesting to note here that, in contrast, avant-garde artists, even if they transformed their methods during the war in certain ways (see Kenneth E. Silver, *Esprit de Corps, the Art of the Parisian Avant-Garde and the First World War, 1914–1925*, London, Thames & Hudson/Princeton, Princeton University Press, 1989), continued to be strongly interested in primitive art during the war. Apollinaire bitterly regretted not being able to continue studying fetishes that were inaccessible in Brussels because of the German occupation. 'Mélanophilie ou mélanomanie', *Mercure de France*, 1 April 1917.

115. Dr Edgar Bérillon, 'La psychologie de la race allemande d'après ses caractères objectifs et spécifiques'. Conférence of the Association française pour l'avancement des sciences, 4 February 1917, Paris, Masson, p. 139.

during the war: 'It is religion itself, considered in one of its essential aspects, that is changed into a sort of recipe against a sudden or a bloody death . . . These papers that were more or less dormant, or sewn into some lining, have been brought out of their retirement, forced like everything else into universal mobilization.'[116]

To hold out at the front, to live in the midst of death, the soldiers needed multiple forms of reassurance: of the affection of their families, from their country, from faith, from superstition. Far from cancelling each other out, these currents reinforced each other in the horror of war. Families, moreover, did everything possible to offer spiritual help to soldiers at the front. Baptisms were performed for children who had not been baptized at birth, as a gesture of piety to preserve their fathers at the front.[117]

Many are the accounts of soldiers who evoke the beneficent protection they have enjoyed: some are convinced their lives were saved by a wallet full of letters from a fiancée that was thought to have turned aside a shellburst; others owe their lives to the intervention of the Virgin or the saints, or to an amulet, or a prayer they had copied down. Jacques Copeau, a non-combatant convalescing in a Paris military hospital, had trouble not showing his contempt for these over-popular forms of devotion. 'Provided you give them something, they are content. That's why many ask for medals, rosaries. One can amuse them like children, with trinkets. They arrange their little things in little cardboard boxes.'[118]

For the historian there is little difference between these wartime beliefs. They reveal the vitality of these men, their strength of life confronting wartime destruction. In the face of an all too rational but totally incomprehensible modernity, the irrational surged back into vigour, in what American observers have called 'emergency religion'.[119]

Spiritualism,[120] belief in premonitory dreams, was part of this pattern. A sergeant told Paul Cazin of a dream early in the war:

116. Charles Calippe, 'Prières efficaces et porte-bonheur', *Revue du clergé français*, vol. lxxxxix, 1917, pp. 241–53 (p. 246).

117. Jacques Ozouf and Mona Ozouf, *La République des instituteurs*, Paris, Seuil, 1992, p. 181.

118. Jacques Copeau, *Journal*, Paris, Seghers, 1992, vol. 1, 13 March 1915, p. 656.

119. *The Committee*, p. 122.

120. It is not surprising to discover two Catholic writers, fascinated by the war as patriots and intellectuals, investigating spritualism. Agostino Gemelli, 'In tema di spiritismo', *Vita e Pensiero*, 1917, pp. 502–16. Stéphane Coubé, anti-spiritualist campaign in Nice then Lent sermons in 1917 at the Madeleine on the same theme: 'Et Satan conduit le bal'. *Le Père Coubé*, pp. 192–9. (See René Guenon, *L'Erreur spirite*, Paris, 1923.)

One night, I dreamed it was over ... We are all going under the Arc de Triomphe ... all the men in the company ... I told them about the dream that evening ... I said to them, 'I saw so-and-so, and so-and-so.' Then the lieutenant asked me: 'What about me, was I there?' Dammit, I hadn't seen him, I was sure of it ... The next day we went up the line. I wasn't thinking about it any more. He was beside me. Suddenly he asks me: 'Was I there, yes or no?' I started to laugh, he wasn't laughing at all. 'All right, Lieutenant, you were there.' He hadn't been ... And he won't be. He was killed.[121]

Studies of spiritualism are well developed in England,[122] but French examples are still little known. In contrast to those who offer criticism without reasoning, Gabriel Marcel discussed his wartime experience of the phenomenon in his autobiography. A non-combatant, he was head of the Red Cross service in charge of informing families of the fate of their missing men. He describes his personal conflict: although not at the front, he had to support his friends, and from their files knew of all the deaths and suffering. 'It could have been extremely dangerous, that is to say that for me it could have turned the war into a completely abstract structure. But what prevented that from happening were the visits I received several times a day, and that overwhelmed me each and every time.'[123]

During the winter of 1916–17, Gabriel Marcel attempted to reduce his inner conflict by participating in spiritualist seances with friends. He recounts in detail how extraordinary coincidences enabled them to discover the fate of certain soldiers at the front by means of the ouija board. In particular, he was able to locate in his well-kept dossiers names mentioned or called up during the seances. Throughout his *Journal de métaphysique* he reflected as a philosopher on spiritualism, clairvoyance amd visions. This is not the place to pursue Marcel's challenging thinking, but the connection should be stressed again between the carnage of the Great War and the birth of an exceptional religious fervour, spiritual investigation and attempts to answer the enduring question 'Why?'. This connection was grasped and articulated by the subtlest thinkers as well as by witnesses with no background whatever in philosophy.[124]

121. Paul Cazin, *L'Humaniste à la guerre*, Paris, Plon, 1920, p. 234.

122. Jay Winter, *Sites of Memory, Sites of Mourning. The Great War in European Cultural History*, Cambridge, Cambridge University Press, 1995.

123. Marcel, *En chemin*, p. 95. André Kahn, temporarily in charge of civilian affairs at the front: 'Having dressed bodily wounds, I am going to dress wounded souls. All day I shall struggle through death certificates and heart-breaking letters from parents. It is as sad as a battlefield, this undertaker's work' (*Journal de guerre d'un juif patriote, 1914/1918*, Paris, Simoën, 1978, 39 and 31 May 1915, pp. 165–6).

124. Gabriel Marcel, *Journal métaphysique*, Paris, Gallimard, 1927. (Notes from 1914–23.)

Intercession

It was entirely natural that men of the Church should wonder about some of these practices. We find in their condemnations (not without a strong analytic spirit, as we have seen) the usual worries of the hierarchy when faced with poorly mastered devotional practices. These 'superstitions' seem simultaneously utilitarian (and thus anti-spiritual) and too imbued with fatalism not to reveal a mental and even moral laziness.

Observers of these practices, by turning themselves into rigorous anthropologists, have enabled us, in our turn, to examine these gestures, these ecclesiastically marginal rites. Further, by analysing them through their subtle reading, despite their ultimate condemnation, they allow us to pursue the analysis further.

Charles Calippe invites us to do so. He believes that these practices are the result of widespread religious ignorance and he wonders if this ignorance is not the prime obstacle to a real religious awakening. 'Why do so many Catholics comprehend so little of the most elementary truths of their religion? And how, by what methods, with what fresh zeal can we anticipate better results?'[125]

Religious Awakening?

Was there a religious awakening during the Great War? The preceding sections offer a partial answer, but have also raised new questions about mentalities during a crisis as violent as the First World War.

The English expression 'revival' (in French, 'réveil', or awakening) refers to an English (later an American) tradition, mainly Protestant, of a periodic religious replenishment of resources, taken on by different branches of Protestantism. These revivals are both quantitative, since more of the faithful are touched by the message, and qualitative, since they concern the renewal and deepening of faith. Revival adepts are usually characterized as 'born-again Christians'. They are born a second time to faith and to religious practice. But the return to a particular practice is not enough to determine a revival: there must be a real reawakening of fervour, and a very visible change in the way of life of whole communities.

125. Calippe, 'Prières', p. 253. It is indeed hardly surprising that the coadjutor of Amiens cathedral took an interest in this so-called 'popular' practice during the war. He was not only the author of two books on Picardy at war, and in particular on the devastation of the churches, but also the author of the anonymous *Journal*, published in 1902-3, in which he developed his social concern over the restoration of souls in a France that had become a 'mission nation'. *Journal d'un prêtre d'après-demain*, introduced by Emile Poulat, Paris, Casterman, 1961.

105

All observers of France in the summer of 1914 spoke of a 'return to the altars'. This movement is quantifiable, for example by the number of confessions and communions made by men at the moment of leaving for the front. Although this 'return', undeniable in the first months of the war, faded a little thereafter, we can still say that firmness, even patriotic and religious fervour, followed a parallel curve. Different certainties came together to create a France determined to win.

Publications appeared quickly to glorify this new religious atmosphere and to explain it. Inquiries were launched in 1915, one by the Catholic Committee for French Propaganda Abroad,[126] another by *La Grande Revue*.[127] Moving from quantitative to qualitative elements, Catholic authors quickly drew general conclusions from their observations at the outset of the war. Written in 1914 or 1915, their books appear in 1916 or 1917, when the military and spiritual reality of the front had already evolved, when lassitude and even disgust for the war were beginning to take over. American translations showed up an even greater discrepancy in their diffusion in the United States. The optimism among clerics at the start of the conflict diminished just as their work was appearing in print and was being read in wider circles. As the deeply Catholic Marc Boasson says so well in 1916: 'With which foot would I not kick the rear of those scavenging scribes who don't blush to wax eloquent over Verdun . . . Silence for all that falls. No talking in the cemeteries . . . Germany is lavish in maintaining the first cemetery, the Père Lachaise of France.'[128]

At a moment when even Barrès was beginning to have doubts, his book *The Undying Spirit of France* appeared in the United States. The writer of the American preface praised the soul of Barrès, 'he who worships before the altar of soldiers martyred for France'.[129] At the end of 1917, however, although the text was certainly capable of galvanizing the Americans who read it while they discovered the war on its own

126. On this Comité Catholique de Propagande Française à l'Etranger and on Editions Bloud et Gay which published its works, see *Histoire religieuse de la France contemporaine*, vol. II, pp. 244-5. The fascinating memoirs of the Dean of the Paris Catholic Institute, who was head of the Committee, have been published: *Les Carnets du Cardinal Alfred Baudrillart, 1er août 1914–31 décembre 1918* (texte présenté, établi et annoté par Paul Christophe), Paris, Cerf, 1994.

127. See these questionnaires and their analysis in Annette Becker 'The Churches and the War', in Jean-Jacques Becker, *The Great War and the French People*, Oxford, Berg, 1985.

128. Boasson, *Au soir d'un monde*, 30 July 1916, p. 149.

129. *The Undying Spirit of France*, New Haven, Yale University Press, 1917.

terrain, Barrès and his French readers had already moved on to another stage. Neither the embittered Marc Boasson nor the new Barrès could be suspected of any lack of religious or patriotic fervour. Boasson, one of the hundreds of Christian intellectuals whose works we possess, speaks in fact of his deepening faith amidst the disasters of war:

> I am terribly changed . . . I am as though crushed, diminished . . . Let us bear all this as best we can. Those who believe in God feel closer to him . . . One has to be very simple to consider religion as a bed of oblivion . . . If God binds our wounds, he does not prevent them from burning. On the contrary, they are supposed to burn, but in feeling them burn we understand the meaning of our suffering.[130]

Far from being a simple and quantifiable 'return to the altars', are we looking here at a qualitative revival? Abbé Brugerette did not hesitate to use the word 'revival' for France.[131] He considered that events were sufficiently extraordinary to be understood only with reference to the American practice. Behind the examination of the movement of religious awakening that was supposedly affecting the French population at the outbreak of war, there were obviously concealed internal and external political goals, and a propaganda intention. Would not the Church that frames this revival be rewarded by its reintegration into the nation? Surely this return of France the sinner to an intense religious life would plead for the entry into war of the 'pure' United States at her side? The religious revival would thus serve the same ends as reports on German 'atrocities' in Belgium and occupied France. We have already seen the insistence of these reports on aspects of blasphemy.

A man in New York in April 1917 made over a million listeners live this mixture of political, social and religious message. He was the great evangelist of revival, the Presbyterian preacher Billy Sunday. In his eyes sin was a personal affair that he worked hard to eliminate by traumatizing oratorical techniques. He discovered that Germany could be worse than alcohol on the road to hell.[132] All his speeches denounced vice as inherent

130. Boasson, *Au soir d'un monde*, 10 June 1916 and 15 November 1916, pp. 127 and 180.

131. J. Brugerette, *Le Prêtre français et la société contemporaine*, Paris, Lethielleux, 1938, vol. III, p. 501. Chapter 6, 'Le ministère paroissial et la vie religieuse pendant la guerre', analyses the results of the survey which was published entirely only for the diocese of Clermont-Ferrand.

132. Until 1917 he believed that 'the war in Europe was a sideshow compared to the damnable effect of saloons'. William G. McLoughlin, *Billy Sunday was his Real Name*, Chicago, University of Chicago Press, 1955, p. 256.

in Germany; the adversary was demonized: 'Hey, Jesus, you've gotta send a country like that to damnation . . . If Hell could be turned upside down you would find stamped on its bottom "made in Germany".'[133] Sermons sometimes written long before the war to convince the faithful of the terrors of hell were resurrected. The Kaiser was associated with the devil as the enemy foreigner, in the way recent immigrants had been treated formerly. 'In those days, all are patriots or traitors, to your country and the cause of Jesus Christ. What grave is deep enough to inter this thousand-footed, thousand-fanged demon? This is the epitaph: here lies Prussian militarism, outlaw and murderer.'[134] Among his listeners, thousands raised their hands when he asked them to sign up for God and their country; some came forward to sign 'pledge cards to Jesus'. It is, of course, hard to believe that real conversions can be produced in what is a veritable spectacle. Sunday's enemies compared him to a clown or to Charlie Chaplin and Douglas Fairbanks, who at that time produced increasing numbers of spectacles for the Committee on Public Information directed by George Creel.[135]

In spite of these critics, a lot of New Yorkers believed in Sunday's message, and the gigantic sums he sank back into the war effort were a strong if indirect proof of their support. Thus the power of a catalyst – here the preacher surrounded by an appealing decorum – brought about a real revival movement: attendance at services, collective and individual prayers. The war was still far away across the Atlantic, but the minds of future combatants and their families had already been prepared for front-line 'miracles'.[136] By no means all the American soldiers who met their French allies on the battlefields, mainly in 1918, had passed through New York and most certainly did not know Billy Sunday even by name. Still, they brought with them the Revival expression that they used at every turn, in speaking of themselves and the French: 'The war spirit has been raised astonishingly. It is the great awakening for us in America.'[137]

This American revival was inescapably linked to the wish to wipe out 'Germany and the Teutonic *Kultur*', and, at the same time, to admiration

133. Meeting on 6 June 1917, New York Herald.

134. *Ibid.*, 9 April 1917 (spoken style).

135. George J. Goddard, *Billy Sunday's Goat, More Harm than Good in Revivals*, pamphlet, January 1917, New York Public Library.

136. This covered the vast majority of Americans, between religion and secular religion. This is assessed by Ray H. Abrams, in his 1933 book *Preachers Present Arms*, New York, Round Table Press Inc.

137. SHAT. Reports on letter censorship, 1st and 4th bureaux, note on opinion in allied nations (15 N 92). 15 July–15 August 1918.

for the spiritual qualities of the French: 'Americans at the front speak with an almost religious feeling of the magnitude of the sufferings borne by our country, and of our manner of bearing them . . . The French soldiers are saints before whom they must kneel.'[138] (Which did not prevent certain Americans from taking up the idea of the war as a punishment of atheistic France.)

Once again, the war can only be understood here on the cultural plane. The postal censors enable us to read extracts from correspondence dating from the beginning of the war, for the Americans, but the end of the war for the French. The anonymous correspondent who described the French soldiers as saints probably knew neither Barrès nor the Catholic culture; but his Protestant or even Puritan culture made him recognize men who were out of the ordinary, 'the Saints'. The battlefields, and beyond that, all of France, had become a new 'city on the hill'.[139]

Yet when American soldiers arrived in France in great numbers, the French had not increased their religious practices; this was no longer the case in 1917 or 1918, as most witnesses testify:

> The religious sentiment that had shown up so keenly in the first months of the war has been considerably attenuated, the constant company of death has led to greater indifference, and life being more uncertain has given many who are fighting the desire to enjoy it without any obstacles, and immediately. Whence comes a sort of fleeting demoralization, counteracting religious tendencies in the great majority.[140]

The facts in this report concerning the home front were corroborated by many chaplains, disappointed by the lack of religious practice among their men, some as early as 1915: 'We are too quickly recalled to reality, especially at Eastertide. We only have to compare the figures of Easter communions (simply the number of hosts distributed, in order to avoid exaggeration) with the total number of the battalion. In my group, 100 out of 1,200 made their Easter communion in the space of four or five weeks.'[141]

138. *Ibid.*, 15 December 1917–15 January 1918 and 15 April–15 May 1918.

139. I refer here to the speech of John Winthrop on the ship *Arbella* off the coast of New England in 1630: 'For we must consider that we shall be like a city on the hill; all eyes are upon us; and if we wrong our God in this task which we have undertaken . . . we shall become the laughing stock of the whole world.' Sacvan Bercovitch has shown clearly how the Puritan message became the core of thought in the United States. *The Puritan Origins of the American Self*, New Haven, Yale University Press, 1979.

140. Report of the *préfet* of the Marne, 30 June 1917 (SHAT 16 N 1538).

141. Geoffroy de Grandmaison and François Veuillot, *L'Aumônerie militaire pendant la guerre 1914–1918*, Paris, Bloud et Gay, 1923, p. 307, Letter from Abbé Roë, 26 May 1917.

These are the same men who seemed like 'saints' to the American observers. For even if they did not pray, or prayed only little, they fought, they held out, they were resigned but 'unbowed'.[142]

In 1915, Marc Boasson was already saying: 'I have the Faith that saves, every time' [J'ai la Foi qui sauve, toutes les fois'].[143] Like him, one can play with the homonyms *foi/fois*. Patriotic and religious fervour were mixed, balanced, multiplied. And the catalysis created elsewhere or at other times by revivalist preachers or missionaries, stressing fear of hell and the sins that lead there, is an effect of the war itself. It is these conditions of fervour that create the awakening, the revival. 'It is certain that the war, for many laggards, will be worth at least ten missions.'[144]

There was no need to arouse fears for salvation; according to Norton Cru, they were inherent at the front: 'All the soldiers, without exception, are afraid, and the great majority show an admirable courage in doing what they have to do in spite of the fear . . . Without fear we would not have stayed alive for twenty-four hours on the front line.'[145] The future Cardinal Liénart commented at length on a letter in which his friend Father Thébaut, killed at the front, confessed: 'I am afraid, I am afraid.' 'There would be no more heroism if man had no feelings.'[146]

For some, this fear, in particular the fear of dying, was seen as the root cause of the brief return to religious practice, which would thus lose all its religious meaning. Marc Boasson attacked this superficial analysis:

> They have spoken of a kind of crisis of fear: a sinister nastiness . . . I defy any of those who have truly felt the taste of the divine come to life again, to have been led there by something that resembled fear. How different it was! An exaltation, on the contrary . . . Such a loss of self that it reached genuine enthusiasm . . . There was an elevation of the human level; man naturally moved upward to meet his faith.[147]

An American chaplain describes his observations of his men at the front in rather similar terms:

> There was more religion in the trenches than anywhere else in the world. Before the 'O Hour' many a boy read his testament and prayed to God . . . The men said their prayers and read their testaments even when they got

142. Becker, *The Great War and the French People*, p. 327.
143. Boasson, *Au soir d'un monde*, 6 November 1916, p. 98.
144. de Grandmaison and Veuillot, *L'Aumônerie militaire*, p. 302. Abbé May.
145. Norton Cru, *Témoins*, p. 28.
146. Mgr. Liénart, *L'Ame d'un régiment, l'abbé Thiébaut*, Lille, pp. 101-2.
147. Boasson, *Au soir d'un monde*, 3 February 1918, p. 309.

within hearing of the big guns. They had a sense of dependance upon One who won't forget . . . I could not find any experience of Christ, or any experience of church among these men. It was a sort of mystic unitarian experience.[148]

This new mysticism was mentioned by numerous witnesses, some seeking to locate the war in a longer evolution of religious sentiment, in the United States as well as in France. 'After decades of materialism, a new mysticism is being born . . . God and immortality have become facts for our everyday life. This mysticism is conscious . . . The evidence of our mature wisdom is that, having experienced the pitfalls we have voluntarily returned to a childlike trust.'[149] Only men still close to their religious origins could react to the war in this way:

> For example, the dechristianization of the peasant soul, even in villages where the church seems abandoned, is extremely superficial. That explains the explosion of religious sentiment we saw breaking out . . . It is because we have observed badly that we are surprised by this, and it is the fault of psychology that we explain it solely by the fear of death.[150]

When chaplains or Catholic observers regret the drop in religious enthusiasm that took place between 1914 and 1918, it is the pre-war period that they tend to blame. The war attenuated and slowed down a phenomenon that seemed inescapable at the start of the century, despite the contrary certainties still evident in *La Revue des Deux Mondes* in 1915: 'Dechristianization is extremly superficial . . . Hence the explosion of religious sentiment we have seen at the front. The thought of a heroic death does not make us religious. It proves we already are.'[151]

Religious and patriotic fervour, fear and courage, certainty of victory and deep fatigue: all these feelings are far from self-contradictory. In the catalysis of the war, they nourished both fighting men and home front, and are symbolized by the most mystic heroic episode of the war, 'Rise up, ye dead!'

148. Emery Shipler, 'War Work in the Diocese of New York'. Reports of Committees on Army and Navy Chaplains. Ms., New York Historical Society, p. 45.

149. Winifred Kirkland, 'The New Death', *The Atlantic Monthly*, May 1918, pp. 577–89 (p. 587).

150. de Grandmaison and Veuillot, *L'Aumônerie militaire*, p. 275. Dr E. Labat, condensing the results of a survey within the Health Corps.

151. E. Labat, 'Notre optimisme', *Revue des Deux Mondes*, 1 August 1915; quoted in 'La Publication du Comité Catholique de Propagande Française à l'Etranger', *La Vie catholique dans la France contemporaine*, Paris, Bloud et Gay, 1918, p. 567. One can well understand why this 'optimistic' article from the beginning of the war was used as such by Catholic propaganda in 1918.

It occurred at Bois-Brûlé in April 1915. A lieutenant, Jacques Péricard, decided to inspect a trench lying extremely close to the enemy lines:

> The trench was full of French corpses. Blood everywhere . . . Little by little I dared to look at these bodies, and it seemed to me that they were looking at me . . . The Boches redoubled their efforts . . . I turned toward the corpses lying there. I thought: 'So their sacrifice is going to be useless? They will have fallen in vain? And the Boches are going to come back? And they will steal our dead?' Rage seized me . . . 'Hey there, get up! What the f . . . are you doing there on the ground? Get up and let's go f . . . those swine out there!' 'Rise up, ye dead! . . . Sudden madness? No, <u>for the dead men answered me</u>. They said: 'We will follow you.' And rising at my call, their souls mingled with my soul and together made a fiery mass, a wide river of fusing hot metal. Nothing could stop me, astound me; I had the faith that moves mountains . . . Twice we ran out of grenades, twice we found full bags of them at our feet among the sandbags . . . it was the dead who had put them there! . . . The whole evening and for many days after, I kept the religious emotion that had seized me at the moment I called on the dead. I felt something comparable to what one feels after making a fervent communion. I understood that I had just lived through hours that I would never experience again, when my head broke through the low ceiling with a rude effort and rose into the heart of the mystery, into the invisible world of heroes and gods.[152]

After Barrès, who popularized the account that first appeared anonymously in *Le Journal des débats*, in two works Victor Giraud took up this 'cry of heroism and resurrection'.[153] Norton Cru, who does not deny the episode, justly attacks those who by distorting the account claim that the dead had really fought among the living.[154] In his narrative Péricard himself gives us the key to the episode. Comparing his state to that of a man who has just made communion, it is certainly a case of 'enthusiasm' in the etymological sense of the word. The divine has taken hold of him, he has taken hold of the divine. The trench of Bois-Brûlé has become a mystical imperative, as Giraud states so well: 'Intimacy with death has made mystics out of us.'[155]

---

152. Narrated by Jacques Péricard, quoted in M. Barrès, *Les Traits éternels de la France*, pp. 25–32. Odelin, *Du théâtre à l'Evangile*, claims that the playwright Emile Rochard had already used the expression several times in his work before the war, for the soldiers of 1870. But he added, 'That does not detract from Péricard, the sublimity is not in the actual word, it is in the circumstances' (p. 265).

153. Victor Giraud, *Pro Patria*, Paris, Bloud et Gay, 1915, 'Pages Actuelles' no. 62, p. 60. *Le Miracle français*, Paris, Hachette, 1918.

154. Cru, *Témoins*, p. 32.

155. Giraud, *Pro Patria*, p. 59.

Intercession

In Grand-Fougeray (Ille-et-Vilaine), the war memorial in the cemetery appears to illustrate the episode of Bois-Brûlé.[156] Above a field of crosses, a gigantic soldier, 'risen in full mystery', is leaning against a cross. Below emerges a fighting man half buried in the earth, beside crosses coming out of the soil in every direction. The long list of the dead men, under the inscription 'In Paradisum deducant vos angeli' (Angels will lead you into Heaven), shows that mystical memory has joined real memory, the memory of 1,350,000 men to be commemorated from then on. The believers of the war would not be the last to live in this memory and through this memory. With the organization of cemeteries, the construction of war memorials and the creation of new stained glass windows for the churches, the entire land of France was becoming this place of mystical memory.

156. I am grateful to Jean-Yves Coulon for having made the monuments in Ille-et-Vilaine known to me, and for permission to quote his unpublished thesis, 'La statuaire commémorative des monuments aux morts de la Première Guerre mondiale en Ille-et-Vilaine', 2 vols, University of Rennes-II, 1991.

3

Memory

Looking beyond the conflict we find Jacques Rivière, bruised by his years as a prisoner, and by deaths among those nearest to him emotionally or intellectually. 'I challenge every combatant, all those who experienced the entirety of the war in their bodies and their souls, to state that they have not felt themselves cut off from a whole area of feeling. We are alive once more but we are no longer the same.'[1]

Georges Valois echoed Rivière, speaking with even greater bitterness:

When men of my generation summon their friends and brothers they see bleeding shadows rise up beside them, with holes in their foreheads and broken bones. That is why we no longer belong to ourselves; we no longer have the right to live for ourselves; we are the executors of the wills of those who died to redeem a century's mistakes.

Gabriel Marcel also recognized all this. In 1971 he acknowledged a whole lifetime's debt to the First World War, in terms of greater humanism but no less redolent of this dramatic weight: 'If I am tempted to say today that the war of 1914 made a different man of me, this is because it undeniably awoke an awareness of the compassion that was probably already dormant within me but which perhaps would not have developed with such intensity without the tragic events in which I participated.'[3] His description of the end of the war, symbolized for him by 11 November 1918 and 14 July 1919 in Paris,[4] shows the same insight: 'Only music, and I am thinking particularly of Beethoven, is capable of translating that conjunction of sorrow and joy which cannot be expressed in

---

1. Jacques Rivière, 'Les lettres françaises et la guerre', *Revue rhénane*, November 1921, pp. 860–9 (p. 865).

2. 'D'un siècle à l'autre', 1921, cited by Michel Toda, Henri Massis, *Un témoin de la droite intellectuelle*, Paris, La Table ronde, 1987, p. 222.

3. *En chemin vers quel éveil?*, Paris, Gallimard, 1971, p. 109.

4. See the Epilogue.

conceptual language.'[5] Norton Cru also understood that for a certain number of combatants music alone would be able to express 'the dark grandeur of the sacrifices'.[6]

Perhaps some of the fervent witnesses we now know so well would simply add prayer. Some expressed their wish to limit commemorations to silence and meditation.

Still, the presence of the dead, the constant 'return' of the dead, was maintained throughout the 1920s by way of channels both official and unofficial. From Abel Gance's film *J'accuse*[7] to Dorgelès's novel *Le Réveil des morts* (The Dead Awaken),[8] works of fiction expressed the feelings of men transformed by the war, who often asserted strongly that the survivors did not always measure up to the sacrifices of the dead. Could commemoration offer an adequate response to the bitterness of the survivors? Words, the sculptured images of war memorials, stained-glass windows, films – all still offer a sense of these endless commemorations. 'In liturgy, commemoration means evoking the memory of the saints in order to honour them, or that of the dead, in order to help them with our prayers.'[9] Thus the Catholic Church enables people to commemorate a lesser saint whose anniversary coincides with that of another one already celebrated, by adding a prayer to the mass. It seems that between 1914 and the 1920s the soldiers of the Great War became such 'saints', evoked more modestly than the official saints of the liturgical calendar, but none the less permanently. This was the wish of Pierre Ladoué, a soldier who wrote from the front of his feelings on the commemoration process to come. For him, families should above all

> establish a cult whose temple would be the soul of children. Thus the memory of the heroes would stay alive. They would not be wholly dead. Even if their remains were lying all confused with the bones of so many others in some distant ossuary, at least their presence would be maintained on the domestic altar, their living, honoured, protective presence: they would be the family saints.[10]

5. Marcel, *En chemin*, p. 119.

6. *Ibid.*, p. 629.

7. An early version of the film, which was made in 1918, came out in 1919. Some of the non-speaking performers who appeared in 'the return of the dead' scene returned to the war where some were killed. In 1937 Gance made a second version of the film. Jay Winter, *Sites of Memory, Sites of Mourning,* Cambridge, Cambridge University Press, 1995.

8. Roland Dorgelès, *Le Réveil des morts*, Paris, Albin Michel, 1923.

9. *Catholicisme*, vol. II, p. 1, 340, col. 2.

10. Pierre Ladoué, *Ceux de 'là-haut'*, 1917, p. 142.

Burial and Consolation

From the beginning of the war the living responded to the dead, no less than the dead to the living: 'Up and on your feet, you who are alive! Stand up to honour the country's brave defenders.'[11] Mgr. Julien was quick to quote Ezekiel[12] in an important address in May 1918:

> Rise up, you dead! . . . Approach from all sides . . . We shall take care not to speak of you as we speak of those who are truly dead. The truly dead are those who are forgotten by mankind. We are here to keep your memory alive in the eternal memory of your country. The truly dead are the forgotten of God. But we are here to win for you the grace of eternal life.[13]

Utterances at religious services for dead soldiers, whether Catholic, Protestant or Jewish, inexorably repeated again and again the idea of a symmetrical relation between the dead and the duty to preserve their memory. Commemoration thus placed itself precisely between death and life, recalling the heroism of the fighting men and consoling those who mourn them.

In 1920, Canon Millot published a collection of speeches and texts for 'services for soldiers who have fallen on the battlefield'.[14] He was inspired to include an index of forty words giving a complete overview of the doctrine of the Catholic Church concerning commemoration: *admiration, âmes* (souls), *amour* (love), *croix* (Cross), *drapeau* (flag), *émotion, espérance* (hope), *exemple, expiation, famille, fleurs* (flowers), *foi* (faith), *France, gloire, guerre* (war), *immortalité, jeunesse* (youth), *justice divine, larmes* (tears), *louanges* (praises), *leçons données par nos morts* (lessons taught by our dead), *mort* (death), *paix* (peace), *parents* (relatives), *patrie* (nation), *prières* (prayers), *protection, purgatoire, reconnaissance* (gratitude), *religion, résurrection, sacrifice, soldats, souffrance, souvenir* (memory), *testament, tombes, union, vie, vertus* (virtues). This list, where the words soul, France, immortality and prayers have the highest number of references, is significant. Death is a sacrifice, life is nourished by one consoling hope, the hope of resurrection, or eternal life.

11. Abbé E. Lemerle, *Tombés au champ d'honneur, Trente-deux allocutions patriotiques*, Paris, Lethielleux, 1917 and 1926, p. 38.

12. 'So I prophesied as he commanded me, and the breath came into them, and they lived, and stood up upon their feet, an exceeding great army.' Ezekiel 37, 10.

13. Mgr. Julien, 'A la gloire des morts de la Grande Guerre', *Le Souvenir Français*, 23 May 1918, p. 2.

14. M. le chanoine Millot, *Nos morts de la guerre, choix de discours pour les services des soldats tombés au champ d'honneur*, Paris, Téqui, 1920.

Giving structure to the memory of the war dead was an ingenious exercise in creating life out of death. In a predominantly Christian society it was natural that the message of Christianity – of sacrifice and resurrection – should coincide perfectly with this effort, to the extent of completely enveloping it: for Memory lies at the heart of Christian sacrifice: 'Do this in remembrance of me' (I Cor. 11, 24–5).

From the time of the first deaths in the summer of 1914, improvised graves, dug hastily during offensives and retreats, were marked with wooden crosses. These became not only the symbol of death but specifically of death in the Great War; before long they became the symbol of war itself, as in the novel by Dorgelès.[15]

Because the cross was the sign of death in western Europe, the respect due the dead was always expressed by it. Although it was not, of course, Christ who was lined up in this way, in rows across the battlefields, nevertheless, as we have seen, it *was* Christ – by imitation. At the inauguration of the Douaumont ossuary in 1932, Abbé Bergey, President of the veteran-priests of France, describes those who

> took up their crosses again and climbed the slopes of Craonne, of Tahure, of Douaumont . . . And so we can apply to them those moving words from the very lips of the divine master: '*O vos omnes qui transitis per viam, attendite et videte si est dolor sicut dolor meus.*'[16]
>
> Oh you who tread today along these roads of Douaumont, of Souville, of Vaux . . . of the Ravine of Death, stop a moment and see if there is a sorrow comparable to the one your heroic little Soldier endured, to save your Country, your name of Frenchman, your worldly goods, your freedom.

The secular Republic, separated from the Church since 1905, buried its war dead under a symbol prohibited on all other public monuments. The proof that the symbol of the Passion is really that of Christian death is the effort that was made to create distinct areas for Jewish and Muslim graves in military cemeteries. The State ordered hundreds of thousands of crosses:

> Notebook of special responsibilities imposed by the contractor of public works . . . for the manufacture of two thousand coffins, small size, and two thousand crosses for the Registry Service of the First district . . . 60 coffins and 60 crosses to be delivered every day . . . The wood to be dried before use

15. Roland Dorgelès, *Les Croix de bois*, 1919. Ironically, this won the 'Vie heureuse' ('happy life') prize in 1919.

16. 'O you who pass along this way, stop and see if there is any pain like mine', *Inauguration de l'ossuaire de Douaumont*, 6, 7, 8 August 1932, pp. 66–7.

and to be of uniform thickness . . . There is to be no faulty construction. The crosses are to be planed on all surfaces.[17]

In their cruel precision – where the civil servant presumably failed to observe the irony of the word 'uniform' – such documents make it possible to overlook the lyricism of enthusiastic testimonials to sacrifice. Minor clerics undertook their labour, without fuss, like the joinery craftsmen whose contract provided for their payment of 2 francs per hour. They had 1,350,000 graves to prepare, repair and make uniform.[18]

Some families would be upset at not being able to bring back to their family vault or parish cemetery the men they had loved when alive and confided to their country but whom they would like to have close to them after their death. A superstition arose in the battlefield: shells that exploded and wounded people passing by were thought to be the revenge of the dead still awaiting burial.

A polemic carried on in all the trench newspapers and heard in the Chamber of Deputies would enable them to have their 'great veterans' exhumed and transported. Three hundred thousand dead were thus legally brought home under the law of 28 September 1920. Ironically, in a certain number of cemeteries where several soldiers from the same village had been repatriated, blocks of graves were created that resemble the official military cemeteries of the front or the hospitals behind the lines, as well as the ossuaries. Uniformity was the inescapable fate of the men who died in the Great War.

The burial of citizens 'who died for France' posed problems because in the 1920s they represented a fundamental political and symbolic stake.[19] The State naturally insisted on keeping together those who had contributed to its victory, and André Maginot became the advocate of this cause. But many families considered that the bodily sacrifice of their sons sufficed: it was time now to reclaim what was theirs. Some spoke

17. SHAT Vincennes, 10 N 194, sale of coffins and crosses, 17 August 1921.

18. The Hollywood script writer Dalton Trumbo wrote a highly pacifist novel in 1939, *Johnny Got His Gun*. The better-known film version dates from 1971. The writer brought in Christ several times, appearing to American soldiers at the front. He was specifically a carpenter, responsible for coffins and crosses.

19. An economic stake too, denounced by Dorgelès in *Le Réveil des morts*, in the shape of the repellent character Bouzier, the businessman-gravedigger: 'Dead men dug up some months earlier . . . were exhumed a second time and it was said that the others, those whose families did not reclaim them, would be buried in their place, to be gathered together at Soupir where there was talk of a national cemetery. But Bouzier had no complaint on the matter; the more often corpses were moved, the more money there was for him' (p. 255).

up abusively with antimilitaristic accusations: 'The dead have a right as well to become civilians again. And your military ossuaries will never be anything but eternal barracks.'[20] One mother was adamant that families would be reunited after death: 'My only consolation would consist of being able to bring together the dispersed remains of my three boys so that they can remain together in the little cemetery near their father. He sleeps peacefully, for he died before having to see the war. Knowing that they are all together, that's all I ask for.'[21] Others, particularly Catholics, wanted to pray over the graves and could not always travel to the battlefields. The difficulties involved in exhumation, even when legalized, and the costs involved in the various procedures, explain why only the wealthiest families – including those of officers – were able to have their dead relatives brought home. Yet this deep need to know where and how the soldiers died and were buried was a constant concern. In each issue *L'Echo de l'ossuaire de Douaumont et des champs de bataille de Verdun* published long lists of 'soldiers found and identified'. The families' enthusiasm for the publication is easily imagined.

For everyone, the period of All Saints is particularly poignant. Both Catholics[22] and Protestants recall that: 'For us, reformed Christians, 1 November is the feast of the Reformation. On that date, we liked to evoke the memory of whose who, in former centuries, died for their faith.'[23] The strategic and diplomatic coincidence that brought victory in November reinforced the greater importance of honouring the dead than of commemoration. Just before the end of the war, a certain Sergeant Y. Villeneuve published a booklet entitled *Pour nos morts. Esquisse d'une organisation nationale de la prière catholique en faveur des morts de la guerre*, in which he suggested that the two feasts of All Saints' and All Souls' Days should become an annual focus of national prayer.

20. *L'Art funéraire et commémoratif*, 1919, no. 2.

21. *L'Art funéraire et commémoratif*, June 1919, no. 2. (Letter in reply to the petition launched by the journal to have bodies transferred.) On the other hand, the former chaplain P. Doncœur insisted in *Etudes* that bodies must be left on 'the field of honour'. 'Don't you want him to remain, as long as France exists, in the national reliquary?' (August 1919, pp. 566–8).

22. Luce Piétri has shown clearly that since the high Middle Ages 'it has been the celebration of all the saints, collectively united in the same love of Christ and already associated with Him in eternal bliss, to be joined after the Last Judgement by the faithful dead who have been remembered the next day'. 'Les origines de la fête de la Toussaint', *Les Quatre Fleuves*, 25–6, 1988, pp. 57–61. This 'remembrance of all the dead' took on even greater significance with the war.

23. Sermon by Pastor Taquet, 1 November 1919, Paris, Fischbacher, 1920, p. 11.

Annual days for the universal Communion of saints, and for the Communion of the saints of France! A brilliant triumph of the twin forms of justice: that of God and that of our nation! A powerful offensive of help for our dead, renewed and promoted further, every autumn! An unparalleled axis of fervour for the religious cycle of French patriotism![24]

The unprecedented crowds of people in French cemeteries on 1 November during the war and in 1919 indicated a nationwide desire to be in communion somewhere, and the places dedicated to death were the natural choice, in a space reserved for meditation or prayer. On 1 and 2 November 1919, the first Days of the Dead after the war, cemeteries attracted visitors in particularly large numbers. The sadness of families, especially of children, is visible in the films that were shot that day for the Gaumont newsreels. In the Paris cemeteries of Père Lachaise, Pantin and Saint-Ouen, and in Lille, the cameramen caught crowds in black, flowers, inscriptions: 'To my fiancé. Souls united in God are never divided.' The most original and significant aspect of this need for commemoration created by the war appeared in the form of focal points for remembering the dead soldiers in various cemeteries: at a sculpture called 'the angel of remembrance' in Montparnasse; on wooden columns at Bagneux; along interior walls at Ivry; at the central round-point in the cemetery of Saint-Ouen. Plaques for soldiers without a known grave are set alongside figures of the Virgin, portraits, flowers, inscriptions: 'for his *Toussaint*' (All Saints) or 'for his birthday'.[25] Thus an 'irregular' commemoration was established at the same time as a collective one, and almost always highly formal commemoration was attempting to respond to endless questions from individuals.

From the beginning of the war, laymen and clergy had been considering possible forms of commemoration. On 16 February 1916 at Bar-le-Duc, the Bishop of Verdun, Mgr. Ginisty, addressed the ceremony of the 'Red Cross and French Memory'. In 1919, Mgr. Ginisty's collected *Paroles de Guerre* were published, including the speech on 'Our battlefields, our fields of the dead' which proposed a full-scale programme of commemoration:

Later, after the victory and the peace, your societies will prepare and direct great pilgrimages across our battlefields ... To honour bodies is good; but

24. Y. Villeneuve, *Pour nos morts. Esquisse d'une organisation nationale de la prière catholique en faveur des morts de la guerre*, Paris, Imprimerie des orphelins-apprentis d'Auteuil, 1918, pp. 92–3.

25. Newsreel film conserved in the Paris film library. *L'Illustration*, 1 November 1919, Pierre Calel, 'Les morts de la guerre dans les cimetières parisiens', pp. 365–6.

souls are beautiful in another way, and worthy of religious interest . . . It is right to engrave names, and to inscribe exploits on parchment, bronze or marble.

And we must turn once more to Religion for inspiration . . . In the great cemeteries of the battlefields, we would like to see a chapel erected . . . and an altar . . . The redeeming blood of the divine Victim would be mingled to some extent with the blood of the saviours of the country . . . Next to the missal, the great Book of liturgical prayer, there would be another, a book of remembrance or illustrated album which . . . would recall the great deeds of the combatants . . . Let us raise the great War Memorial in the Panthéon, nothing could be better! . . . But the first precious casket for these treasures of glory is the funeral chapel that guards the hero's ashes

Next comes his parish, his original church where his name on the Roll of Honour will be read aloud with honour every Sunday and be cause for public prayer.

Finally his family and home. There the portrait of the valiant warrior will be enshrined . . . But there is another monument finer than marble, more durable than stone . . . This is faith, admiration, gratitude; it is the prayers and sacrifice of a whole people; and the sanctuary where it is to be erected is the heart of the nation. There is the true mausoleum of souls . . . In all its divers forms your great work, my brothers, . . . will contribute . . . towards its construction. Thus, thanks to you, victors over death and oblivion, our heroes will live on, and their memory will be blessed across the centuries.[26]

Battlefield chapels, war memorials, prayers at funeral services and family reunions, 'local memories, national memories',[27] all the ingredients of commemoration are already inscribed in this text from the bishop of no less a place than Verdun, speaking several weeks before the beginning of the most famous battle of the war. The date is important for two reasons: because it proves that the organization of the remembrance of war is inherent in war itself, and because it is supported by a precedent, that of the commemoration of the war dead of 1870-1. Mgr. Ginisty's conclusion is enlightening:

And the Church in her turn offers God her remembering and her memorial. To the glory of the Sacred Heart - which loves the French and which, with the Holy Virgin and the incomparable Joan of Arc, has saved them once more - she dedicates the national Monument of her faith, of her gratitude and of her love. Begun in tears and the humiliations of defeat, nearly half a century

26. Mgr. Ginisty, *Verdun! Paroles de guerre*, Paris, Téqui, 1919, pp. 24-9.

27. Here I am borrowing the title of an article by Antoine Prost, 'Mémoires locales et mémoires nationales. Les monuments de 1914-1918 en France', *Guerres mondiales et conflits contemporains*, no. 167, July 1992, pp. 41-50.

ago, it will be accomplished in the joy of triumph and revenge, and the gold of its domes and its cupolas will shine in the sun of victory, of peace and of the 'Sacred Union' of the French people. Amen.[28]

The religious plan for commemoration was based primarily on the certainty of a resurgence: from the defeat of 1871 to the coming victory. The monuments would no longer bear the inscription 'Gloria Victis', for soldiers dying 'Pro Patria' and revealing their country's failure.[29]

The second certainty is the 'Sacred Union'. Reminder of the sacrifices of the dead passed through exaltation of the living, through the political insistence necessary to victory called union, which was consecrated by the unique importance of its cause. In all political parties as in all the Churches, during and after the war, this insistence on the role of the dead in the France of the future was constant. In an article of 2 November 1914, Charles Maurras established this programme:

> In the aftermath of the final victory, we must take care to mingle constantly with our cries of joy the tears so long restrained . . . What finer France will we recreate on tombs almost as venerable as altars? . . . Universal mourning will then be the greatest intercessor among us . . . and the noblest incentive . . . Yesterday we were seeking the necessary sacrifices through vigilance and foresight in the name of a somewhat abstract fatherland. Tomorrow the dignified procession of the dead will be irresistible.[30]

The sculptor Jean Ajalbert was deliberating the same subject at the same time and published a book in which he asked numerous personalities in the world of art and politics: *Comment glorifier les morts pour la patrie?* (How to glorify the men who died for their country?) His conclusion was similar:

> Through the centuries, their imposing image must possess posterity, which is too inclined to forgetfulness . . . Just as rough crosses in the fields perpetuate the religious aspect of the past, so inscriptions repeated from north to south, from east to west would create for the entire land a new moral ambience . . . They would repeat and maintain the Sacred Union, setting rich and poor side by side in the ordeal, priest and schoolteacher, squire and cowherd.[31]

28. Ginisty, *Verdun!*, pp. 28-9.

29. On memorials to the war of 1870-1 see: Annette Becker, 'Monuments aux morts après la guerre de Sécession et la guerre de 1870-71: un legs de la guerre nationale?', *Guerres mondiales et conflits contemporains*, no. 167, July 1992, pp. 23-40.

30. 'Notre jour des morts', *Action française*, 2 November 1914.

31. Jean Ajalbert, *Comment glorifier les morts pour la patrie?*, Paris, 1916, p. 3.

In the best days of the Sacred Union, before 1917, it seemed normal to see lay and even anticlerical personalities of the greatest importance sharing, in broad terms, the views of well-known representatives of the world of religion. Victory once achieved, would it allow commemoration by the Sacred Union?

Battlefield Ossuaries and Local War Memorials: the *Union Sacrée* in Stone?

In comprehending the memory of war, we must distinguish between the battlefields where the soldiers fell, where they disappeared or were buried – all in the north and east of France – and their places of origin, in terms of their various local, professional and religious communities.

Because the war memorials of the communes, built for the most part between 1919 and 1924, are the most visible in the entire country, situated out of doors rather than inside buildings, they are the best known. Their common denominator, the commune, is obviously the most widely shared element. Unfortunately no organized comprehensive study of France's 35,000 (or 36,000?) communal war memorials has yet been undertaken. However, substantial departmental studies will make up for this lacuna.

In choosing to draw a parallel between communal monuments on the one hand, and the four national battlefield ossuaries / necropolis cemeteries on the other – Douaumont, Lorette, Dormans, Hartman-willerkopf, together with the commemorative chapel of the battle of the Somme at Rancourt – we are superimposing a national framework, common to the commemoration of all soldiers, on to the local map grid. The great ossuaries share with local war memorials the task of commemorating the men who were lost. Some are empty tombs, cenotaphs; others contain thousands, even tens of thousands of men whose identity has been consumed in earth and fire. The communal war memorials, like those of parishes and professional bodies, show names whose bodies are unknown: the ossuaries contain heaped bodies without names.

Each of the five ossuaries lies at the centre of a vast necropolis where identified men are buried. In the spirit of the 1920s, local and battlefield commemorations were thus complementary. The Unknown Soldier of the Arc de Triomphe in Paris was chosen on 10 November 1920 at Verdun. Republican determination left no doubt over the ceremonial transferral of the unknown soldier to the Arc de Triomphe on 11 November 1920, two years after 1918, fifty years after 1870.[32] The decision to transfer the heart of Gambetta to the Pantheon at the same moment says much about the political effect that was being sought.

> What would have become of Gambetta's labours if the unknown soldier had not been there from 1914 to 1918 to oppose his breast to the barbarian hordes? . . . Glory to you, humble martyr whom we know only by the name of French Soldier. Who are you, poor comrade? Where do you come from? No one knows . . . We know only one thing, that you were our saviour.[33]

Syncretism and ecumenism enabled everyone to find 'his' soldier and to bury him his own way: the victim of sacrifice was being celebrated, or his death was being sanitized.

Do the monuments in the communes allow the same patterns of analysis? Although between a third and half of the war memorials were placed in front of village-halls or schools – Republican sites *par excellence* – there is still much to be explained which lies partly or wholly outside the Republic. Is it because the war (and its intrinsic cult of the dead) opened the way to a renewed spiritual element that only the Churches really knew how to channel? The fervour hovering over the commemoration of the war matched the magnitude of the drama.

During the war, certain sectors of the front had already been labelled 'sacred', as, for example, by the Catholic military doctor Vallery-Radot: 'Holy land of France . . . earth held tight in the grip of war, sacred land.'[34] After the war the words Artois, Somme, Verdun, Marne were inscribed on war memorials: no longer names of battles, these are names with a religious resonance, uttered with the same fervour as the names of the dead men lost in their soil. They have become a metonymy of sacrifice.

Moreover, people began to go on pilgrimages to these battlefields, particularly for All Saints' Day and at Christmas, as here at the temporary ossuary of Douaumont:

> An uninterrupted procession of pious visits . . . at the time for exchanging New Years gifts . . . Today again we think of the hero and we want to do

32. See the Ph.D. thesis of Avner Ben Amos, *Molding the National Memory, the State Funerals of the French Third Republic*, 3 vols., typescript, 1988, to be published by Oxford University Press, and his article, 'The Sacred Center of Power: Paris and Republican State Funerals', *Journal of Interdisciplinary History*, XXII: I (Summer 1991), pp. 27–48.

33. J. Mermet, 'Le cinquantenaire de la République', *Le Progrès de l'Oise*, 10 November 1920. For more details on this, see the Epilogue.

34. Pasteur Vallery-Radot, *Pour la terre de France par la douleur et la mort*, Paris, 1919 (written in 1914-15).

something . . . Here is a wartime godmother who lost her godson at Verdun and who does not want the year to end without sending her offering in his memory . . . Here is a widow, asking for a taper to burn before Our Lady of the Seven Sorrows during the midnight mass.[35]

And a little of the soil was brought back and enclosed in an urn at the foot of certain monuments. With the earth of Verdun or of the Somme, places could be consecrated that experienced the war only as 'a long litany of men killed and yearned for by their families'. Pilgrimages always meant the purchase of souvenirs, and mass-produced little terracotta sets of the Way of the Cross, complete with helmets and palms, were rapidly available from shrewd merchants. 'This milestone contains a bit of sacred earth from Verdun.'[36]

The designers and constructors of the very large memorials tried to avoid this type of commercialism, but the projects were costly and often required funding campaigns undertaken by various promoters. Mgr. Ginisty went all the way to the United States to ensure the construction of the Douaumont beacon. American generosity is clearly visible in the building, and the great bell bears an engraving: 'I owe my existence to the generosity of Madame Anne Thorburn Von Buren, who gave me in order to render thanks to God for the great victory of Verdun, and in memory of the French and American soldiers who fell on the battlefield.'

The bishops were indeed involved in the origins of the commemorative ensembles of Lorette (Mgr. Julien), Dormans (Mgr. Tissier[37] and Verdun (Mgr. Ginisty). The strongly Catholic du Bos family founded the Rancourt-Bouchavesnes memorial to commemorate a kinsman fallen in battle. The commemoration committee was placed under the patronage of the Bishop of Amiens.[38] Only the local committee establishing Hartman-

35. *L'Echo de l'ossuaire de Douaumont*, November–December 1922, p. 240.

36. The literature of pilgrimage also proliferated. Emile Poiteau, *Pèlerinages en Artois*. (Commemorative poetry.) The Lorette foundation, held in the Pas-de-Calais departmental archives, contains several folders of commercial advertisements for 'religious statues, statuettes and Christmas figures' and other 'general merchandise of religious objects' (42 J. 128–9). The very detailed accounts of the Association show that sacred images, decorated ashtrays and other objects of commemorative kitsch were the public's preference. Dorgelès also described, in *Le Réveil des morts*, traders with supplies of mortuary articles for the pilgrims.

37. The bishop of the 'Miracle of the Marne' and author of 'La vie religieuse' in *La Vie catholique dans la France contemporaine*, Paris, Bloud et Gay, 1918.

38. Philippe Trépagne, 'La Mémoire des batailles de la Somme dans l'entre-deux-guerres dans le département de la Somme', MA degree dissertation, supervised by Nadine Chaline and Stéphane Audoin-Rouzeau, University of Picardy, 1992.

willerkopf, in Alsace, did not see itself as a purely religious project, although the great majority of its members were Catholic.

All the sites selected have acquired an aura of heroism and sacrifice. They emphasize the front line, described by Dupouey as a 'long mystical line'. At the harshest, most dreadful points of the offensives, at these geographical witness-stands of death, there is a wish to recall, as prominently and forcefully as possible, the reality of the Great War. The decision to raise an ossuary over an immense necropolis at these focal points was inevitable: 'To preserve the memory of those whose heroism won the victory, and to raise a national monument of gratitude to God and to the heroes who saved the country.'[39] The secretary-general of the Douaumont Ossuary undertaking, Henri de Montherlant, described what visitors would see: 'They will find hope sitting there, like the angel on the tombstone. And hope is never a lie. The earth of the Campo Santo in Pisa was brought back from Golgotha. The earth of the holy field of Douaumont is natural calvary soil.'[40]

Each site is thus presented as a *campo santo*, a holy field where cemetery, ossuary, Catholic chapel (Verdun, Dormans, Lorette, Rancourt) or ecumenical chapel (Hartmanwillerkopf), cloister, beacon or lantern of the dead, are all related and associated. 'The only homage worthy of their memory would be the construction of a village church in order that prayers could be sent up for them, from the very earth their devotion has given to their Country, and the construction of a commemorative monument.'[41]

The complete agreement between the Ministry of Pensions, charged with national necropolis organization, and the private committees interested in commemorative monument construction was not without various difficulties and polemics similar to the problems disturbing communes as they built their own war memorials. Aesthetic and monetary concerns triumphed over ideology. On the necessity of building monuments to these 'sacrificed men', to these 'martyrs', there was virtual unanimity throughout the nation, including the terminology to be used. From Georges Duhamel's *Vie des Martyrs* to the pacifist lyrics of the *Chanson de Craonne*, 'We are the sacrificial victims', the phrases were

39. Mgr. Tissier, cited by Jean-Pierre Verney, 'Les nécropoles nationales françaises et les monuments des champs de batailles', in Annette Becker and Philippe Rivé, *Monuments de mémoire, monuments aux morts de la Grande Guerre*, Secrétariat d'Etat aux anciens combattants et victimes de guerre, 1991, p. 107.

40. Henri de Montherlant, *Chant funèbre pour les morts de Verdun*, Paris, Grasset, 1924, p. 44.

41. The Rancourt project cited by Trépagne, *La Mémoire*, p. 69.

used in the passive sense for what was claimed as strongly active by the mystics of patriotism and/or faith.[42]

Faced with difficulty in completing the monuments, in 1929 France even introduced 'National days for the completion of the four great monuments of the front'. Under the patronage of the President of the Republic, all the marshals of France, the cardinals and archbishops, the pastors and the Chief Rabbi, flags, insignia, pictures or postcards were sold on 4 and 28 July to help raise the funds required.

As for the design and ornamentation of the great monumental ensembles, the power of Christianity was never in doubt. All are ex-votos, and – taking up the excellent typology used by Jacques Benoît for Sacré-Cœur of Montmartre – ex-votos of stone, of prayer (all the faithful who come there to pray), and of imagination (iconography and décor).[43] The high tower of Douaumont even adopts the form of a gigantic crusader, with its four crosses dominating the horizon and windows like helmet slits.

On the lantern tower of Lorette, the inscriptions chosen by Mgr. Julien take the form of prayer quatrains:

> You who pass as pilgrims near their tombs,
> Climbing their calvary and its bloody roads,
> Hear the clamour of the hecatombs:
> 'Be united, people, be human.
>
> Bones that once a proud breath rendered living,
> Scattered limbs, nameless remains, human chaos,
> Sacred medley of a vast reliquary,
> God will recognize in you the dust of heroes!'

42. Since the exception proves the rule, it should be pointed out that a few refusals of commemoration came from socialists (or Communists after 1920) who preferred to use the money for social aims, as in Lens in the Pas-de-Calais. In Lyon the ARAC (veterans) refused to cooperate in the construction of the city's monument in striking terms: 'Would you consider, Monsieur le Maire, putting up monuments to Leprosy? You may say that it is a matter of commemorating the dead and not the war: but since one cannot have the one without the other, we disapprove of any commemoration . . . So the country having once been covered with 'Gloria Victis', it is now to be saturated with 'Gloria Victoribus' while, on the other side of the Rhine, 'they' will be doing the same, but the other way round . . . And what about the inaugural speeches? Has your classicism been able to calculate the mass of solemn and venomous public sites that all the grumblers will spill out at the foot of their memorials at the same moment, perhaps, where before our new monuments the relentless eloquence of our "professors of energy" will be poured out?' 12 April 1920, Municipal Archives, Lyon, 'monuments aux morts'.

43. Jacques Benoist, 'Le Sacré-Cœur de Montmartre', introduction.

[Vous qui passez en pèlerins près de leurs tombes, / Gravissant leur calvaire et ses sanglants chemins / Ecoutez la clameur qui sort des hécatombes / Peuples soyez unis, peuples soyez humains. / Ossements qu'animait un fier souffle naguère, / Membres épars, débris sans noms, humain chaos, / Pêle-mêle sacré d'un vaste reliquaire, / Dieu vous reconnaîtra poussière de héros!]

The choice of artists to decorate the chapels was carefully thought out: at Douaumont the great Catholic painter George Desvallières[44] was given responsibility for the stained glass, while at Lorette the glassmaker Charles Lorin offered a window in memory of his son Etienne, killed in 1917. He in turn chose Henri Pinta, one of the decorators of the basilica of Montmartre, to execute his sketches. A Romano-Byzantine basilica was thus built on the exact site of the chapel erected in 1727 by the painter Nicolas Florent Guillebert in gratitude to the Virgin for his recovery at the Italian sanctuary of Loreto, a chapel pulverized by the battles of this latest war. 'From now on this earth is twice holy and twice sacred.'[45]

Ecumenism is present too, particularly at Hartmanwillerkopf. In the centre of the crypt, a wide bronze disc, 'PATRIE', is surrounded by the lines of Victor Hugo: 'Those who died in piety for their country / Have the right for their tomb to become a place of prayer.'[46] Three altars stand against the walls – one Catholic, with a Virgin and Child by Bourdelle, one Protestant and one Jewish. Inscriptions drawn from Saint John ('I am the Resurrection and the Life') or from Ezekiel ('With the four winds blow, O Spirit, blow upon these bodies and make them live again') emphasize the shared power of the Old and New Testaments. 'Each year three ministers of different faiths, but having the same God and the same dead, will officiate in this sacred place.'[47]

The monument of Hartmanwillerkopf was conceived in a spirit of ecumenism and of the *Union sacrée* at one and the same time, since the interdenominational crypt is placed under an altar to the nation, itself surrounded by a military cemetery dominated by the slopes of the Vieil-Armand, an immense cross on its summit. The aim was to group on a

44. We will return later to this important commemorative artist.
45. Mgr. Julien, *A la mémoire des 100,000 héros tombés à Lorette*, Arras, p. 5, and Paris, Téqui, 1920.
46. 'Ceux qui pieusement sont morts pour la patrie / Ont droit qu'à leur cercueil la foule vienne et prie.' These lines are often inscribed on communal war memorials or recited at 11 November ceremonies. It is interesting to note that the lines were written by Victor Hugo in 1831 to commemorate Parisians killed in the 1830 revolution. Their 'nation' had suffered attack not from a foreign power but from 'despotism'. The use of the lines after 1871 and 1918 gives them a very different meaning.
47. *Les Nouvelles de Strasbourg*, 7 July 1936.

single axis 'the battlefield dominated by the cross, the field of rest dominated by the flag, and the field of honour dominated by the Altar of the nation'.[48] Reports of the annual ceremonies always devote a large part to the three religious services.

Although Catholicism predominates at Douaumont, there are Jewish and Muslim commemorative monuments. The universality of the Catholic Church is emphasized: 'Chapel offered by the Catholics of France, Belgium, Canada, Switzerland, the United States'. Similarly, at the time of the dedication of the Dormans ossuary in September 1931, the Catholic Primate of England, Cardinal Bourne, was present and called on the union of France and England 'for the salvation of civilization'.

The speeches delivered by the different faiths evoked ecumenism and the *Union sacrée* in parallel:

> We shall go to the monument of the Marne victory (at Meaux) as to a sacred place, as one goes to pray on the tombs that are dear to us . . . For us it will be a place of interdenominational pilgrimage, where the prayers of all will mingle, where religion, no less than our country, will bring to all those who fell on the battlefields the immense homage that is their due.[49]

The creeds are assimilatory even unto death: 'We no longer ask, "Are you republican, monarchist, socialist, Israelite, free-thinker, or Catholic?" but simply: "Are you French?" . . . When each of us rises up he is no longer anonymous . . . obscure. He becomes a giant and dominates history . . . That is what our union can accomplish. To forget that would be to betray our dead and betray France.'[50]

When the Lorette chapel was consecrated in 1927, a 5,000-strong choir performed the Requiem Mass of Alexandre Georges in the open air. The programme described the work at length:

> The Requiem. The entire first part reflects anguish. The three movements of the prelude express the collapse and misery of a whole nation after the bloody days . . . The Kyrie . . . The parallel in the minds of venerated mothers seeing on this Lorette plateau the Golgotha of their children who died for their country . . . The *De profundis* . . . The brutal emotion seizes you, as all the higher brasses sound 'to arms' before the final Requiem, as at its opening all

48. *L'Alsace française*, 9–16 October 1932, p. 852.
49. *L'Univers israélite*, 1932. Cited by Laundau, *th.cit.* vol. II, p. 448. Michel Lagrée has studied an interesting example of the *Union sacrée* as seen by Catholics, with the example of wood carvings created during the 1920s by the Breton former chaplain Prudent Quémerais, 'The Influence of Catholic Sport in France between the two World Wars: an Iconographic Example', *Sport histoire*, no.1, 1988, pp. 115–20.
50. *Inauguration de l'ossuaire de Douaumont*, p. 70.

the flags are flown at half-mast, as its last words, 'Requiem Aeternam', seem to linger in the throats of the performers effaced before the voice of the essential and inevitable soloist, the cannon.[51]

In the conception of these monuments, in the choice of their architects and decorators, and even in their inaugural ceremonies, there is a clear intention to blend the cult of the war dead with an affirmation of religious faith.

Which faith? Certain themes are doubly striking, both because they repeat those that were dominant during the war (the imitation of Christ, from the Passion to the resurrection, and the imitation of the Virgin, of the 'Stabat Mater') and because these themes also appear on the war memorials of the communes. Yet, with a few exceptions, these were not the consequence of the Churches' direct will or action.[52]

The Land and the Dead

The vast majority of the war memorials of the French communes have the formal simplicity and modesty of expenditure represented by a simple stele or obelisk. Placed in cemeteries with a cross on top, such monuments had been made for centuries to honour individual memories of the war dead. After the War of 1870, they were still usually confined to cemeteries in collective commemoration of the dead who had been buried elsewhere. With the Great War, the incidence increased quantitatively and qualitatively: more steles commemorating more dead, and more often placed in the centre of the village. By law the stele could not have a cross on the top of it unless it stood in the cemetery or near the church. In the strongly Catholic west, in Alsace and in Lorraine, more monuments were erected in the cemeteries or the parish grounds than elsewhere in France. This enabled the inhabitants to Christianize their monuments as much as they wished.[53]

51. Archives of the Pas-de-Calais, Lorette foundation. Alexandre Georges, a native of the Pas-de-Calais, a veteran of the 1870 war and choirmaster to the Comtesse de Paris, had composed a cantata 'La revanche' (Revenge) and 'songs of war'. During the Great War he composed religious music. He was thus particularly well suited for this 'Lorette Requiem'.
52. See Annette Becker, *Les Monuments aux Morts, mémoire de la Grande Guerre*, Paris, Errance, 1988, ch. IV, 'La patrie comme passion'.
53. In Vendée and Loire-Atlantique 65 per cent of the monuments are in cemeteries, in the Pas-de-Calais the figure is 38 per cent. Articles by Florence Regourd, Yves Pilven de Sevellec and Bénédicte Grailles respectively, in *Monuments de mémoire*. In the Vaucluse, out of 148 communes with at least one memorial (there are frequently several, in particular one inside a church, see below), and 86 in cemeteries. (J. Giroud, R & M Michel, *Les*

However, in many small villages the space surrounding the church, town hall, school or cemetery was extremely small. The position of the local war memorial offers a form of résumé of the life and death of the soldiers. Probably baptized and married in the local church, they attended the school in the commune before dying for it: 'The commune of X to its children' is by far the commonest inscription to be found in the Republic. All these memorials without sculpture are funerary monuments, symbols of sacrifice, that could be called Republican if placed near the town hall, or Christian if surmounted by a cross. The explanations for this sacrifice are not in competition: the cults of the Republic and the Churches are complementary, just as the combined efforts of all contributed to the victory.

By 1922, when 11 November became a national holiday, the ceremonies had become a cult whose striking parallel with Catholic liturgy has been described by Antoine Prost.[54] Yet this syncretic cult was not enough for the more religious of those who attended, since in the immense majority of cases a religious service either preceded or followed the ceremony at the memorial. This enabled priests and pastors to recall the message of their Church and their doctrine in regard to death and war. Often, quoting letters from dead soldiers, they would cite passages that were veritable spiritual testaments. In some communes combatants' letters were engraved on the monument, making it simultaneously a testament and a means of making them live again.

> Martyr, in Greek, means witness: a witness faithful unto death. At the side of the Christian martyrs there are the martyrs of patriotism . . . To give one's life: all is there. What does death matter if I have been useful? I am not sent in order to be killed, but to fight; I offer my life for future generations. This is not death, it is a new posting.[55]

Without waiting for memorials to be built, a committee had met to prepare a book of the last letters 'written by French soldiers killed in

---

Monuments aux morts dans le Vaucluse, Paris, Scriba, 1991) Bernard Cousin and Geneviève Richer investigated the memorials in the Bouches-du-Rhône on this point, which they describe as 'laicized and patriotic'. 'They have no religious imprint, unless it is considered such that more than half the memorials stand in cemeteries'. *Marseille*, 1st quarter, 1977, pp. 18–26.

54. Antoine Prost, *In the Wake of War, 'Les Anciens Combattants' and French Society 1914–1939*, Oxford, Berg, 1992. (*Les Anciens Combattants et la société française*, Paris, 3 vols, PFNSP, 1977.)

55. Address by Pastor Taquet, p. 13. The letter quoted here was written by G. Groll, assistant secretary of the Christian Union of Young Parisians.

the field of honour'.[56] The introduction by Marshal Foch, President of the Committee, stated: 'This is one more monument to the undying glory of the French soldier.' The book contains, in alphabetic order, the last letters of several hundred soldiers whose unfailing patriotism ignores political and religious divisions. Written between 1914 and 1918, they were published in 1921 as a tribute to the *Union sacrée*, the Sacred Union, in the same way as the monuments. Alphonse Dupront's characterization of the Sacred Union, 'loyal respect for each of the mystical or rational sources of its moral strength',[57] is perhaps too fine to describe adequately such post-war attempts to preserve the memory of what could no longer be saved in reality.

Commemoration as Resurrection: Imitating Christ and Mary

The second category of commemorative monuments consists of war memorials decorated with sculptures by artists, sometimes of national but most commonly of regional reputation, or else bought from foundry catalogues. Although abstract art was in its early phases, it was never chosen for a monument. Instead, we see the mark of the neo-classical taste of the greater or lesser notables responsible for ordering the monuments, inheritors of the 'statuemania' of the nineteenth century. But Nathan Rapoport, who was in charge of creating a memorial to the Warsaw Ghetto after the Second World War, had this to say about his choice of the figurative style:

> Could I have made a stone with a hole in it and said, '*Voilà*! The heroism of the Jews'? No, I needed to show the heroism, to illustrate it literally in figures everyone, not just artists, would respond to. This was to be a public monument, after all. And what do human beings respond to? Faces, figures, the human form. I did not want to represent resistance in the abstract: it was not an abstract uprising, it was real.[58]

Similarly, the fighting men of the Great War had waged a 'very real' war, and they intended this to be evident to future observers. The monuments represent above all the '*poilus*', victorious or dying, attacking or exhausted; they are the supreme subjects of commemoration: regardless

56. *La Dernière Lettre*, Paris, Flammarion, 1922.
57. *La France et les Français*, Paris, Encyclopédie de la Pléiade, 1972, p. 1503.
58. Interview by James E. Young in 1986: 'The Biography of a Memorial Icon', in *The Texture of Memory, Holocaust Memorials and Meaning*, New Haven, Yale University Press, 1993, p. 168. (The monument was built in 1948 in Warsaw. A replica was recast in Yad Vashem, Jerusalem, in 1975.)

of any individual feelings about war in general, face to face with the
poilu there is unanimity of respect and sorrow. The memorials express
the universal desire for resurrection. From the grains of wheat more or
less discreetly present, to Christ himself represented beside or above
the *poilu*, all the symbolic forms available to express resurrection were
spelled out by the sculptors.[59]

We have already seen that Charles Péguy's poem *Eve* and its theme
had become topical during the war, and in commemoration it appears
again and again. At the age of fourteen in 1917, Jean Cavaillès concluded
an essay thus:

> Oh grains of wheat, the blood of so many heroes has fertilized the soil; to the
> golden liquor of the sun is joined the red liquor of men ... Through your
> abundance, nourish all of France and especially those of its children who are
> fighting to save you ... May your seeds infuse in their hearts an ever greater
> ardour to hasten the victory and drive out the invader.[60]

One of the most prolific French creators of war memorials was the
sculptor Maxime Réal del Sarte.[61] Former President of the *Camelots du
roi* (young royalists associated with *Action française*) and a military
veteran, he had suffered heavily in the war, losing a brother and his own
right arm. It is hardly surprising that this great Catholic, responsible for
most of the statues of Joan of Arc erected in the 1920s, should have
created many war memorials. A personal friend of Maurras, he did not
hesitate to represent him as a soldier on the Rouen memorial. Réal's first
monument, erected at Saint-Jean-de-Luz and dedicated to his brother
Serge, is called 'The Soil of France'. Many French communes commissioned the same model, which he adapted to their wishes without
changing its theme: a young woman or some children meditating beside
a tomb nearly hidden by stalks of wheat. Suffering and prayer may be
stressed more or less strongly, but the symbolism of resurrection is always
the main element. The comment of one observer to Réal del Sarte was
apposite: 'Are you not the image of France herself, who, though mutilated,
shines anew? ... Eternally, generations will come to kneel at the foot of

---

59. Dorgelès presents one of the rare exceptions in *Le Réveil des morts*: 'Crosses had
sprung up everywhere. No more trees in the orchards, no more wheat in the fields, but
graves and ever more graves ... And Jacques ... sought the place that André had chosen
to die in there, when unknown hands had thrown fistfuls of men to the wind, all these
blue seeds that would never germinate.'

60. Jean-François Sirinelli, *Intellectuels et passions françaises*, Paris, Fayard, 1990,
p. 36.

61. See Annette Becker, 'Réal del Sarte', in Becker and Rivé, *Monuments de mémoire*,
pp. 239–41.

your monument.'[62] Clemenceau liked his sculpture; he saw in it 'the whole soul of France', while the Bishop of Dax was certain that 'to sculpt like that is to practice a vocation of true religious quality'.[63]

The title that Réal chose for his work is unequivocal. Just as in 1909 he was already singing the song of the *Camelots du roi* ('Tomorrow on our tombs the wheat will flourish more beautifully'), he stated now that the blood of heroes would revive the soul of France.

This lyricism in stone was accompanied by numerous similar speeches throughout the 1920s and 1930s. The expression 'French soil' was reiterated constantly and Abbé Bergey used it as the basis for a veritable parable of the war:

> And here is what I saw: when one of my soldiers fell, the tall stalks of wheat would separate as though with infinite respect, to receive the body... And when, in the evening, we went... to gather up our comrades, we could not find them in the inextricable web of the wheat... The earth did not want to give them up to us. She was keeping her little ones to herself, who before dying had come to declare their love to her. They have saved the soil of France.[64]

Mgr. Julien, wondering what monument 'would be worthy of their sacrifice and their triumph', concluded with the wish: 'May the French soil... remain the principal witness of their heroism and martyrdom... Let the trees of the forests, themselves mutilated, extend their arms like crosses, in memory of the tree of immortal hopes planted once and for eternity by the Divine One who was crucified on the sorrows of the earth.'[65] Many communes followed Mgr. Julien's concept, placing the Saviour and the saviours of France side by side on their memorials. The soldier may be fighting, or wounded, or dying at the foot of the cross, or his gaze may be meeting the eyes of Christ, as if a mission calvary were the surest way to recall the combatants of the Great War. The most touching monuments are those representing the Entombment: there is an infinite play of reflection between the memorial – by definition an empty tomb – Golgotha and its three crosses, and these *poilus* weeping for their comrades, inert sculpted bodies, endless lists of names. There must be no confusion: we are concerned here with communal rather than parish monuments. And if they are more numerous in departments

62. Jean Ybarnegary cited by Anne-André Glandy, *Maxime Réal del Sarte, sa vie, son œuvre*, Paris, Plon, 1955, p. 122.

63. *Ibid.*, pp. 122, 115.

64. *Inauguration de l'ossuaire de Douaumont*, p. 63.

65. Mgr. Julien, 'A la gloire des morts de la Grande Guerre', *Le Souvenir français*, 23 May 1918.

Figure 11. War memorial of Campbon (Loire Atlantique). Entombing Christ, entombing a soldier.

where Catholic practice is the strongest – in Brittany with René Quillivic's fine sculptures, or in Alsace where, faced with the ambiguity of the uniform worn by 'fallen children' who might have been in either the French or the German army, the resurrection was an even more overwhelming aspiration – no region in France was exempt.

The sculpted decorations of the ossuaries and war memorials devote much space to the Virgin, to her sorrows and courage, and by extension to those of mothers, relations, and fighting men.

The reconstructed chapel of Lorette was naturally intended to be dedicated to the Virgin. The prayers dedicated to her here were remembered. The text on the new pediment now reads:

> To thee who from the womb of sorrows
> Gave birth to holy hope,
> To thee this temple born of tears
> Is offered by the women of France.

[A toi qui du sein des douleurs / Enfantas la sainte espérance / A toi ce temple né des pleurs / Offert par les femmes de France.]

At Dormans, situated (at the suggestion of the devout Marshal Foch) at the heart of the two battle areas of the Marne – that of 1914, the 'miracle', and that of 1918, the 'victory' – the Virgin is present everywhere, as at Hartmanwillerkopf, where Bourdelle has her displaying her new-born son. 'Queen of martyrs, console the afflicted.'

In cemeteries and in public squares, Mary suffers and consoles. The *Pietà*, the mother of sorrows, is the form of Christian iconography most often utilized for commune monuments. Whether Mary herself is holding a *poilu*, or whether she is being imitated by an allegorical figure of the town or of a very real mother – from Vendée, Flanders, Savoy, Brittany or the Auvergne – the artists and their commissioners leave no doubt as to the real subject.[66] The most astonishing example of this recycling of Christian imagery is the entirely masculine *Pietà* in the Czech cemetery at La Targette (Pas-de-Calais). The Czech volunteers of the battle of Lorette have imitated Christ; have they not also made possible the 'resurrection' of their nation? Thus we are shown a visual summary of wartime Christianity, where a *poilu*/Mary is holding a *poilu*/Christ. The survivor shows his grief, but in the hope of resurrection. 'The Church does not forbid tears, it only forbids us to weep as those do who have no hope.'[67]

---

66. See *Monuments de mémoire*, and the illustrations in this volume.
67. Mgr. Morelle, 5 December 1918, special service for the war dead, Guingamp.

Figure 12. War memorial of the Czech cemetery in La Targette (Pas-de-Calais). 'They chose to die for liberty' (1925).

Figure 13. War memorial, Metz. Metz being German from 1871 to 1918, the soldier/Christ of this *Pietà* has no uniform. He had been fighting in German uniform before the city was returned to France with the lost provinces.

Here we find Réal del Sarte again, sculptor of tears and hope. The *Action française* activist illustrates a poem by Charles Maurras for a monument placed by some municipalities in their cemetery and by others in the open public square. At Sare, the entire sonnet is engraved as an inscription: 'I have sought thee under the thundering sky . . .' The text and its sculpted illustration show a tragic interchange between the shroud and the winding-sheet, between the crown of thorns and the laurel wreath, between earthly pain and heavenly reward:

> . . . Sacrificed that my hand may crown,
> My brow is girded with thy green laurels.

The municipality of Courchelettes in the department of the Nord decided that its dead soldiers must always be visible. The names of its eighteen men who 'died for France' were inscribed on street signs with the 'date of their sacrifice', and set on a great cross over the words 'Courchelettes does not forget'. The signs were then divided between different streets. These sacrificial plaques had become relics twice over; for all the inhabitants were thus protected by their martyrs.[68]

The Memory of the Churches and of Churches

Although the Churches, as participants in the national struggle, found an appropriate space in national commemoration and although, as noted above, they exercised significant influence on certain aspects and themes, this did not seem adequate. Parishes, congregations, seminaries, Catholic or Protestant professorial faculties, religious schools, were coherent groups which had all lost members to the war. As in the Ecole Normale schools for teachers, on the railways, in the postal service, in the police stations, etc., the obsessional commemorative mentality of the 1920s dictated that these institutions, formed around the doctrine and culture of the Churches, should each honour their dead in their own way. This was imperative for two reasons: first, because these institutions, which had felt marginalized and even rejected since 1905, had during the war justified their place in the nation, and second, because 'infamous rumour' had proved they were not totally safe from suspicion.

By facilitating the repeated proclamation of their particular sacrifices, the commemoration of their dead was to perpetuate their efforts. In the regions of the north and east where churches of all creeds had been ravaged by the war, their reconstruction and in particular the replacement

68. *L'Illustration*, 5 July 1919.

of thousands of stained-glass windows, offered excellent support. In fact, although worship was rapidly re-established in most of the devastated parishes (235 churches had to be rebuilt in the Pas-de-Calais, for example), it returned mainly in improvised locales, barracks often offered by English and American Catholics to their suffering co-religionists. Not until the 1920s were the necessary funds available for complete reconstruction and interior decoration of the churches. In most dioceses of the north and east of France, the bishops created cooperatives, in imitation of those formed at the same time for the rebuilding of damaged villages.[69]

The Churches were thus at the origin of a highly visible and public commemoration and also of a more secret version, either inside a building which must be entered in order to grasp its commemorative aspect (stained glass, parish memorials) or because it existed only in hearts and minds.

Like all institutions and corporate bodies the Catholic Church, the different Protestant sects and the Jews all had their Book of Remembrance. In 1918, the pastor Albert Valez was already gathering the names of every pastor who had served with the troops. He recalled the ecumenism of the war: 'Like the priests and the rabbis, our pastors did their patriotic duty... In devotion and heroism, the ministers of the divers sects were equals.'[70] Each French diocese published its Book of Remembrance, preferably bearing a preface written by its bishop, or by a nationally known Catholic like Henry Bordeaux or Jacques Péricard. All the religious schools did the same. These formal records are lists of individuals with the common bond of their shared involvement in the same institutions and their shared destiny: death in the Great War. This obsession with repeatedly naming the war dead, as though to exorcise their disappearance by way of this eternal written presence, exerts a kind of fascination.

It still concerns a resurrection, that of a specific lifetime. To take the single example of Dupouey, that naval officer's name is inscribed in the

69. Their loans were secured by the war-damage indemnities guaranteed by the State. See *Reconstructions et Modernisation, la France après les ruines, 1918–1945*, Archives Nationales exhibition catalogue, January–May 1991. Jean Guérin's book on the cooperatives bears the highly symbolic title of 'The Awakening of the Stones': *Le Réveil des pierres. Histoire d'une coopérative, 1919–1929*, Robert Bourson, Compiègne, 1930. On the reconstruction of the churches, see Nadine Chaline's paper at the Conference 'The Battle of the Somme in the Great War', Péronne, Historial de la Grande Guerre, July 1996. (Proceedings to be published.)

70. Albert Valez, *Nos pasteurs au feu*, Paris, Comité protestant français, 1918, p. 3.

Books of Remembrance in the Collège Stanislas and the Naval Academy, on the memorials of these institutions, on the plaques of his parish church, on the war memorial of his native commune, and again of the commune where he lived – at the very least. On 11 November, at the moment of the roll call of the dead, his name is spoken aloud at many different memorials.

As signs of belonging, the Books of Remembrance were also used to demonstrate qualities special to each institution, even to each region: 'Why so many heroes in Lozère? For this diocese furnished more priests than the average . . . He who is generous with God is generous with his parents, his friends, his nation . . . All love comes from God, and all love outside of him is a lie and an illusion.'[71] *Le Livre d'or des maîtres de l'enseignement libre catholique* proclaimed that these teachers in schools with religious rather than republican sympathies 'were able to uphold the symbol of the Christian teacher, the glorious soldier or the hidden hero'.[72] Similarly, although 450 out of the 900 practising Protestant pastors were mobilized, and although 35 of them died, that might appear a modest number compared with the lists of Catholic clergy who lost their lives. So the sons, daughters and wives of pastors are added to the Book of Remembrance: 'It is the particular glory of the pastors not to give themselves alone but also to give their sons to the country and the Kingdom of God.'[73]

The most important work, for the Catholics, was the enumeration of the clergy of all the allies in the two enormous volumes of the *Livre d'or du clergé et des congrégations*, under the eloquent title *Preuve du sang* (Proof of Blood). The book, undertaken as early as 1915, was designed to counter the effects of 'infamous rumour'. After the war, complete lists of volunteers and dead were drawn up. Among all the statistics, a palpable desire to persuade is evident: one column is reserved for the names of those 'cited and decorated', one for the number of citations, another for the number of decorations. The figures are presented as scientific proof of the immense role played by the Catholic Church in the war. The introduction of each volume reinforced the historical argument by refuting 'infamous (and political) rumour', attacked by Cardinal Luçon in these words: 'Thus, by the grace of God, the war which

71. J. Péricard, preface to *Le Livre d'or du diocèse de Mende*, Mende, Evèché de Mende, 1930, p. VII (58 deaths out of 297 mobilized priests and seminarists).
72. Paul Escard, *Livre d'or des maîtres de l'enseignement libre catholique*, Paris, Société Générale d'Education et d'Enseignement, 1922.
73. Valez, *Nos pasteurs au feu*, part 2, 1920, p. 5.

cost us so much blood and left us so many ruins, has at least had the happy result of bringing people and religion closer together, casting light on the beneficent function of its teachings and reconciling the people to the priest by establishing contact between them once more.'[74] In 1925, the Archbishop of Reims still thought that Freemasonry, 'an impious sect that never produced anything useful for humanity',[75] was conspiratorial, and the Book of Remembrance became an urgent plea on behalf of the Catholic Church: 'The people of France will not hesitate: they will not deny the religion of their fathers; they will remain faithful to Christ, friend of the Franks.'[76] The war dead were being used as soldiers all over again: religious and political struggles had not been concluded with the Armistice and neither domestic nor foreign politics would leave them alone. This is true for all parties, all creeds and all countries involved – with consequences we know only too well. Commemoration served above all to define a territory, that of the dead; yet everyone was also trying to take advantage of their past lives, to reanimate them in new battles, whether peaceful or bellicose – capitalizing on the sacrifices of the dead.

In two articles printed in *Etudes* in 1917, 'the war memorial' was described as 'physical consecration and spiritual and moral remembrance'.[77] One can read into this a fear widely held by the survivors of the drama of the war: that the sacrifice, the millions of dead, would ultimately be revealed as useless, and that the victory itself would be perverted and betrayed. This fear too is at the root of the commemorative fervour. Those who have returned have no wish to betray those whom they left 'in hell'. Perhaps suffering the guilt of the survivor, they feel the urgency of working on behalf of the dead. And adherents of the different creeds have not forgotten the intense fervour of war. This is the ardour that was to live again in memory and action. 'If they could come back in twenty years . . . let them find a France that is once again the eldest daughter of the Church.'[78]

This ardour expanded through the next generation, heirs brought up in the cult of the departed: 'Call the new-born baby after your family's

---

74. *Livre d'or du clergé et des congrégations; la preuve du sang, 1914–1922*, Paris, Maison de la Bonne Presse, vol. I, 1925, vol. II, 1930, vol. I, p. XIII.

75. *Ibid.*, p. XIV.

76. *Ibid.*, p. XIV. This text by Cardinal Luçon should naturally be read in the context of the coalition of the left in general, its anticlericalism, and the action of General de Castelnau. See *Histoire religieuse de la France contemporaine*, Paris, Le Seuil, T.IV, pp. 282-94.

77. Joseph Dassonville, 'Le monument aux morts', *Etudes*, nos. 152 and 153, 1917.

78. *Ibid.*, account by a Catholic sergeant in 1917, who was killed later, p. 471.

dead soldier.'[79] Here we find an echo of pre-war populationist campaigns, the fear of demographic decline as decline, pure and simple; a fear strengthened by millions of dead and wounded. But it goes even further: France can only grow demographically stronger through the moral force of the departed, breathed into heirs that the survivors will have for them and through them, as one bishop expressed it: '*Voix d'Outre-Tombe*: "Be fruitful and multiply" (Genesis I, 28)'.[80]

In 1925, Abbé Keller, following the demographic logic of these injunctions to the limit, founded a 'low-cost housing corporation' with the aim of building a housing project, in rue Saint-Yves in Paris (14th *arrondissement*),

> the *cité* of Remembrance, a vast workers' enclave with low-cost housing where, in a Christian atmosphere, the war dead will live again thanks to the families with their many children, who will be sheltered by their memory and who will be adopted by their survivors in their name. This social ex-voto will be the worthy and generous continuation of the heroic deeds of those who fell.[81]

Placed under the high patronage of His Eminence Cardinal Dubois, Archbishop of Paris, 'The City of Remembrance' gradually took shape through the strenuous efforts of Abbé Keller in buying the terrain, finding architects and construction companies, and above all in finding the money needed for the venture. The allotment letters resembled those produced for the construction of the great ossuaries, with which Abbé Keller made an eloquent comparison:

> This will be the essential complement to so many chapels and ossuaries erected in memory of the dead of the Great War. THERE they fell, defending the land of their ancestors against the invader, and the whole moral patrimony that constitutes the nation. HERE we shall build homes to shelter in a Christian atmosphere the families with many children which have always been (and will be once more tomorrow) the backbone of the true France.[82]

The '*cité*' was planned as a rectangle of buildings punctuated with back-yard gardens. The plans reveal its design in the form of a great church, with the chapel forming the choir. Even the decoration with pious images has been foreseen: 'Each home will bear the name of a soldier who died

---

79. *Ibid.*, p. 274.

80. Mgr. J. A. Chollet, *Nos morts de guerre, consolations et enseignements*, Paris, Lethellieux, 1932, p. 323.

81. Extract from subscription leaflet published by Abbé Keller, 1925. Historical archives of the diocese of Paris.

82. *Idem.*

for France; his portrait and a brief notice about him will be found in the main room.' Those who pledged 30,000 francs or more to the project had the right to designate a name, and it is hard to escape the suspicion, given the size of the amount, that these generous benefactors were interested in the second goal of Abbé Keller, a political one: 'to facilitate the impact of parish clergy on a population very heavily influenced by communism'.[83] When in 1927 the first families settled into rue Saint-Yves, the building work was not complete and Desvallières had not yet painted the chapel frescoes, but already 700 children had become 'the adoptive descendants' of the same number of dead soldiers.

The hundreds of commune war memorials representing an 'imitation of the *poilu*', with admiring children responding to their fathers' involvement, transmit exactly the same message. This also clearly explains the presence of children at the 11 November ceremonies, and in particular their part in calling the roll of the dead.

It was once more to young people that Abbé Bergey addressed his appeal for the priesthood:

> Now we must replace our dead, and urgently, amid tombs that are still fresh, become the messengers of reconciliation and peace . . . We are the wounded, the mutilated . . . And we must stretch our efforts to fill the empty places in our ranks, to serve the souls that need us! We anxiously await your coming as relief troops, young men! For our cassocked dead you must be the grains of wheat that breathed in the dying sigh of my soldiers, the breath that over their stiffened bodies wildly sang the radiant song of new harvests![84]

The systematic use of the capital letter for 'the Dead' places them apart, separate from the ordinary dead: these men have died for their country, and for God.

They died for a flag, which although it was the tricolour – the national flag, thus republican – takes on a mystical meaning with Catholic orators: 'Blue from the dust of battle, white from the dust of marching, red from the martyrs' blood.'[85] This new interpretation of the three colours also enabled monarchists to accept the national flag. The flag is never separated from the cross, nor is it ever forgotten that 11 November is the Saint's Day of St Martin, of the blue cope.[86] The coincidence of the calendar itself accomplished much.

---

83. Letter from Abbé Keller to the Archbishop of Paris, 20 June 1930. Archive cited.

84. Address cited, p. 72.

85. Abbé E. Lemerle, *Tombés au champ d'honneur, trente-deux allocutions patriotiques*, Paris, Lethellieux, 1917 and 1926, p. 33.

86. Millot, *Nos morts de la guerre*.

St Martin, the soldier who became a monk and then a bishop, the man of charity who shared all with the poor and prayed ceaselessly – who better to become the patron saint of the soldiers of the Great War? Was not the army of the Roman Empire, according to the dictionary of spiritual matters, 'the natural school of asceticism, community life, mutual help, for the sense of sacrifice'?[87] The veterans of the First World War themselves would soon subscribe to this legend, which they had sometimes managed to oppose during the war itself. The motto of the *Union nationale des combattants* (National Union of Veterans), 'United as at the front', certainly resembles the hagiography of St Martin.

Religious commemoration created a veritable catechism in words and images. The priests, and particularly the bishops, were chiefly responsible for the discourse, but it fell to the artists to represent this catechism in stone, bronze, painting or glass, more rarely in music. In 1917, Mgr. Batiffol, President of the Society of the Friends of Liturgical Art, was already describing 'the spiritual task of artists':

> You are all invited to rebuild those of our churches that have fallen on the field of honour . . . The deliverance must not leave us with improvised churches which would perpetuate an impression of invasion in their aggressive ugliness . . . Preserve the memory of our dead in the churches . . . I fear that there will be secular monuments erected to them in our big cities, which will be vulgar and soulless.[88]

We have seen that the worries of Mgr. Batiffol were not justified by the communes' war memorials: if they are at times 'secular', or even occasionally 'vulgar', in any event they are never 'soulless'. But could the Churches' own commemoration satisfy him?

The religious pattern of commemoration of the fighting men followed on naturally from the thinking underlying devotions in wartime. Ex-votos placed in the churches after 11 November 1918 are no different from those already noted. We could expect to find on the one hand the imitation of Christ and the Virgin, on the other hand an outline of the most important devotions of the war period, intended for the national saints, the Sacred Heart and Thérèse and Joan. The museum in Fourvière contains a remarkable chalice: the parents of an aviator killed in 1916 wished to recall his sacrifice by means of the liturgical object destined to commemorate the sacrifice of Christ. The bowl is engraved with a propeller and a machine gun – reminders of the war – and St Michael

---

87. *Dictionnaire de spiritualité*, Paris, Beauchesne, vol. X, p. 690.
88. *Revue du clergé français*, vol. XCII, pp. 81–7.

on a tank, with the dedication: 'In memory of Henri Blanchon, killed in combat on 10 July 1916'. The chalice becomes a monument to this death.

When it came to parish war memorials, there was near unanimity: everywhere there was at least a commemorative plaque 'To the children of the parish of X who died for their country' or 'for France'. Under the dedication, the list of names; sometimes the initials R.I.P. or P.P.E. further reinforce the funerary function of the plaques.[89] What marks them out as different from the rolls of honour in churches, whether Catholic or Protestant, in synagogues, or on the war memorials of the communes? The presence, occasionally, of the cross or the star of David. There were few manufacturers competing in the commemoration market and it is hardly surprising that they should propose very similar plaques to the mayor and to the priest.[90] The enamelled plaques with photos of the parish dead which are displayed in some churches are often the same as the plaques displayed on the commune memorial.

On the other hand, some individual sculptors created original works, such as a scene in the parish church of Hem (Nord), where a mother weeping before a tomb sees St Michael appear: 'Mother, your child is not lost.'

Some sculptors or marble-engravers specialized in parish monuments, applying the principles of mass production. Their principal creation was the two sets of sculptures to be found in Catholic churches all over France: one featuring angels crowning victorious *poilus* who are often soldier-priests, and the other of descents from the cross and entombments. The duality of the war was illustrated by the sculptor Michelet, who carved the two angels of the Te Deum and the De Profundis in the crypt at Dormans: the angel of victory expresses gratitude to God, while the angel of the prayer for the dead is sleeping [*dormant*], a reference to its location in Dormans. On the tympanum two more angels lay a *poilu* in his tomb to await the hour of resurrection. The most moving moments of the New Testament have been chosen for these groupings. Some parishes commissioned a *poilu* guarding a trench and Golgotha at one and the same time. The theatricalization of the war is complete: the battlefield of the sacrificed soldiers is reconstituted under the Cross. One of the most popular soldier-sculptures in the catalogues, from the Jacomet de Villedieu company (Vaucluse), was thus adapted for an environment

89. *Requiescant in pace*, rest in peace; *priez pour eux*, pray for them.

90. Maurice Agulhon has shown that at the end of the nineteenth century, companies specializing in the production of religious statues began to supply *mairies* with figures of Marianne, the female figure representing France. *Marianne au pouvoir*, Paris, Flammarion, 1989.

other than the public square. The weeping Virgin, St John or Mary Magdalen participate in this silent mystery where the sacrifices of the war renew the sacrifice.

Some parishes, not content with reserving a mere chapel of the church for the memorial, completely transformed the nave so as to turn the whole structure into a memorial to the war dead. This is evidently what happened in certain reconstructed churches in the north and east of France. The architects of St Laurence of Neuville-Saint-Vaast, in the Pas-de-Calais, for example, conceived a neo-Gothic construction where sculpture, inscriptions and stained glass form a complete plan of commemoration.

Other symbolic churches were redecorated after the victory: at Floing, near Sedan, as at Mars-la-Tour, the last commune in Lorraine to remain French after German annexation of part of the region under the Treaty of Frankfurt, the insistence on the Christian heroes of 1914–18 sought to counteract completely the sorrowful monuments erected after 1871.

The stations of the cross were similarly represented during the 1920s. Either plaques were set up to the parish dead and its soldier-priest between two stations, or a whole new set of stations was ordered. Two artists were well known for their stations of the cross, in which *poilus* imitate Christ: Maxime Réal del Sarte and George Desvallières. At Laventie (Pas-de-Calais), Réal took on an important commemorative project: the commune memorial in front of the town church, a *Pietà* showing the Virgin and a *poilu* leaning against a war cross with a few stalks of wheat growing at its foot to the left of the church,[91] Bernadette praying to the Virgin; in the church, a 'war' Way of the Cross and an altar with a *Pietà* above it.

George Desvallières, a reservist captain, volunteered though 50 years old. He had two young soldier sons, one of whom was killed in 1915. He experienced the war as an artist: 'The war. I realized that I saw with an artist's curiosity. . . I recited a De Profundis for the poor men who were dying. I did no sketches except for a few while resting. I told myself: "If I survive, I will do nothing but pink and blue Holy Virgins." '[92] For

---

91. The departmental fine arts commission approved this choice even though, as its comments show, it did not understand Réal del Sarte's symbolism: 'We must have confidence in the artists to carry out their concept, which should remain simple and beautiful, whatever peronal preference I may have for the elimination of accessories such as the war cross and the wheatsheaf.' Quoted by Bénédicte Grailles, 'Les Monuments aux morts de la Grande Guerre dans le Pas-de-Calais', MA dissertation supervised by Annette Becker and Catherine Dhérent, 1991. Vol I, p. 14.

92. Albert Garreau, *Georges Desvallières*, Paris, Les Amis de Saint François, 1942.

him the war was the time of his rededication (following his conversion to Catholicism before the war[93]), and of compassion for the sacrificed men of the war, until the end of his life. Influenced by Gustave Moreau, for whom he, together with Georges Rouault, was 'the depository of his pictorial testament',[94] Desvallières, immutably bound by his wartime vow, stated and restated through his drawing and painting that 'although war is abominable because people kill each other, it is admirable because people die for each other there'.[95]

His nod to the St Sulpice style of art should not be misunderstood. Before the war Desvallières was vice-president of the *Salon d'Automne*, and defended the most revolutionary artists, the Cubists; his friend and patron was Jacques Rouché, a graduate of the *Polytechnique* who had moved into revolutionary theatre, and was named director of the Paris Opera in 1913.

Like Paul Claudel, Jacques Maritain, or his friend Maurice Denis with whom he was to found the *Ateliers d'Art Sacré* in 1919, Desvallières was convinced well before the war that religious art was born of faith. His new artistic orientation was uniquely thematic: henceforward he would try to transmit the twin messages of faith and of mass death, according to Maritain's precept: 'If you want to create a Christian work, be Christian, and seek to make a beautiful work with your heart in it; do not try to "act Christian".'[96] Desvallières's commemorative painting of the sacrifices of war is not 'blue and pink'. It is extremely sombre, like Rouault's work in the 'Miserere',[97] and the blood flowing from the wounds of his soldiers is not the charming bright poppy red of the symbols of a sanitized heroism. From the stained glass of Douaumont to the stations of the cross at Wittenheim, near Mulhouse, or from the Church of the Holy Spirit in the 12th *arrondissement* of Paris to the fresco cycles of the Chapel of Remembrance in rue Saint-Yves in Paris, to his masterpiece, the Saint-Privat Chapel, belonging to J. Rouché, near

93. Born in 1861, he was converted in 1905 out of friendship for Léon Bloy, one of the great agents of conversion to Catholicism. In January 1914 he became a member of the Third Order of Dominicans. Jean Philippe Rey, 'Desvallières et la guerre de 1914–1918', *Société de l'histoire de l'art français*, 1988, pp. 197–211.

94. *Gustave Moreau et la Bible*, catalogue for the exhibition at the National Museum of the Bible Message, Nice, 1991, p. 16.

95. Garreau, *Georges Desvallières*, p. 120.

96. Jacques Maritain, *Art et Scolastique*, Paris, Librairie de l'art catholique, 1920, p. 113.

97. This set of engravings, executed by Rouault during the war, was not exhibited or published until 1948.

the Pont du Gard, Desvallières recreated Calvary and the resurrection of his son Daniel, and of all the war dead. Christ himself comes to take his companions of 1914–18 from their freshly dug tombs at the front. The inscription on the Chapel of Remembrance in Paris mingles sacred dates and acts: 'He was born 1914 He suffered 1916 [Here the altar is placed] 1917 He died 1918 He rose again'. The Saint-Privat Chapel presented a whole figurative theology of the war: Original Sin which brought about the war, the Sacred Heart and Calvary, Sacrifice and Redemption: 'The sacrifice of the soldiers becomes the remedy for sin. The communion of saints is re-established, the chosen couple (*poilu* and nurse) intercede on behalf of the inhabitants of the earth.'[98] The stained-glass windows of Douaumont, of the same period, developed the same themes, including in particular the nurse, the 'white angel' often praised by the soldiers but rarely commemorated. 'Did Desvallières succeed in the eyes of his contemporaries? A woman said to me one day, '"You are a sadist, you take pleasure in horrors and blood". "Why no, there is a certain idea of sacrifice that costs very much and in which one finds an exaltation, a purification of the soul."'[99] His art, 'born out of the war', but also revealing him, in its form, to be a student of Moreau, was to some extent doubly displaced: neither the partisans of Saint-Sulpice art nor the new avant-gardes born, like his, out of the war – Dadaism, followed by Surrealism – could understand him. Yet in 1929, Robert Vallery-Radot dedicated an issue of *L'Art et les artistes* to his work in which he had no hesitation in writing:

> Desvallières is the only painter who could show us the meaning of the war . . . This war not only put man to the test by fire and steel; it slowly tortured him through dreary imprisonment for four long years . . . In this abandonment of the whole being, this Christian saw the Man of sorrows reveal his face crowned with thorns and offer again his despised gifts: poverty, charity, obedience, in other words, the cross.[100]

Desvallières systematically placed representations of the Sacred Heart in all his compositions, either in the form of insignia attached to the tricolour flag, or as Christ himself showing his heart. All Catholic commemoration emphasized the Sacred Heart, following directly in the tradition of its wartime cult. As Jacques Benoît commented aptly, 'the

98. Rey, 'Desvallières', p. 203.
99. Garreau, *Georges Desvallières*, p. 105.
100. Robert Valléry-Radot, 'Desvallières', *L'Art et les artistes*, no. 100, October 1929, p. 28. I am grateful to M. G. Paladilhe, great-nephew of G. Desvallières, who kindly approved this section devoted to his great-uncle.

consecration of the basilica so long deferred . . . can be seen as the true victory ceremony celebrated by Catholics in Montmartre'.[101]

In certain big cities with several parishes, it was usually the church of 'the Sacred Heart' that became the place of commemoration for all the Catholic dead of the city. In Paris it is the crypt of the Montmartre basilica and not Notre-Dame that functions as monument to the war dead. This is also the case in Lille, where the women of the *Association des enfants de Marie* made a solemn vow to build a church dedicated to the Sacred Heart if Lille were preserved from the Prussian invasion. Moreover, one of the stained glass windows installed in 1893 represents 'repentant France offering the basilica of Montmartre to the Sacred Heart'.[102] After the war, this church was a natural choice for the construction of a gigantic Golgotha, watched over by a *poilu*. The ex-voto church took on greater sanctity with the remembrance of the war dead, in imitation of Jesus Christ.

In Avignon, 'city of popes', was it not their duty to raise a votive church? The vow was taken in 1915, and made good between 1921 and 1925. This votive church is dedicated to the Sacred Heart, as the archbishop of Avignon explained:

> Already, perhaps, public monuments have been raised to our heroes, here and there, where people will come from far and near to celebrate their memory . . . But there is an object higher, more vast, that we have aimed at in building and promising a church to the Sacred Heart of Jesus. Our purpose is to establish and perpetuate here a form of cult of the prodigies that Christ accomplished to save France . . . To this cult of divine favours we wished to join the memory of the heroic soldiers used by God to realize in France his designs of love and goodness.[103]

Built despite financial difficulties, this church was destroyed by shelling in 1944. Today a stele placed in the garden of the reconstructed church, between rue 11 novembre and rue Foch, is a reminder: 'Votive Church dedicated to the Sacred Heart in memory of the soldiers of the diocese of Avignon who died for France. 1914–1918'.

It was unthinkable for the departments of the west to keep aloof from this double cult of the Sacred Heart and the war dead. In 1919 they decided to build the Church of the Sacred Heart at La Roche-sur-Yon,

101. Benoît, *op.cit.*, p. 656. On this, see the Epilogue.

102. Hervé Oursel, 'Les vitraux de l'église du Sacré-Cœur à Lille', *Revue du Nord*, no. 261/2, 1984, pp. 599–618.

103. Quoted by Giroud and Michel, *Les Monuments aux morts dans le Vaucluse*, pp. 49–50.

the 'Vendéen Montmartre'.[104] Going beyond votive churches, Bretons and
Vendéens do not hesitate to place the Sacred Heart outside, in the public
square itself, in the form of war memorials situated even at some distance
from church or cemetery. Plaster statues placed on boulders represent a
Saint Sulpice-style Christ showing a bleeding heart whose model can be
found in the basilica grounds at Paray-le-Monial. Two monuments occur
frequently in the Vendée and in Loire Atlantique: one, close to the
imagery of the war, represents a large Christ with the Sacred Heart
coming to the aid of a chaplain attending the last moments of a wounded
man. Above a tree stripped bare by the war, an angel brings the martyr's
palms and the crown of victory (Le Plessé, Loire Atlantique). The other
is a great altar at which France on her knees is praying to the Sacred
Heart. Four angels spell out the dates of the encounter: 1914–1918
(Avessac, Loire Atlantique). At Les Essarts in Vendée, on a similar
monument, Marguerite-Marie Alacoque supports a dying man and
presents him to Christ.

The Sacred Heart itself is rare in the form of ornamental sculpture on
war memorials, but the votive churches and stained glass representing
Marguerite-Marie Alacoque at Paray, or on the battlefields, should not
be ignored as part of this desire to use the image of the Sacred Heart in
commemoration. Although its devotees failed to win the State authorities
over to their cause, either during or after the war, when Clemenceau
refused to attend the consecration of the Montmartre basilica, still the
imagery of commemoration was to anchor the Sacred Heart very strongly
in French Catholicism. Moreover this 'campaign' ended in a spiritual
victory of the first order, since Marguerite-Marie Alacoque was canonized
in 1920.

Bernadette, Joan of Arc and Thérèse were to benefit in the same way
through commemoration of their acts of protection during the war. We
are already acquainted with the ex-votos; sculptures, paintings, artificial
grottoes and stained glass became the most common forms of the
commemorative cult, mingled with the cult of the intercessors to whom
the soldiers had prayed so devoutly during the war. Imitation Lourdes
grottoes constructed in parish church enclosures or against the walls of
churches are not a post-war novelty. Much like the sculpted Golgothas
whose origins go far back in modern times, they are substitutes for
all the pilgrimages that cannot be made to Jerusalem or Lourdes.

104. Florence Regourd, 'La mort célébrée, typologie des monuments aux morts de la
guerre 1914–1918 en Vendée, *303, la revue des pays de la Loire*, no. XI, 1986, pp. 64–78
(p. 66).

Memory

Unfortunately no complete list of all these grottoes has yet been drawn up, but investigations in various departments show that they proliferated during the 1920s, very often through the execution of vows made during the war. Thus we have the grotto at Chaumont (Haute-Marne), as the consequence of a vow dating from the battle of the Marne.[105] Similarly, 'imitation grottoes bring Lourdes to Brittany'.[106] Some become important places of pilgrimage during the war, before being transformed into war memorials by the addition of lists of the dead. We find war memorial-grottoes like these in all the departments, although naturally they are more numerous in the more Catholic regions. Bernadette and the Virgin often appear in the form of statues, with the presence of the soldiers reduced to their names alone; sometimes a war *Pietà* – Virgin and *poilu* – is there to strengthen the parallel. Generally, ex-votos on the walls of the substitute grotto emphasize the intervention of the Virgin of Lourdes in a wartime miracle. Some grottoes are there in addition to the parish monument in the church, while others fulfil this office alone. Still others are the only monument in the village.

Since people gave thanks to the Virgin of Lourdes in grottoes throughout France, Lourdes itself was bound to construct a war memorial. Mgr. Tissier, Bishop of Châlons, gave the address at the laying of the first stone during the national thanksgiving pilgrimage of 1919. For him, glory, faith and gratitude should be mingled: 'Coming here to pray to the Queen of Heaven, posterity will be proud to salute her guard of honour in passing.'[107] The finished monument recalls the challenge of a German newspaper at the start of the war: 'With so many French bones broken, the Holy Virgin of Lourdes would have much to do to mend them all.' On the victory monument, Our Lady of Lourdes makes sport of the blasphemy, and repulses the enemies while protecting her French soldiers. A vault beneath the altar is filled with soldiers' souvenirs – rosaries, medals, letters, etc. The possessions of soldiers who had prayed so often to the Virgin of Lourdes during the war were transformed into relics to be looked at but not touched. The Lourdes monument is a contemporary reliquary: it is not the bones of martyrs that are kept there, but the traces of their souls.

The soul of Joan of Arc, mingled from the beginning with the soul of France, also appears in the memory of the war. Present on commune

105. Philippe Bruneau, 'Les grottes de Lourdes', *RAMAGE*, no. 4, 1986, pp. 151–65 (p. 162).
106. Michel Lagrée, *Religion et cultures en Bretagne, 1850–1950*, Paris, Fayard, 1992, p. 308.
107. Mgr. Tissier, *Nos tributs de gloire*, Paris, Téqui, 1920, p. 287.

monuments all over Lorraine, she had also long since acquired the status of national heroine. Alone or with a *poilu*, she is on memorials everywhere, in the spirit of the books by Ernest Lavisse: 'In no other country does one find a story to equal that of Joan of Arc. All French people must love and venerate the memory of this girl who loved France so much and who died for us.'[108]

Once more in these post-war years, a national and a Catholic cult were so intermingled in the cult of Joan that all could find what they wanted there. Lavisse, who inspired commune war memorials representing Joan, was 'indifferent to religious problems' for his 'gospel of the Republic'.[109] Réal del Sarte saluted her canonization in 1920 which he saw as a result of the devotions of the soldiers. On the commune monument of La Baule he sculpted a Joan who has become Mary, holding on her knees a soldier who has become Christ: the crown of thorns surrounds the helmet.[110] At Rouen in 1924 he built a monument to the mutilated and the widows of the war, with an immense figure of Joan, like a Virgin of consolation, protecting under her great mantle a widow in tears with a baby in her arms, and a wounded soldier whose amputated leg is replaced by laurels.[111]

It is naturally in the churches that we find most of the Joans and, as one might expect, in Domrémy itself, where she is crowning a victorious *poilu* above the altar, while a second soldier reposes in a tomb below. The imitation of Joan has made a saint of him.

In other regions the war dead are commemorated with the help of local or national saints with strong regional connections, like Joan in Lorraine. Saint Remy occurs most frequently on the commemorative windows of Champagne, and Saint Yves in Brittany. Like the inscriptions in Breton, Basque, and old Provençal, the regional costumes worn by Savoyards, Auvergnats, Alsatians, etc. provide the war memorials of the communes with regional claims to glory, while provincial saints are

---

108. Ernest Lavisse, *Histoire de France*, middle course, Paris, Armand Colin, 1912 edition.

109. Pierre Nora, 'Lavisse, instituteur national; le "Petit Lavisse" évangile de la République', in *Les Lieux de mémoire*, vol. I, *La République*, pp. 247–89 (p. 270).

110. The same motif reappears in a bronze plaque at the foot of the magnificent monument in Les Eparges, which appears to resemble a sphinx with the inscription on its chest, 'I believe'. In 1936, Maxime Réal del Sarte lost his son Philippe. The death announcement bore the same design. But this time, a 'true' Virgin and a 'true' Christ were represented. Philippe Réal del Sarte was born after the war, in 1921. I am grateful to M. Pilven le Sevellec for having sent me this remarkable document.

111. *Grand Hebdomadaire illustré de la région du nord de la France*, 16 November 1924.

represented among the soldiers. The latter are thus commemorated in four concentric circles, each recalling the reasons for the struggle: God, France, the region or village – so many monuments and stained glass windows show the dying soldier dreaming of his village, represented by the parish church – and finally, the family.

The Breton 'Sanctuary of Remembrance' at St Anne d'Auray represents the most ambitious example of regionalist commemoration. In the chosen place, a 'Breton 'national' pilgrimage'[112] – the wall of the enclosure inscribed with the names of the 240,000 Bretons who died in the Great War, the chapel crypt with its five altars, one for each diocese, the inscriptions in Breton and French – everything combines to make this immense esplanade attached to the old church into a symbol of the Breton Catholic presence in the French nation. Planned in 1921, its crypt blessed in 1927, inaugurated in 1932 in the presence of a crowd of tens of thousands, the chapel/war memorial of St Anne d'Auray tells (thanks chiefly to the sculptor Le Bozec) of a Brittany in despair over so many losses, and proud of having lost them thus. On the sculptures as in the speeches can be found the poet Jean-Pierre Calloc'h, killed at the front in 1917, who gave his life 'For God and Brittany'.

> I am the Great Watcher, standing over the trench.
> I know what I am, I know what I am doing . . .
> It is the beauty of the world that I guard tonight.[113]

In the crypt, a stained-glass window stylistically resembling certain painters of the school of Pont-Aven blends the old devotion to St Anne, mother of the Virgin, with remembrance of the Breton soldiers and sailors of the war. Such windows of remembrance can be found in several Breton churches – about fifteen, to my knowledge, in the five departments. At Saint-Michel Chef Chef (Loire Atlantique), at Saint-Jean-sur-Vilaine or La Bazouge-du-Désert (Ille-et-Vilaine) and at Tréguier, *poilus* fight the Germans, or expire on the upturned earth. The windows are generally divided into two registers, like the ex-votos. Set above scenes of war, Christ welcomes his new 'saints'. Either the Virgin, Marguerite-Marie Alacoque, Joan of Arc, a military chaplain or a nurse accompanies the soldiers.

---

112. Lagrée, *Religion et cultures en Bretagne*, p. 302.

113. A. Morio *et al.*, *Le Mémorial de Sainte-Anne d'Auray*, Lorient, Imprimerie de Bretagne, 1971, p. 14. On Calloc'h and the war, see Tim Cross, *The Lost Voices of World War One*, Iowa City, University of Iowa Press, 1988, pp. 270–5. His death undoubtedly meant the great loss for France of a 'Breton Claudel'.

Figure 14. Window of remembrance, Saint-Jean-de-Vilaine (Brittany). Christ and Saint John appear with the parish church to 'the dead children' of the village.

Figure 15. Window of remembrance in the Church of Pierrefitte-Nestalas (Hautes Pyrénées). The Virgin appears in the trench, while a chaplain speaks to the soldiers. Photograph by Gérard Boutté.

Windows of remembrance of this type exist in most regions of France, in greater or lesser numbers. Obviously the reconstructed churches of the north and east contain the greatest number, and Lorraine, Picardy and Artois are particularly rich in this domain. Certain windows form veritable strip cartoons, summing up the whole spirituality of remembrance. In the church of Isbergues (Nord), we see a *poilu* praying at the foot of a calvary, and the same man dead on the knees of his mother/the Virgin in mourning. Below, a long list of the parish dead is inscribed in the same pane of glass.

Thanks to the remarkable inventory made in Pas-de-Calais, it is possible to make an instructive and exhaustive study of the department's various stained-glass windows created at the time of the reconstruction.[114] Of a total of 260 churches inventoried, 38 contain remembrance windows properly so called; but a grasp of all the spiritual effects of the Great War involves looking beyond the remembrance windows alone, since they are part of a wider category. Thus I have listed the different themes of all the stained-glass windows in the reconstructed churches of the Pas-de-Calais. It goes without saying that Christ is present in every church; the Virgin too is everywhere, represented in scenes of Jesus's childhood, or at the foot of the cross. Four intercessors, four women who lived between the fifteenth and the twentieth centuries, are the subjects of 88, 76, 69 and 61 windows respectively: these are Marguerite-Marie and the Sacred Heart, Bernadette and the Virgin of Lourdes, Thérèse de Lisieux and Joan of Arc. St Martin and St Michael appear about 20 times each, while St Geneviève and the Virgin appearing at La Salette and at Pontmain occur only 2 or 3 times.

Let us now consider the 38 windows of Remembrance: they show the Virgin 17 times, Christ 15 times, and Joan and Thérèse only 4 and 3 times each. St Michael, St John, St Vaast and Clovis each appear once.

This rich sample from the Pas-de-Calais, confirmed by more scattered examples from the rest of France, strikes me as extremely interesting. Commissioners of works commemorated the Catholic war dead in the way that the men themselves had chosen to address God during the war. That the majority of these commissioners were themselves soldiers, widows, orphans, helps to explain this accord between wartime and post-war devotions in remembrance.

On the windows of remembrance proper, the *poilus*, the Virgin and Christ take up all the available space. We find the intercessors around

114. Patrick Wintrebert, *Le Vitrail dans le Pas-de-Calais de 1918 à 1939*. Catalogue of the exhibition organized in 1989, Archives of the Pas-de-Calais.

them, on the other windows, and providing them with a protective frame.

To reassure, to console, to say that all these sufferings had not only not been in vain, but that they were enabling a sanctification of man – is this not the main function of these glass creations, and indeed of all commemoration? 'For those who do not know, they appeared to die, they are at peace.'[115]

115. Stained-glass window in Mont-Notre-Dame (Aisne). See Jean-Pierre Blin, 'Le vitrail commémoratif de la Grande Guerre', in Nadine-Josette Chaline (ed.), *Chrétiens dans la Première Guerre mondiale*, Paris, Cerf, 1993, pp. 167–96.

Epilogue: Death, Thine is the Victory

The victory celebrations of 14 July 1919 in Paris live on in the collective memory as the greatest post-war national demonstration, eight months after the signing of the Armistice and a few days after the signing of the peace treaty. This was the victors' enthusiastic response to the 'enthusiastic' departures of 1914.[1] A few years later, during a veterans' pilgrimage to Lourdes, Jacques Péricard recalled these two moments, separated by five years of war:

> [this] emotion is one that I have felt only twice in my life, first at the time of mobilization in 1914, at the sight of the French soul reappearing in its magnificent unity; and for the second time at the Victory Parade when, under the guidance of its 1,500,000 dead, the French Army advanced through the Arc de Triomphe to carry out into the world the flame of Peace and Brotherhood.[2]

Poincaré had proclaimed the *Union sacrée* in August 1914: despite setbacks during the war and upsets after it, was it still intact on this great day of 14 July 1919? Experts in the history of Bastille Day indicate, correctly, that the choice of the national day for these celebrations marked the 'apotheosis' of the day uniquely recognized by every French citizen.[3]

For greater understanding, this reading of the central events of July should perhaps be extended to two other commemorations in 1919. On 14 July, two groups of French people, one tiny (socialists, particularly their militant pro-Bolshevik element), the other vast (Catholics, Protestants and Jews), criticized certain aspects of the festivities to the extent of rejecting them *en bloc*. The socialists prepared a day of demonstrations and strikes on 21 July while the Catholics deplored the excessively secular aspect of the commemorations.

Socialists and Catholics had two opportunities to commemorate the end of the war in their own way: on 31 July the socialists recalled the

---

1. We would prefer the phrase 'firm and resolute' used by Jean-Jacques Becker, *1914, Comment les Français sont entrés dans la guerre*, Paris, P.F.N.S.P., 1977.

2. Jacques Péricard on the International Pilgrimage of Catholic war veterans, Lourdes, 22–4 September 1934, *Pèlerinage international des anciens combattants catholiques*, Lourdes, 1934, p. 13.

3. Rosemonde Sanson, *Le 14 juillet, fête et conscience nationale, 1789–1975*, Paris, Flammarion, 1976. Jean-Pierre Bois, *Histoire des 14 juillet, 1789–1919*, Rennes, Ouest-France université, 1991.

assassination of Jean Jaurès five years earlier, and on 16–19 October Catholics consecrated the basilica of the Sacré Cœur in Paris, the ceremony originally planned for 17 October 1914 having been delayed for five years by the war.

Apart from the inherent differences between the three ceremonies, the religious fervour present in each of them arose out of the war, was born in the war, and was consolidated by the millions of dead and wounded. The following year, on 11 November 1920, the French Republic continued its spectacular honouring of the war dead by the interment in Paris of an Unknown Soldier while celebrating its own fiftieth anniversary. The inscription chosen for the tomb, which was placed (not without problems) beneath the Arc de Triomphe in the Place de l'Etoile, is a reminder that the victorious Republic was indeed identified with the Nation. 'Here lies a French soldier who died for the country. 1914–1918'; '4 September 1870, proclamation of the Republic. 11 November 1918: return of Alsace-Lorraine to France'.

In 1920, as in 1919, polemic and religious devotion lay at the heart of the commemorative ceremonies. As was widely evident, most French people, like the writer-soldier Henry Malherbe, considered that 'Only the memory of our dead can defend us, can save us, can renew us. To recreate society and promote our long-standing destiny, let us accomplish the hopes of our fallen brothers. And let us swear on their memory to be righteous men henceforward.'[4] Should we not consider carefully these various and diverse 'righteous men', through the 1920s and 1930s? The commemorations of 1919 and 1920 enable us to follow this fervour and its contradictions closely.

14 July 1919: the Official Commemoration

The extraordinary extent of the celebrations involving millions of Frenchmen – Parisians and others who flocked in to the capital in great numbers, an estimated extra 2 million people – made the day of 14 July a remarkable popular success.[5] The selection of 14 July, proposed by the government to the Chamber of Deputies on 27 June, had been confirmed without opposition. The various French messianic messages,

4. Henry Malherbe, 'Le retour des vainqueurs', in *La Grande Guerre vécue, racontée, illustrée par les combattants*, 2 vols, Quillet, 1921. Vol. 2, p. 413, the final words of the last page of the text.

5. The only comparable event is the state funeral of Victor Hugo in 1885. See Avner Ben Amos, 'Les funérailles de Victor Hugo: Apothéose de l'évènement-spectacle', in *Les Lieux de mémoire*, vol. 1, ed. Pierre Nora.

the result of the long history of the Christian monarchy and the French Revolution via the principles of 1789, are clearly shown in this account in the newspaper *Le Temps*:

> Those who have witnessed this day of great memory and infinite hope can confirm the perfect harmony between the images of a past superbly rich in history and legend, and the heroic realities of the unique moment when the unwearying effort of the French nation manifested itself. A nation which is always ready for combat and for labour, for the advancement of universal civilization, and for continuing human progress, devoted to justice.[6]

On 14 July 1919, the immense parade which passed beneath the Arc de Triomphe[7] glorified the army above all. The army parade was a reminder that love of one's country means above all being ready to die for it in battle, in the cause of defensive patriotism. It is 14 July and the tricolour flag is truly at the heart of this France. Paris is decorated with tens of thousands of flags and tricolour ribbons, erected by the authorities or hanging from private houses.[8] On 13 July President Poincaré had awarded their swords to the three Marshals, Joffre, Foch and Pétain, the 'saviours'[9] who next day led troops from all army corps the length of the Champs-Elysées. After the cavalry and the infantry, tanks and aircraft showed the public the birth of modern warfare.

The front page of *La Croix* condensed this enthusiasm for the army into a series of heavy headlines: 'THE DAY OF GLORY! A triumphal procession. The reapers of victories, our allies, our soldiers, our sailors, are acclaimed and covered with flowers.'[10]

Although the socialist daily paper *L'Humanité* disputed the wisdom of the decoration, 'a work of vandalism . . . the Champs-Elysées now looks like . . . a race-course promenade',[11] its journalists were none the less impressed by the extraordinary number of participants and could only report the mass enthusiasm at the parade, however much they deplored its carnival aspect.

The keynote of the evening celebrations was the parade of Florentine illuminated clusters. These were thousands of bulbs set on floats, arc lights forming the names of the great battles of the war, and portraits of

---

6. *Le Temps*, 15 July 1919, p. 1, 'Le retour des vainqueurs'.

7. The Unknown Soldier was not interred there until 1920.

8. There were also among them, of course, the flags of the Allies, just as their troops paraded with the French troops.

9. *La Croix*, 15 July 1914.

10. *La Croix*, 15 July 1919, front page.

11. *L'Humanité*, 13 July 1919, p. 2.

the nation's leaders and its generals. The sites of military martyrdom –
Artois, Verdun, the Marne – were transformed into luminous garlands.
This would have been startling if illuminated tributes had not become a
standard element of the Third Republic's 14 July celebrations. Fireworks
experts would suggest sophisticated themes, the 'great patriotic decorations' in which '*Vive la France*', 'Glory' or 'the Nation' lit up the sky,
together with tricolours and guns. It was even possible to buy the famous
Longepied group, 'Pro Patria', a war memorial to the 1870 war in a
magical fireworks version.[12] Did joy, illuminations, cheering at the
military parade really indicate the only note of the day?

A poem on the front page of the newspaper *Le Figaro* gives a good
insight into the state of mind of millions of French people who came
together to acclaim their living heroes when so many others were dead:

> Alone . . .
> My husband, my brother, died out there, gloriously.
> I weep for them, my sorrow is profound.
> And yet one day others will come, that day is near.
> That day I must be in the front rank to greet those who return, sublime.
> That day my mourning veil will no longer cover my face, my dark shadow
>   must not sadden those who pass . . .
> That day I will have kisses for them and flowers, that is how I shall celebrate
>   my dead, for they are dead so that these shall return.
> They will pass by, fine and great, at the centre of cheers and shouting.
> They will pass by.
> When the last one has passed I shall come home to my empty house,
> I will put on my black veil again and I shall weep.[13]

The night of 13–14 July was dedicated to the dead; before the victory
could be celebrated, it was right to begin with them. People watched all
night through at the foot of the cenotaph. The base of this vast empty
coffin, whose gilded plaster further reinforced the notion of the almost
obscene temporary nature of life, bore the words: 'To those who died
for the nation'. All night long floodlights and purple flares illuminated
veterans who came to meditate.

---

12. I am grateful to William Maufroy, Valenciennes municipal archivist, for having helped
me to find out about these fascinating civic fireworks celebrations. The example quoted is
from 1893, Valenciennes archives, shelf 3D 269. William Maufroy, 'Les cygnes et la
République: les feux d'artifice au service du ralliement valenciennois', *Valentiana*, no.
13, June 1994, pp. 9–18. Patricia Bracco and Elizabeth Lebovici, 'Les feux d'artifice, pigeons-
voyageurs de l'idée républicaine', *Monuments historiques*, no. 144, 1986, pp. 26–30.

13. P.B., *Le Figaro*, 14 July 1919, p. 1.

The day of 14 July was dedicated to the living. No one, however, was misled: the military parade was led by a thousand mutilated men who represented the million very seriously war-wounded men. One-armed men guided the blind, other veterans pushed invalid chairs. Jean Galtier-Boissière painted this terrible parade which brought together all the horrors of the war. His red, white and blue palette had difficulty in emphasizing the sombreness.[14] Death hung over the victory.

The public decided to gather at the cenotaph and at the statue of Strasbourg, transformed into a war memorial, in the Place de la Concorde. Hundreds of thousands paraded past in silence or in tears. They wanted to pass as close as possible to this coffin which held nothing, the symbol of the gap left by 1,350,000 missing men. The dead stole their day of glory from the survivors. But the survivors knew well that it must be so:

> Look back; the *Union sacrée* has cemented our victory. . .Look forward: let it be known that on the path that we must take in days to come, France still united will grow greater in peace . . .Yes, indeed, everyone must read the list of martyrs, must have been there. Let them still be there . . .if they wish that France, tested and glorious, may be France restored and always hospitable.[15]

The *Union sacrée* consists of two words, '*union*' and '*sacrée*'. It was in disunity that the criticisms of the pattern of 14 July, and more generally of the government in office during 1919, were expressed, from 14 July onwards, and organized what could at first sight be taken for 'counter-commemorations' although the 'sacred' element was strongly present.

The Socialists, 14–31 July

L'Humanité launched a tirade against the Church authorities, against the militarization of the ceremonial, and also against the lack of moral content. 'Salvoes, fanfares, military parade, dancing, fireworks and . . . carousing – that was the Victory Festival!'[16] At the foot of the same account on the front page, beneath the ironic heading 'A Very Full Day', two drawings appear: the nation's most important leaders, notably Poincaré and Clemenceau, guard the cenotaph, then in the evening they let themselves go in frenzied dancing. Far from seeing the fundamental duality of the day, the joy of victory and the sadness with which it has been so dearly bought, *L'Humanité* chose to emphasize the intrinsic

14. The picture hangs in the BDIC, Les Invalides, Paris.
15. *Le Temps*, 13 July 1919, 'La fête triomphale', p. 1.
16. *L'Humanité*, 15 July 1919, p. 1.

hypocrisy of a régime which took little note of its fellow-citizens, in peace or in war. In a violently anti-militarist editorial, André Morizet launched an attack on this hypocrisy which in his eyes corrupted the State:

> As these lines are being read, innumerable detachments of genuine combatants will begin to assemble along the Paris avenues to watch the magnificent collection of the men who sent them into battle . . .However . . .the great leaders can be assured that their swords are not rusted into their scabbards and will look for the sweeping gesture used for salutes in the cinema world . . .Among the ripple of the banners finally brought out of the hiding places where the colonels kept them, they will face the enthusiasm of the crowds and the cheers will gun down their close-packed crowd.[17]

Here can be seen the strongly reciprocated wartime hatred of the soldiers and officers on active service for the shirkers of the headquarters staff. But it goes further than that. Behind the denial of a victory so unjustly snatched from those who won it can be seen a political goal. The false joys of victory are an unbearable disorder. The festivities are an insult to the dead because they betray them. On the same day, the Socialist Party's national council examined the clauses of the peace treaty, and it can easily be imagined that they would reject it. Surely the false celebration of a false peace indicated that only the socialists who supported the Bolsheviks would know how to lead the nation and honour the dead:

> The victims, the dead, will receive deeper and more enduring homage . . . there will be the difficult but persevering effort . . . of socialists of all lands who unanimously wish to replace the present disorder with a new order which will totally exclude any future possibility of bloody conflicts.

> Today these views will be completely hidden masked beneath the flags and banners.

> Tomorrow, when the illuminations are extinguished, the horizon will become clearer.[18]

The 14 July ceremonies took place in a desperate social climate: after a highly activist 1 May, strikes and demonstrations proliferated during May and June, based on the high cost of living and the reluctance of managers to introduction of the 8-hour day. When the first visitors reached Paris in the days before 14 July, café waiters were on strike. They returned to work on 13 July, having won their claim for the 8-hour day. The socialists prepared what was to be a great day of demonstrations

17. *L'Humanité*, 14 July 1919, p. 1.
18. *Ibid.*

and strikes on 21 July, protesting against the high cost of living and against intervention in Russia.[19]

Yet, faced with the millions who cheered the official parade, there must be questions. According to *L'Humanité*, a counter-parade organized by the united federation of war-mutilated men attracted only 250 people,[20] and the newspaper was almost forced to rejoice that the brawny intervention of the police allowed it to make an issue out of the occasion: 'See how the poor survivors of the war . . . were treated on the day of the victory celebration by the infamous police of the infamous Clemenceau.'[21] Here the pre-war 'strike-breaker' image is superimposed on the 'German-breaker' image. If these 250 war veterans genuinely disturbed the peace-keeping forces when they arrived to lay their wreaths in the symbolic Père Lachaise cemetery, it was because the fear of revolution was indeed present. To assess these days accurately we must remember that we are still in July 1919 and only the historian can know what happened afterwards.

The next event concerning the socialist commemorations was on 31 July, when socialists associated the memory of Jaurès's assassination with the millions of deaths that followed.

> He fell, bloodstained, in his ruined dream,
> In the instant when death unleashed
> Reared over the world its great gleaming scythe . . .
> – Lay in its coffin the murdered Peace,
> This dreadful night, with him![22]

At the moment when the editorial team of *L'Humanité* had its strongest intellectual representation, it is not surprising that many of them paid homage in its pages to the socialist graduate of the Ecole Normale Supérieur who created it.[23] As for the public ceremony on 31 July, far removed from the 'vulgarities' of the crowd on 14 July, it took the form of a concert and poetry performance. The great hall of the Trocadero reserved for it, with seating for only 6,000, was sold out in advance.

19. In the face of the genuine lack of popular support, and the divisions in the socialist movement, the day was in fact cancelled on 18 July. Annie Kriegel, *Aux origines du communisme français*, Paris, Flammarion, 1969, pp. 86–91.

20. *L'Humanité*, 15 July 1919, p. 2.

21. It appears that their appeal had appeared only in the pages of *L'Humanité* in the preceding days. Genuine censorship or indifference on the part of the other newspapers?

22. Maurice Pottecher, 'Chant funèbre pour le tribun tombé', *L'Humanité*, 31 July 1919, p. 1.

23. Christophe Prochasson, *Les Intellectuels, le socialisme et la guerre, 1900–1938*, Paris, Seuil, 1993, p. 201.

The account emphasized that those who had listened to music by Wagner and Doyen and texts by Victor Hugo, Romain Rolland, Anatole France and Stefan Zweig, had taken part in the 'people's true celebration':

> We can confirm this, we who without believing in our eternal life never cease to behave as if we were eternal; the dead were present among us in all purity . . .Dead brothers, we have not forgotten the pact that links us, nor the sound of your final words.
>
> This was no cenotaph; for our soul is not in an empty tomb . . .Those who danced in the streets during the funeral watch or who felt their debts to the victims purged because they saluted them with the same sword that had led them to their death, hear the account of another festival.[24]

Once again we can see the Socialist Party's anti-militarism and ethical, indeed moralizing, élitism. Intellectuals set the tone (politically speaking) but also showed the route to distinction in the cult of the dead. That German art should be honoured, with the selection of Wagner and the Austrian Stefan Zweig (although a personal friend of Romain Rolland) is revealing of what separated militant pacifists from those who had piled up captured enemy guns in heaps along the Champs-Elysées on 14 July.[25]

But the most striking feature of this ceremony of 31 July is the extreme fervour with which it was announced and followed up:

> We are convinced that our readers will contribute in their meditational fervour, matching a solemnity which is religious (in the best sense of the word) even more than political . . .If there may be nobler duties than visiting a grave, there is certainly none more noble than that which consists of bringing back the dead into the choir of the living, to draw from this union the lesson which concerns the future.[26]

The vocabulary is chosen with care from the range of the sacred, etymologically that which binds mankind together. What remained of the *Union sacrée* in 1919 was that great breath of devotional fervour for France which arose in 1914 and was felt with intensity and spiritual distress through the war years. As the socialists separated definitively from those with whom they had fought the war, was there not a sort of regret for the times when it was still possible to believe in a just fight in the crusade for France?

24. *L'Humanité*, 2 August 1919, p. 1.

25. On Zweig and France, see Monika Natter, 'Les médiations françaises de Stefan Zweig', *Austriaca*, no. 34, June 1992, pp. 43–52.

26. *L'Humanité*, 31 July 1919, p. 1.

Epilogue: Death, Thine is the Victory

The Catholics, 14 July–16 October 1919

As for the Catholics, they claimed to sustain their belief in these days of crusade. As we have already seen, the journal *La Croix* enthused over the victory celebration, this 'Festival of the Giants'.[27] Yet 'shadows' were discussed by the editors of the Catholic paper. Its provincial readership made it regret the excessively Parisian nature of the ceremonies and the disregard for the martyr-cities of the front. Its fear of revolution made it devote much space to social agitation, behind which it denounced German influence: 'Militarily defeated, it is clear that Germany leads this whole dance.'[28] This stab in the back had the reverse advantage of setting all socialist militants and the C.G.T. in the camp of anti-patriots, traitors to the endangered Nation. The most important factor for a paper with such a name, however, whose front page bore a Christ on the Cross with the caption 'Adveniat regnum tuum', was the excessively secular tone of the ceremonies. 'Today the soul of France shimmers in its banners, a magnificent national unity. Let it be more than an ephemeral bloom . . . We have one regret: there was a serious lapse. From the official design, from the solemn programme, God was absent.'[29]

For the Catholic commentators, this (deliberate) omission was the greatest offence to the spirit of the *Union sacrée*. Victor Bucaille, writing in *Le Figaro*, makes a point of this aberration, contrary to what happened during the war. He stressed the many signs of religious revival at the front and behind the lines, and of ecumenism in the face of death: 'A matching respect for beliefs animated the chaplains of the various faiths . . .to guide souls in search of eternal life.'[30] If it can be imagined that the portion reserved for the living, in the army, was secular, any commemoration of the dead without a Church presence seemed an insult, in particular on the watch-night at the cenotaph. 'In this respect, Jews, Protestants and Catholics suffer with equal sadness.'[31]

Naturally, religious services were organized in the synagogues and churches. The deeply Catholic Marshal Foch was present at the Mass in Les Invalides, but in his private capacity. The State authorities rejected any association with the Churches as institutions. It may well be observed,

27. 12 July 1919
28. *La Croix*, 12 July 1919, p. 1.
29. *La Croix*, 15 July, p. 1.
30. *Le Figaro*, 14 July 1919, p. 2.
31. *Ibid.* It may be noted that only *Le Figaro* posed the question in an ecumenical form. The Catholic newspapers and periodicals mentioned only the insult to Catholicism, not to religious feeling in general.

with benefit of hindsight, that all approaches to death took on religious overtones, that the purple flares chosen for the cenotaph were the colour of mourning in the Catholic liturgy. That in no way seemed adequate to practising observers of the various religions, particularly the Catholics.

> Those who were going to defend their threatened nation were not asked what religion they adhered to, or whether they had any religion at all. By linking their memory with the glory of today, we should respect the faith by which they lived . . .The government would have honoured itself if it had made this gesture; it would not in any way have been contrary to its professed neutrality, for the neutrality of a State can be the respect of various beliefs; it is not necessarily repudiation.[32]

The Catholics would have liked to see an altar under the Arc de Triomphe: 'What powerful reality would have taken the place of an empty symbol.'[33] Above all, they took the pretext of this 14 July to express yet again the impression that they had been cheated by the *Union sacrée*, orchestrated as it was by the anti-clerical directors of the Third Republic: 'The *Union sacrée*, for Catholics, consisted of this: forgetting that the government had stripped the churches, seized the funds for masses, ousted the religious community, priests and bishops, from their dwellings, broken with the Pope: to give this government blood, gold, silence . . .for five years [it] was nothing but a magnificent opportunity for renunciation.'[34] In fact on 2 July, in the Chamber of Deputies, the problem of re-establishing the bonds with the Holy See had been taken up and rejected.

The ceremonies of 14 July thus served to reveal the dissent between the Catholic Church and the government. Behind the anti-clerical Clemenceau lay the Law of Separation, the crisis of inventories, wicked rumour, the refusal, finally, to associate the symbol of the Sacred Heart with the fight for France.[35]

The consecration ceremonies for Sacré-Cœur in Montmartre (the Martyr's Hill) were to enable the strength of Catholicism to be demonstrated in October of the same year. As Jacques Benoît said so accurately, 'The consecration of the basilica, so long delayed . . . can be seen as the true feast of the victory celebrated by Catholics in Montmartre.'[36] The

32. *Ibid.*
33. Paul Dudon, 'La voix des morts de la Grande Guerre', *Etudes*, 5 August 1919, pp. 256–70 (p. 264).
34. *Ibid.*, pp. 262–5.
35. See Chapter 2.
36. J. Benoît, 'Le Sacré-Cœur de Montmartre', p. 656. *Les Lieux de mémoire*, III. Les France, 3. De l'archive à l'emblème, articles by François Loyer, 'Le Sacré-Cœur de Montmartre', and by René Rémond, 'La Fille aînée de l'Eglise.'

basilica was consecrated on 16–19 October. The solemn consecration took place on the Thursday, Friday was the feast of the Blessed Marguerite-Marie, Saturday was for remembrance of the war dead and to pray for them; the ceremonies ended on Sunday, the day for thanksgiving. Facing these hundreds of thousands of the faithful crowding round the building, all the official speeches, whether from the Papal Legate, His Eminence Cardinal Vico, or the French bishops, took up the same message: France, chastised in 1870–1, by defeat, the Commune and the abandonment of the Papacy, owed it to herself to recognize the coexistence of the victory and the consecration of the basilica: 'France penitent, devoted and grateful'. The consecration proved that the suffering of the French in the Great War, the death of 1,350,000 of their nation, had not been in vain: the hope that guided them had won its reward.

> In 1870 there was no more hope. And that is what created the horror of the situation . . . It was then that the Catholic faithful made their national vow to construct a church dedicated to the Sacred Heart . . . the work took fifty years. But what is fifty years in the life of a nation? History will not see between the war of 1870–1 and the war of 1914–18 the enormous hiatus that we find so striking today. It will link the two together. The second is the consequence of the first, Alsace-Lorraine lost by defeat and returned to us through victory.[37]

And so, to the tune of 'Pitié Mon Dieu', the congregation sang: 'Our thanks to you, O God, God of mercy, O victorious God, You who have saved France, keep her in your Sacred Heart.'

The consecration of Sacré-Cœur was the key moment in France's return to normality, from defeat to victory, from the rending apart to the hope of reconciliation, not without irony on the part of *La Croix*:

> In 1870, on this same Montmartre hill, Clemenceau watched the bloodstained flower of the Commune surging and seething. He would have been very surprised if he had been told then that, fifty years later . . . the force of Christ would appear there, that a whole nation would watch its triumph eagerly, and that he himself would watch it all with a calm and, who knows! perhaps kindly eye.[38]

The Pope, whose awkward fate formed the third element of the 1870–1 vow, was present through the intermediary of his legate and in the announcement of celebrations to take place in 1920 in Saint Peter's church in Rome, for the canonization of the Blessed Marguerite-Marie Alacoque and Joan of Arc. The canonization of the two French women

37. *La Croix*, 15 October 1919, p. 1.
38. *La Croix*, 18 October, p. 1.

was hastened by the war and by devotion to them in the front line and in the rear, as also happened with Thérèse of Lisieux. Did not Pope Benedict XV favour France in his letter of thanks to the Cardinal Archbishop of Paris?

> May Our Lord Jesus Christ .. be with you . . .At the prayer of your compatriot the Blessed Marguerite-Marie . . .from the heights of this magnificent temple that you have created in honour of His love, may He embrace and shower with grace not only France but the whole human race, so that what the wisdom of Man has begun at the Congress of Versailles, divine charity may bring to perfection and completion on the Mount of Martyrs.[39]

It is unnecessary to go into the ceremonies in greater detail to understand the clear parallel between the victory celebrations in June and the Catholic ceremonies in October. Contrary to what might appear from a superficial reading, there was no competition between the certainty of the victory of France as civilized and/or Christian, lay republican and/or religious. The 'Martyrs' Mount' received the martyrs of the Great War. The church crypt would soon be transformed into a memorial to the Parisian dead of the war.

11 November 1920: the Symbol of the Unknown Soldier

On 11 November 1920 the great spontaneous and official ensemble of rejoicing and mourning, begun on 11 November 1918, came to a conclusion with the interment of the Unknown Soldier beneath the Arc de Triomphe. The French ceremonies took place against a background of similar international events: all the combatant nations, victors and vanquished, buried an unknown soldier with great ceremony during the 1920s, following the double precedent on 11 November 1920 in London and Paris. These national funeral services for all those who had been reduced to mangled remains on the battlefields, but with sufficient scraps of uniform for their nationality to be identified, were the commemorative innovation of the Great War.[40] The symbolic tombs established in Rome, Washington, Lisbon and Brussels in 1921, Prague and Belgrade in 1922, then in Bucharest, Budapest and Warsaw in the following years, formed the kernel of national commemoration. In particular, all the new states emerging from the empires that collapsed in the war nationalized their

39. Quoted in Yves de la Brière, 'Chronique du mouvement religieux, au Sacré-Cœur de Montmartre', *Etudes*, November 1919, p. 360.
40. Ken Inglis, 'Entombing Unknown Soldiers: From London and Paris to Baghdad', *History and Memory*, vol. 5, no. 2, 1993, pp. 7-31.

dead with the interment of their own Unknown Soldier.[41] It can easily be understood that the German republic, born in defeat, could not reach a commemorative consensus.[42] In other countries too, there was no shortage of debate,[43] and the French example enables us to analyse the controversies as they continued and accompanied the 1919 ceremonies. Although agreement over the interment of an unknown soldier and the date of 11 November brought almost complete unanimity, the site selected for repose of the body and the organization of the ceremonies led to substantial debate in the Chamber of Deputies and in public opinion.

It was the spectacle of the fervour at the foot of the cenotaph, the immense empty tomb whose affective charge on 14 July we have noted, which created the notion of another tomb, equally full of the symbol of death but this time containing a soldier brought back from the battlefield. The date of the transfer, 11 November, and the site for selection of the unknown man, Verdun, followed naturally. An unknown hero would be brought to the centre of power, in the capital, from the heart of the citadel in the supreme site of the war, of mythic significance after 1916, Verdun.[44] After 14 July 1919, 11 November 1920 was the inevitable date for such a ceremony; but 1920 was also the fiftieth anniversary of the Third Republic, and the coincidence of these dates led France into an important debate.

Macabre minds, so marked by the war that they could no longer envisage any ritual other than interment in a symbolic setting, introduced the notion of taking Gambetta's heart from his grave and setting it in

41. Australia has offered a dazzling endorsement of the practice, on 11 November 1993. Just as the Prime Minister, Paul Keating, was working for the establishment of a republic, the Australian soldier exhumed in the Somme and reinterred in Canberra in the Australian War Memorial confirmed that the Unknown Soldier in Westminster Abbey had never, since 1920, represented the entire British Empire.

42. Volker Ackermann, 'La vision allemande du soldat inconnu: débats politiques, réflexion philosophique et artistique', in Jean-Jacques Becker, Jay Winter, Gerd Krumeich, Annette Becker and Stéphane Andoin-Rouzeau (eds), *Guerre et cultures, 1914–1918*, Paris, Armand Colin, 1994, pp. 385-96.

43. For the United States, see my article, 'Les deux rives de l'Atlantique, mémoire américaine de la Grande Guerre', *Annales de l'Université de Savoie*, January 1995, pp. 23-36.

44. The selection of the coffin of the Unknown Soldier from eight others by Corporal Auguste Tain is too well known to describe again here. See Inglis, 'Entombing Unknown Soldiers'. On the myth of Verdun, Antoine Prost, 'Verdun', *Les Lieux de mémoire* (ed. P. Nora). The British Unknown Soldier was embarked on the destroyer HMS Verdun on 10 November to be brought to Westminster.

the Pantheon with the unknown soldier. The heart of the great republican patriot of 1870 would lie beside the great unknown patriot who had sacrificed himself for his nation, the republic which had won back the lost provinces. 'To great men, from the grateful nation'; the Pantheon seemed the obvious place. This misjudged the French nation's perception of the supreme national effort between 1914 and 1918. The veteran soldiers and their families (in other words, most of the French nation) were convinced that the soldiers of Verdun, of Artois, of the Marne, etc., were not 'important' young men, the élite with an almost routine future before them as successful military, political, literary or scientific pupils who had reached the Pantheon during the earlier decades of the Third Republic.[45] Thus it was that the Ministry of Public Education, charged with organizing the ceremony for 11 November, came to divide the events: 'transfer to the Pantheon and interment beneath the Arc de Triomphe of the remains of an unidentified soldier killed during the Great War'.

On 8 November, only three days before the planned ceremony, the Chamber of Deputies held an extraordinary session designed to vote through the law and credits necessary for its application. The members of the government were convinced that the proposed law 'would benefit from the moral truce which in peace is the equivalent of the wartime *Union sacrée*'.[46] This did not take into account the socialist group, whose spokesman, M. Bracke, denounced the manoeuvres of the government: while giving the impression that it wished to associate the fiftieth anniversary of the Republic with the transfer of the Unknown Soldier, it was turning the whole event 'into a military festival of General Headquarters staff. The feeling of the people is sufficiently clear for you to have to hide the living staff behind the symbolic corpse of the dead.'[47]

This speech was followed by rough arguments which ended in a break in the session. The respect due to the dead was forgotten by both Right and Left, each of whom used the dead for their own political game, some pressing for the Republic's fiftieth anniversary to come first, others for military honour. The President of the Council, Georges Leygues, finally spoke, with several interruptions from the monarchist Léon Daudet. For Leygues, the Republic would be properly honoured on 11 November because it had

45. Avner Ben Amos, 'Les funérailles de Victor Hugo'.
46. *Le Temps*, 10 November 1920, p. 2.
47. *Ibid.*

172

restored the nation . . . and formed generations with hearts of iron who without weakening endured the most formidable challenges that a nation had ever had to undergo . . . In transporting the remains of the Unknown Soldier to the Arc de Triomphe, from the sacred mountain, for so many centuries the setting where different spirits developed to offer France such greatness and drive . . . we will conduct the body of the soldier to the place where it should lie: beneath the triumphal arch raised to the nameless armies, to the crowd of unknown heroes, sons of the Revolution . . . who bore in the folds of their banner and spread across Europe the new principles proclaimed by France at the end of the eighteenth century, which have created the modern world.[48]

As on 14 July of the preceding year, the French revolutionary messianism was intense. It did not convince the editors of the newspaper *La Croix*, supporting the Republic rather than its secular values: 'At the moment of danger one can see appearing magnificently this spirit of sacrifice inculcated in the French soul through twenty centuries of Christianity [*sic*], and which forty years of secularism could not stifle.'[49] Republican Catholics, in contrast to the monarchists of *Action française*, none the less associated themselves fully with the ceremonies planned for the Unknown Soldier. On 29 October, His Eminence Cardinal Luçon addressed a letter to all French bishops, advising them to participate in the various festivities by means of a religious ceremony, 'to mark the participation of the clergy and Catholics in this national demonstration and to meet the benevolent attitude of the present government'. The Cardinal of Reims referred to the *rapprochement* between France and the Holy See which, still considered impossible in 1919, was now confirmed: the Doulcet–Gasparri agreement on the exchange of a Papal Nuncio and an ambassador on 28 May 1920. The 11 November ceremonies were thus used by the authorities of the Catholic Church to press their advantage in negotiations. On 30 November, the Chamber voted for the re-establishment of the French embassy in the Vatican, to which Charles Jonnart would be appointed in 1921, to work on all matters still in abeyance.[50]

In this way, the Republic's fiftieth anniversary occurred at a key moment in its relationship with the Catholic Church. Quite straightforwardly, the Church authorities set aside their complaints, still so vehement in 1919, particularly because the transfer ceremony was not

48. *Ibid.*

49. Article by Jean Guiraud, 'La République et la Victoire', *La Croix*, 11 November 1920, p. 1.

50. Jean Vavasseur-Desperriers, *Charles Jonnart. Recherches sur une personnalité politique de la IIIe République*, Lille, Presses du Septentrion, 1996.

associated with them as they would have liked, while the Archbishop of Paris was invited to bless the coffin of the Unknown Soldier in the afternoon of 11 November.

Although Catholics made up the majority of the nation, who could say that the Unknown Soldier had not been Protestant, or Jewish? Yet it was a Protestant minister who had been pressing for this ultimate use of the Arc de Triomphe since 1915: 'Jesus Christ will have the final word. Beneath the triumphal arch He will bring about a new era with humanity humanized.'[51]

The perpetuation of the *Union sacrée* was confirmed, at least where death was concerned, when the strongly Catholic Jacques Péricard was authorized to manage the ritual of the flame at the Arc de Triomphe from 1923 onwards. Although the Catholic Church had not achieved the full political breakthrough that it hoped for, the war – through the sacrifices of the dead and their commemoration which it had skilfully channelled – had at least enabled it to win back a more important place in the nation. The socialists, for their part, persisted in their opposition. As in 1919, as in the Chamber of Deputies, and even more radically because, as we have seen, *L'Humanité* was in the hands of the 'hard' socialist faction, the newspaper which was to pass a month later to the brand-new Communist Party derided the governmental ceremonies.[52] Caricaturists and editorialists let themselves go once more against militarism, favours to Catholics, the hypocrisy of the government in its organization of the 'funeral masquerade of 11 November'. 'Mortgage your unknown dead man . . . steal our comrade from us, and order funeral dances, funeral feasts, funeral plundering . . . Like the dead stone figures from the *danse macabres* . . . your Unknown Soldier takes your hand and leads you to the hole where History intends that you and your cardboard laurels should go and rot.'[53] These socialists fought for a republic that would grant an amnesty to the mutineers of the Black Sea and the striking railwaymen, following the example of the amnesty for the Communards – by which Gambetta had distinguished himself in 1876.

Paradoxically, but in direct line with 1919, *L'Humanité*'s highly intellectual journalists used religious metaphors with which to belabour the 'Pharisee' hypocrites and to align themselves with the true, the only

51. Pasteur Wilfred Monod, 'Le prix du sang', in *Pendant la guerre*, Paris, Fischbacher, 11 July 1915, 1916, p. 47
52. The Congress of Tours opened on 26 December 1920.
53. Paul Vaillant-Couturier, *L'Humanité*, 10 November 1920, p. 1.

combatants, their brothers, their comrades. The unknown man described by the socialists was a Christ of scorn and grief who suffered under spitting and blows. The worker and peasant membership of the *Fédération des mutilés* found Pauline accents to rally to the anti-militarist and socialist cause: 'Whoever you may be, friend, labourer, peasant, Catholic, Protestant, Freemason, atheist or Jewish worker, your religion is your own: that of the anonymous instrument that we represent in the hands of beneficiaries without honour, of men who profit unto death . . . and even beyond . . . Beloved comrade, anonymous victim immolated by all the sacrilegious profiteers, sinister vampires, preordained assassins.'[54]

The socialists continued to promote themselves as the representatives of all those who felt cheated by the war and above all by the consequences of victory, snatched from the combatants by the politico-militarists. They called for a boycott of the planned demonstrations, did not vote the credits for the celebrations in the National Assembly, but had to yield to the evidence: their readers, like most Parisians, pressed into the large crowds all along the route, and, far from ignoring such useless ceremonies, they offered comment in lengthy columns.

For the Unknown Soldier was acknowledged by the French people. On the evening of 10 November, the unknown man arrived by a special train from Verdun and was laid for one night in the Place Denfert-Rochereau in Paris, close to Gambetta's heart. A funeral watch was arranged. The next day the cortège moved to the Pantheon where Gambetta's heart was interred after a speech from the President of the Republic, Alexandre Millerand, who linked the Republic, the Unknown Soldier and individuals from all elements of the Third Republic – Gambetta naturally, Ferry, Waldeck-Rousseau, Jaurès and de Mun.

The political ecumenism of the *Union sacrée* reclaimed its rights, with some jeering from *L'Humanité*: 'What should we really think of the republican hero whose venerated guts are promenaded around and who will end up by establishing the new cult of the secular and republican Sacred Heart?'[55]

From the place of the colonel-hero of the 1870–1 war in the Pantheon to the Arc de Triomphe, the chosen Parisian topography served the organizers' designs admirably: to create an indissoluble link between the revenge prepared by the Republic and the victory, not forgetting the enormous price paid by the French in general and their élites in

54. *L'Humanité*, 11 November 1920.
55. Victor Méric, *L'Humanité*, 12 November 1920.

particular. The unknown man's coffin, borne on a gun-carriage draped with the tricolour, was surrounded by war-handicapped men who, as on 14 July 1919, recalled above all the drama of the war. The war had destroyed men, had destroyed families; the commemoration should bring them to life again: the interment of the Unknown Soldier, his adoption by the whole nation, were his resurrection, he was France's Christ: 'What we revere in him exceeds any earthly measure: this is a human wrapping which lost its flesh and shredded away in a shroud of mud, this is a handful of bloodstained earth raised up by a new miracle, by giving him the face and soul of France.'[56]

The Unknown Soldier was also accompanied throughout his day by a fictional family, a war-widow, a father who had lost his son, a child who had lost his father. The war had reversed the logical order of the succeeding generations, the commemoration would serve as a remedy: each one adopted the unknown man as the lost father or son.[57] The correspondent of the socialist paper who said he had followed the cortège 'out of professional duty' finally gave the most poignant description of the unknown man, so well known by the millions who had loved him, been close to him and lost him: 'Perhaps he fell near me in Artois, in Champagne, or at Verdun. Perhaps he had shown me pictures of his father and mother, his wife and his children, during our long watches in the trenches?'[58]

Two years after the armistice of 11 November 1918, the ceremonies of 11 November 1920 – more political but, thanks to the essential Catholic rallying to the events, more united than those of 1919 – brought out into the Paris streets tens of thousands of people in tears, sure that they were watching their own lost one passing. The Republic could celebrate itself energetically, but fervour remained with the anonymous masses who had defended and saved it.

For many years not a single provincial visitor, not a single foreigner, could visit Paris without going first to the tomb beneath the Arc de Triomphe. Beyond any official ceremonies and military parades, the Unknown Soldier wholeheartedly combined the values of sacrifice and of intense distress connected with the war. And by a reversal which would have delighted those who disparaged the ceremonies, the tomb

---

56. 'Deo Ignoto', *Le Temps*, 11 November 1920, p. 1.

57. Maurice Leblanc then wrote a very typical detective story, *La Dent d'Hercule Petitgris*, in which a mother was 'saved' by the certainty that her own son was indeed the Unknown Soldier. (Bouquins, Laffont, 1988). I am grateful to Frédéric Gugelot for having pointed out to me this fine literary example for my researches.

58. Gabriel Reuillard, *L'Humanité*, 12 November 1920, p. 2.

also became one of the focal symbolic sites of pilgrimage. In 1935 Jean Giraudoux gave his character, Andromaque, the task of expressing this 'Arc de Triomphe' pacifism:

> The soldiers who paraded beneath the triumphal arches are those who have deserted from death . . . The men who were killed are not at peace in the ground. They do not blend into it for rest and eternal dwelling. They do not become part of its territory, its essence. When a human skeleton is found in the soil, there is always a sword at its side. It is a bone of the earth, a sterile bone. It is a warrior.[59]

In 1942 the writer Henri Calet, who was captured in 1940 and escaped after seven months of imprisonment, used a devastating fictional form to describe his experience of the collapse of 1940. At the end of the book his hero/double returns to Paris:

> I ended at the Etoile. I crossed the *Place*, disowning my actions a little to myself, I stopped beneath the Arc and there I said a modest Hello to him as I passed, without drums or bugles, to the other man, the one who was killed last time. For myself and for the two million comrades. I understood better what he had gone through before he was buried. A few flowers were wilting on the stone – faded flowers which smelt of decay. We were from the same family, those who are gathered together every twenty years on the battlefields for strange harvests . . . for whose sake, for what did we suffer, he and I? He represented two million dead and I, two million humiliated – without going any further into our history. For France. But why did she wish us so ill?
>
> Grey-uniformed soldiers stopped to salute him, magnificently. Here too we were not alone.[60]

Here we can see (and through what gifted writing) the final result, during the Second World War, of the Great War survivors' repugnance at their crusading energies in a cause that they could no longer decently defend. Between 1918 and the very early 1940s, the survivors of the '*Der des der*' ('The Last of the Last'), combatants and civilians, created a conceptual screen designed to diminish or even efface their wartime fervour. These forms of pessimism have been studied more often than the earlier fervour. Is it not more stimulating to concentrate on lost faith, or cynicism, than on the banal optimism of simple faith?

There is a parallel to be drawn here with the creation of forgetfulness, even denial, of the atrocities and exactions perpetrated by the various

---

59. Jean Giraudoux, *La Guerre de Troie n'aura pas lieu*, Act I, scene 6, Paris, Le Livre de poche, pp. 97–8.

60. Henri Calet, *Le Bouquet*, Folio/Gallimard, p. 292.

armies of invasion and occupation between 1914 and 1918. Relationships established from 1915–16 onwards contained irrefutable proof; they also included narratives which were sooner or later recognized as myth – as, for example, the anecdotes described in Chapter 1 concerning children or the crucified Canadian. Allied propaganda, particularly British, French and American propaganda, had room for every crime, real or imagined, to the extent that after the war and before recent research carried out by John Horne, Allan Kramer, Stéphane Audoin-Rouzeau and myself in northern France, these 'atrocities' were often considered to be invention pure and simple.[61] At both ends of the political spectrum, the baby had been thrown out with the bathwater: surviving pacifist combatants, particularly the militants among them, saw the war itself as an atrocity, so that it was unnecessary to make assertions which were more or less propaganda. This inevitably distracted the nation from the true fight to be fought, the war against war itself. Atrocity propaganda then became the pacifists' scapegoat, the over-simplified explanation for the national will to fight, the consent to this tragedy which led to 10 million deaths: they had been misled; it would not happen again.

As for that other veteran of the Great War, who became a politician and then Head of State, he was also convinced, as he explained clearly in *Mein Kampf*, that the superiority of British propaganda, particularly in the invention of atrocities, should not be overlooked in the forth-coming struggle.

> The English propagandists' brilliant knowledge of the primitive sentiment of the broad masses is shown by their atrocity propaganda, which was adapted to this condition. As ruthless as it was brilliant, it created the preconditions for moral steadfastness at the front, even in the face of the greatest actual defeats, and just as strikingly it pilloried the German enemy as the sole guilty party for the outbreak of the War: the rabid, impudent bias and persistence with which this lie was expressed took into account the emotional, always extreme, attitude of the great masses and for this reason was believed.[62]

And yet, between 1914 and 1918, the Serbians discovered, at the same time as the inhabitants of northern France, the Belgians, the Polish, the Russians, the Germans in East Prussia and above all the Armenians, that

61. John Horne and Allan Kramer, '*German Atrocities*', *1914 to the Present*, Cambridge, Cambridge University Press, 1998; Stéphane Audoin-Rouzeau, *Le Fils de l'Allemand*, Paris, Aubier, 1996; Annette Becker, 'Life in an Occupied Zone: Lille–Roubaix–Tourcoing, 1914–1918', in Hugh Cecil and Peter Liddle (eds), *Facing Armageddon. The First World War Experienced*, London, Leo Brassey, 1996.
62. Adolf Hitler, *Mein Kampf*, 1925, English translation, London, 1969, pp. 167–8.

the war now extended beyond the battles of soldiers and the patriotic culture of wholly mobilized nations. War in occupied territory became total. In 1939 Hitler was able to jeer at the wavering European memory of the massacre of the Armenians: 'After all, who now talks about the annihilation of the Armenians?'[63] In face of the certainty of impunity among the murderers who thought that the battle of memory would always be won, we should wonder, sadly, whether the struggle of pacifists has not also contributed to this clouding of memory. The conceptual screen set up during the 1920s and 1930s by militants determined to condemn the war as an atrocity, rather than the atrocities within the war, has had more than a modest share of responsibility for this forgetfulness.

This idea of the manipulation of opinion based on false accounts of atrocities reappears in the mockery of intense patriotic fervour during the war. How in fact should we read the first lines of an article like this one, published in the United States in 1918:

> Germany's ambition was to do evil well; and this she has accomplished with astuteness and far-reaching efficiency, enabling her people to play their atrocious parts without revolt or shame. But in France it is the soul which dominates her martyrdom . . . Never in the history of man has the superior force of the soul been so clearly exemplified. All religions are an expression of faith, though dogma through the ages has dimmed in purity. But this war has cleared the spiritual vision in France, and beauties of the soul, once dim and evasive, have become real and near, lending the individual a dignity and poise which renders life a privilege and death merely a natural and kindly deliverance from an inadequate body.[64]

And yet the rest of the article describes the devotions and superstitions, at the front and behind the lines, with which the readers of this book have become familiar. It was not the devotions linked to the war and to death which disappeared during the 1920s and 1930s: it was the possibility of recognizing, in nations traumatized by the disappearance of their crusading expectations, that such devotions had even existed. And yet in the face of death, traditional beliefs, anchored in the most ancient faith of mankind, continued to express themselves.

---

63. Hitler is supposed to have said this on 22 August 1939. Even if it is apocryphal, as some historians think, it is entirely in accordance with his nature to have said it.

64. Nina Larrey Durya, 'The Soul of France, Some Spiritual Experiences and War-Time Superstitions', *Harper's Magazine*, September 1918, p. 457.

Conclusion

What is the date of the prayer that concludes this book? It was probably written just after the death of Maurice Gallé, a cadet in the 106th infantry regiment who was killed at the age of 22 on 25 September 1916, near Bouchavesnes on the Somme. Since the last three stanzas refer to the final victory of France, it seems likely that they were added after 1918.

We know that Germaine Franchemont, the young victim's grandmother, composed this text and repeated it day after day in her grandson's room.

There is no need to analyse it, or to demonstrate how the whole of this book is summed up simply in this terrible text. The memory that I have sought to define is there, within a family, in the bruised and exalted love of a grandmother who was destined by the Great War to outlive her own grandson.

To My God

For the twenty years of happiness you gave me
Through my dear little boy
I thank you, Lord.

For his sweet childhood
For his loving growing up
For his fine and pure youth
I thank you, Lord.

For these two years of the right
For me to enjoy his presence
When my good fortune brought me a thousandfold intimate joys of which
    he was the cause
I thank you, Lord.

For his courage when he left his beloved home on 16 December 1914,
Not knowing when he would come back
Leaving his Mother so sick and finding his grandmother dead in Paris
I thank you, Lord.

For all his many qualities
That brought him love and trust from all, his seniors and his soldiers,
In his new path in life,
I thank you, Lord.

For his delight at coming home on leave
For Christmas 1915 and New Year 1916
I thank you, Lord.

Because in 1915 after the September attack in Champagne
He saw that you might want to ask of him the sacrifice of his life
And because he accepted
I thank you, Lord.

Because it was given him to take part
In the apotheosis of the year with his *poilus* on 14 July 1916
And because he trembled with enthusiasm
I thank you, Lord.

Because on 25 September 1916
He volunteered for a particularly dangerous mission
And was known as a magnificent French officer
As a pure Christian knight
I thank you, Lord.

Because he gave up his holy soul
On a fine day such as he loved
I thank you, Lord.

Because you have permitted us to know exact details
Of his last moments
And because we know he did not suffer
I thank you, Lord.

Because he fell on French soil
Because we have been able to visit his grave
And water with our tears the sacred earth he watered with his blood
I thank you, Lord.

Because his sacrifice and that of his brothers in arms
Has saved France and has put her in the first rank of nations
By saving along with her the whole world
I thank you, Lord.

Because you granted him the finest death
And opened your Paradise
Where I imagine him as a Saint
I thank you, Lord.
Amen.[65]

How many times did Germaine Franchemont repeat this prayer? Probably until the day she died. The fact that we do not know the exact date

---

65. Musée Gallé, Creil, Oise. Quoted with the permission of Nathalie Garreau, author of an MA dissertation under the supervision of S. Audoin-Rouzeau and N. Chaline, University of Picardy, 1992, 'Impact de la Première Guerre mondiale sur les Gallé, famille de Creil'.

emphasizes the difficulty in ending this book. At what point does one stop? When all the Germaine Franchemonts and all the mothers, wives and comrades of the trenches have disappeared, and along with them the fervour of the war and post-war days that enabled them to hold out during the battles and the anguish of separations. Already by the end of the 1930s, a part of this world had disappeared; then along came the Second World War, bringing its new portion of sufferings and responses.

But the last remaining veterans, the childless widows, and the children of the war who are themselves all old people now, still continue today to perpetuate the memory of the conflict's deepest shocks. Soon, when they are gone, the Great War will at last be over.

Index

(Page numbers in italics refer to illustrations)